KEATS AND SHAKESPEARE

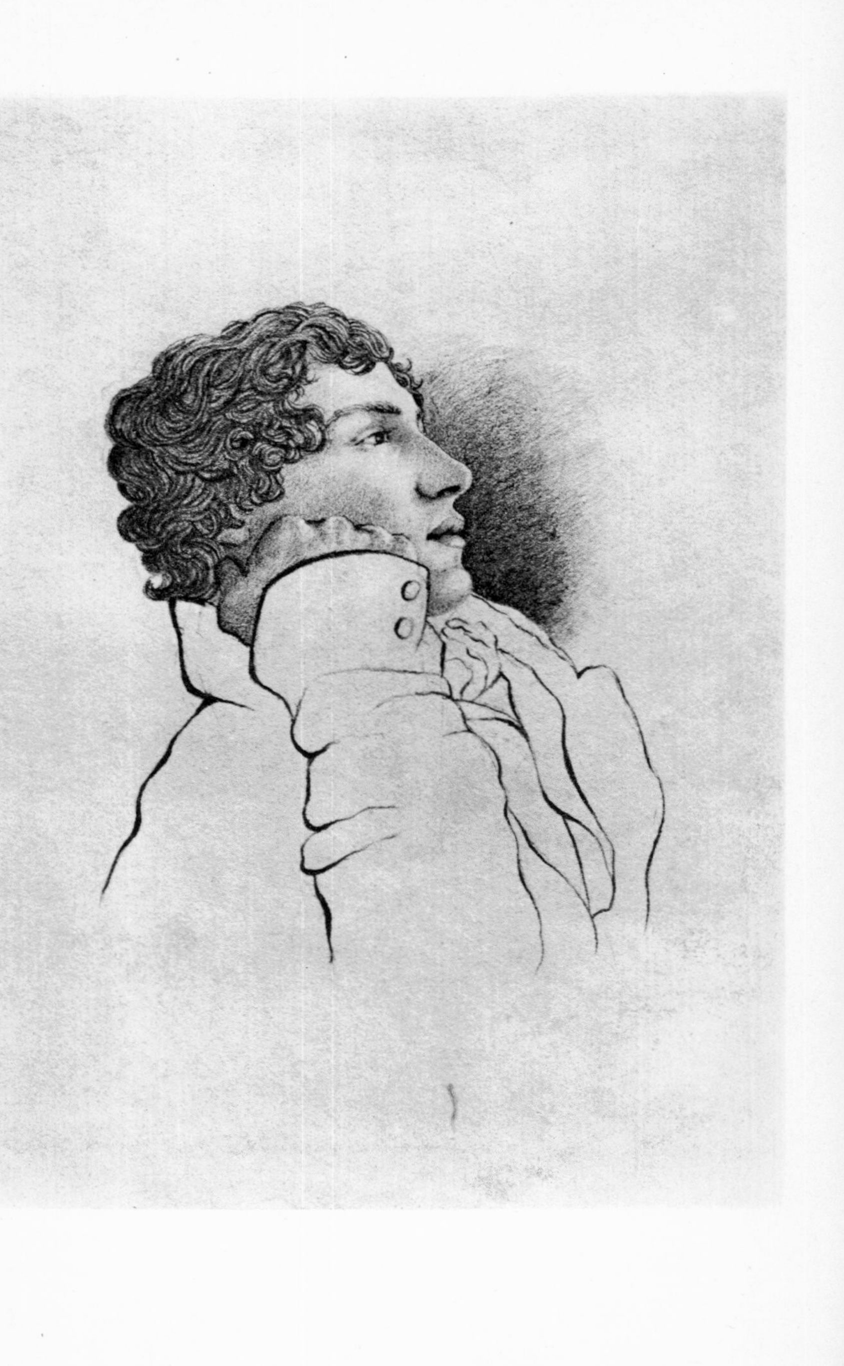

KEATS AND SHAKESPEARE

A Study of Keats' Poetic Life from 1816 to 1820

by

JOHN MIDDLETON MURRY

OXFORD UNIVERSITY PRESS
LONDON: HUMPHREY MILFORD
1925

This book is printed in England at the Westminster Press, London. The type used is Monotype Plantin Light-face and the paper Dutch mould-made. The frontispiece is a collotype reproduction of a pencil sketch of John Keats, made by Charles Brown, probably in July 1819, and now in the National Portrait Gallery, and is printed by Frederick Hall at the University Press, Oxford.

'He is; he is with Shakespeare.'—Matthew Arnold: 'Essay on Keats.'

'They are very shallow people who take everything literally. A Man's life of any worth is a continual allegory, and very few eyes can see the Mystery of his life—a life like the scriptures, figurative—which such people can no more make out than they can the Hebrew Bible. Lord Byron cuts a figure but he is not figurative—Shakespeare led a life of Allegory: his works are the comments on it.'—Keats' Letter to George Keats: 18th February 1819.

'When in the reason's philosophy the rational appears dominant and sole possessor of the world, we can only wonder what place would be left to it, if the element excluded might break through the charm of the magic circle, and without growing rational, might find expression. Such an idea may be senseless, and such a thought may contradict itself, but it serves to give voice to an obstinate instinct. Unless thought stands for something that falls beyond mere intelligence, if "thinking" is not used with some strange implication that never was part of the meaning of the word, a lingering scruple still forbids us to believe that reality can ever be purely rational. It may come from a failure in my metaphysics, or from a weakness of the flesh which continues to blind me, but the notion that existence should be the same as understanding strikes as cold and ghost-like as the dreariest materialism.'—F. H. Bradley: *Principles of Logic*.

'I should observe perhaps that if Keats' position as formulated above is accepted, the question still remains whether a truth which is also beauty, or a beauty which is also truth, can be found by man: and if so, whether it can, in strictness, be called by either of those names.'—A. C. Bradley: *Oxford Lectures on Poetry: Keats' Letters*.

'Ethics and æsthetics are one.'—Ludwig Wittgenstein: *Tractatus Logico-Philosophius*.

PREFATORY NOTE

I REGRET that Miss Amy Lowell's new biography of Keats was not published before this book was completed. By the courtesy of her English publisher, Mr. Jonathan Cape, I was permitted to read the rough proofs of a part of her first volume, to which I owe my my knowledge of the story of Charles Brown's 'marriage' to Abigail Donohue and of the text of Keats' letter to Haydon of 22nd January 1818, concerning *Hyperion*.

This book is not a biography of Keats. If Miss Lowell's second volume is as good as her first, the biography of Keats has been written once for all; and I sincerely hope that Miss Lowell's critical idiosyncrasies will not blind English opinion to the enduring merits of her work. Neither is this book a criticism of Keats, in the ordinary sense of the word. I should call it simply an attempt to show what Keats was, by telling the story of his inward life, as revealed in his poems and letters during the four years of his poetic career.

Above all, this book is not the exposition of a theory. In criticism I have but one theory, namely, to be loyal to the reality of the man whose works move me profoundly. If in any vital point I have misread the reality of Keats, then, so far as I am concerned, this book is nugatory. In an introductory chapter I have given the history of how it came to be conceived and undertaken.

I wish to express my gratitude to the Master and Fellows of Trinity College, Cambridge, but for whose invitation to deliver the Clark Lectures for 1924, on which this book is based, the book itself could not have been written.

Abbotsbury, *25th November* 1924.

P.S.—Since the above was written, the two volumes of Miss Lowell's *John Keats* have appeared. Unfortunately, her second volume is by no means as good as her first. I am afraid I owe to it nothing except the necessity of elaborately correcting one very serious mistake in it concerning the composition of *Hyperion*. Miss Lowell's second volume contains in an appendix a valuable fragment hitherto missing from Keats' great journal-letter of February-May 1819.

CONTENTS

CHAPTER I

INTRODUCTORY

AFTER many attempts, I could discover no better way of indicating the scope and character of this book than by giving a short account of the process by which it came to be what it is, which is something very different from what I originally planned.

When the invitation to deliver the lectures on which the book is based reached me, my mind was full of a subject which is not easy to describe: I will call it briefly the history of the human soul since the Renaissance. For some years there had been gradually forming in my mind a conception of the main movement of the human soul since that great moment when the human mind—which is not the same thing as the human soul, or the two heroes of this book would never have been what they were—broke away from the bondage of a religion become a formalism, and entered upon that adventure, of which we are the inheritors. I mean the adventure of the individual mind exploring the universe for truth.

The process of this adventure, which is not yet at an end, and which in a sense may be only beginning, had gradually come to shape itself in my mind as a movement from the rejection of religion to the rediscovery of religion, or rather, from the rejection of a religion petrified by its own formalisms to the rediscovery of the essential reality of religion. From that bare statement—which I must leave for the moment unjustified and with its central term undefined—it is obvious that the history of the human soul since the Renaissance is, for me, something very different from the actual spiritual history of the vast bodies of men and women who compose the nations. Rather than such a history, it is the spiritual history of various outstanding men who have, for some reason or other, imposed themselves upon the memory of mankind.

That, it may be said, is a singular fashion of conceiving the history of the human soul since the Renaissance. And I admit that it is singular; but I also contend that it is not unreasonable. The history of the most remarkable and individual human souls since the Renaissance is, of course, not the same as the history of the human soul since that event; it is, I believe, truer and more essential than such a history could ever be, if it could be written at all. For the most striking fact about these great individual souls, it seems to me, is not so much their greatness or their individuality, as the manner in which they have imposed themselves upon the memory of mankind. Shakespeare himself is not so marvellous as the fact that he has not been forgotten. By what means and with what fidelity he is perpetuated—whether by the effort of a few men and women in each generation, as the sceptic might assert, or by the natural process of something we may call the unconscious soul of a nation—I cannot pause to inquire. But there is some quality, some significance, some value in these great individuals which the world will not willingly let die.

That is enough. These souls whom the general human soul can hardly be said to have understood, have yet been revered by it. And of these souls whom it reveres, it most reveres those who have uttered themselves through the written word. After all, it may be said, the others have left nothing of themselves behind: there is nothing of them to be remembered. It is the poets, and the poets alone—and let me say now that I use this word poet of the truly creative writer in whatever form—who have built for themselves monuments more durable than brass. That is the simple explanation; and yet I wonder whether it is the true one, or one that is wholly true. Perhaps something more mysterious is at work, and the old conception of the *vates sacer*, the sacred poet, touches it more nearly than the fact of being bibliographically extant. Many things are written, few are remembered: and of those few fewer still are remembered passionately, as though to forget them were to die.

The history of the souls of those men whose writings are thus passionately remembered is to me, by the very fact of that passionate remembrance, not indeed the outward and visible but the inward and spiritual history of the human soul. For these are the men who have uttered a truth so mysterious that it cannot be wrenched apart from the words in which they uttered it; it cannot be made current or passed from lips to lips save in that living flesh of speech with which they clothed it. Not this abstraction nor that commonplace can contain their wisdom; it is what it is and cannot be translated. Through their words men have touched what they do not understand, yet cannot forgo. Shall we take our courage in our hands and say mysteriously that they have touched their own souls? There is nothing men understand less than their own souls, or more passionately desire to remember.

For, after all, it is with something which is not their minds or their bodies that men respond to the words of the great poet. It is from some secret depths that the strangest and most fundamental judgement comes. 'This is beautiful;' yes, at a pinch we may conceive that it is the mind that tells us this. 'This is valuable;'—again it may be the mind. But 'This is *true*'—of something the like of which we have never seen or known—the mind never said that. Great poetry is the utterance of that to which the human soul responds, of that which the human soul endorses. So that the history of the souls of the great poets is the most essential history of the human soul itself.

There is no logic in that conclusion, for it assumes that the true poet utters his own soul. That to me is a simple and fundamental fact, though it is tacitly denied by half the criticism that is written. I assert it unequivocally. Without this fundamental belief literature would be meaningless and monstrous to me, an irrelevant and futile thing. To know a work of literature is to know the soul of the man who created it, and who created it in order that his soul should be known. Knowledge of a work of literature which stops short of that may be a profound, an inspiring, a bewildering knowledge, but it is not the real knowledge. The writer's soul is that which moves our souls. That is the truth which, in my belief, must be accepted; when that is accepted we can advance towards some understanding of the mystery why the words of the poet are his soul, and why the greater the poet the more completely are his words his soul.

It was not strange, therefore, that one who conceived the history of the human soul since the Renaissance in these peculiar terms, and found the secret vicissitudes and victories of the general soul writ large (or writ exceeding small) in the souls of the great poets, should have come to conceive of the soul of the greatest of these poets as prophetic of all that history. Yet, I confess, it took me a long while to come to that conclusion. Shakespeare was, for many years, far too big for me to comprehend. That movement of the soul from the rejection of religion to the rediscovery of religion, which I found so plainly marked in the greatest of his successors, was in him but fitfully revealed. In Shakespeare I was lost; and I had wandered in his works as in a great and trackless forest for many years before I became possessed with the conviction that he also had gone the same way as his successors, but that he had gone further than they. He was the greatest adventurer of all; his was the greatest soul; his path the most dizzy and mysterious; he was himself verily 'the prophetic soul of the wide world dreaming of things to come.'

Filled with this conviction, when the invitation came to me to deliver the lectures upon which this book is based, I welcomed the opportunity of giving in them a first rough sketch of the development of Shakespeare as I had come to conceive it; and I set to work gaily and confidently. I wrote an introductory lecture on the large and general movement of the human soul since the Renaissance, and announced my purpose of following it out in detail in the work of Shakespeare. But when I began upon this part of the work I found myself faced with an unexpected and insuperable difficulty. I suddenly realized that in my study of Shakespeare I had come to take for granted all manner of conceptions which I could not possibly expect an unprepared audience, however sympathetic and generous, to take for granted; I had gradually grown accustomed to a kind of thinking which is not the ordinary kind of thinking at all; I had formed the habit first of making certain translations between poetic thought and rational thought, and then of discarding these translations altogether; I had come to assume a whole system of correspondences between purely poetic imagery and the steps of discursive thinking—correspondences, I insist, and not equivalences—which I could not reasonably require other minds to assume without a demonstration which to be convincing must not be incidental. Above all, by my study of Shakespeare, I had slowly and only half-consciously formed convictions as to the nature of the human soul and the human universe, which are different from the opinions generally held to-day.

I saw that my one chance of making intelligible these slowly formed convictions of mine concerning Shakespeare was to use the greatest of his successors, John Keats, as though he were a mediator between the normal consciousness of men and the pure poetic consciousness in which form alone Shakespeare remains to us. There was, to my own sense, nothing in the least arbitrary in this method. I myself had made my final approach to Shakespeare through Keats; I had long since formed my own conclusions with regard to Keats, in some ways novel enough, but which, in so far as they could be expressed by saying that Keats was potentially, at least, our next greatest poet after Shakespeare and the only poet who is *like* Shakespeare, had the support of Matthew Arnold's great authority.

That Keats 'is with Shakespeare' is an assertion which means to me something different from what it meant to Matthew Arnold, because Shakespeare himself means something different. But the admission of a similarity by a great critic whose methods are other than mine was important to me. It confirmed me in the belief that Keats was indeed the natural approach to Shakespeare. Accordingly I once more concentrated upon a study of Keats: I carefully re-read the whole of Keats—letters and poems together—in chronological order, and I found, at once to my excitement and dismay, that my old conclusions with regard to Keats, though substantially true (in my own view, of course) were woefully crude and inadequate. It was as though in years past I had apprehended only the skeleton and not the living man. I could scarcely believe my own eyes when I found the most essential clues unmarked by my pencil in the little five-volume edition of Buxton Forman which I have always used. What evidence I had missed! What obscurities I had suffered to remain obscure, whereas now they seemed to me clear as day! That was the excitement; but the dismay was equal. It was utterly impossible to expound Keats in one or two chapters as I had hoped. It was out of the question to make use of Keats merely as an approach to Shakespeare. In order that he could serve as an approach to Shakespeare, he had to be understood completely in and for himself. He also was complete, he also was a 'pure poet' of the highest order. I must put Shakespeare out of my mind and devote myself to Keats alone.

Accordingly I began upon the new task, and this time I pushed on, as well as I could, to the end. I made it now my sole object to re-create the movement of Keats' soul during the brief years of his poetic life. Some may call it an imaginative reconstruction; if it is not also an imaginary one that will be to its advantage. I do not believe it is imaginary; I have based my narrative squarely on the facts. I have seldom had recourse to conjecture, or to what I should call conjecture. That the result of my examination is different from that arrived at by others is due, I should say, simply to my having approached the facts without any *parti pris.* I have not been influenced by any conception of an ideal Keats, and I have never taken it upon myself to say, for instance, that this mood is unworthy of Keats, or that judgement of his upon his own work untrue. In other words, I have tried to understand Keats as he was, not to fit him to some pattern of my own. In this attempt I have found myself continually forced to the conclusion that he meant what he said, where other critics have concluded that he meant something else; and above all I have found it impossible to accept the view that Keats' mind and powers were denatured by disease, or that the love-passion in which his later life was thrilled and disquieted was morbid or grotesque or humiliating. The more deeply I have read into Keats' life the more obvious it has been to me that Keats was a hero of humanity, and that an attitude of condescension or patronage towards him is utterly impossible. The thing that Keats actually was is infinitely more perfect than any perfection we can invent for him. The proper attitude of criticism towards Keats is one of complete humility.

As invariably happens, when I came to work on the actual material of his life and work, I found that certain threads, of which my conscious mind had been ignorant, began to show themselves clearly in the pattern that was shaping itself. One of these was so remarkable that I was rather frightened than rejoiced by it. I had, as I have said, approached Keats because he was essentially like Shakespeare, because in the ordinary sense of the phrase we know far more *about* Keats than we do about Shakespeare, and because I felt that an understanding of Keats would serve as a natural stepping-stone to to a comprehension of Shakespeare; and, as I have said, I found that the reality of Keats was so absorbing and complete that it demanded to be treated as an end in itself and not as a means. I put Shakespeare out of my mind, and concentrated whatever powers of understanding I possess upon Keats alone.

What was my amazement when I discovered that Keats himself was far more conscious than I had ever been of the strange relation between himself and Shakespeare! At all the crucial moments of his life his reference and appeal lay to Shakespeare, not to that inanimate Shakespeare which is the name given to a volume of printed words, but to a real presence, a living being whom Keats believed that he intimately understood, and who made demands upon Keats' loyalty from which in his moments of extreme agony he struggled in vain to escape. Shakespeare veritably was Keats' forerunner and secret-sharer not merely in literature, but in life. That opposition between literature and life is, in the case of pure poets such as Shakespeare and Keats, impossible finally to maintain, but I must use it now, as I use many other distinctions of which it is not the least object of this book to prove the ultimate unreality. So I will speak for the moment of Shakespeare the poet and Shakespeare the man, and say that the most intimate motion of Keats' inward life gradually revealed itself to me as a motion of loyalty to Shakespeare the man. What was to me astonishing was to find proof that Keats was conscious of it.

After all, I suppose there was nothing to be astonished about. If I was right in my view of Shakespeare, and right in my view of Keats as the only poet who was essentially like Shakespeare, then the intimate connection between them was of such a kind—Shakespeare the forerunner and Keats the spontaneous follower in the exploration of life—that it was not possible that Keats should have been unaware of it. That I think is true. But it is necessary to emphasize the epithet ' spontaneous ' in my description of Keats as a follower of Shakespeare. Indeed, it is not possible to follow Shakespeare otherwise than spontaneously, as perhaps I may succeed in showing. The basis of the likeness between Shakespeare and Keats lies in a similar completeness of humanity confronted with the same world of experience. They are as it were seeds of the same species growing in the same environment, except that one is forced into maturity by an excess of heat years before the other. But their similarity is really that of the same germ reacting to the same conditions. Shakespeare followed a predestined path ; so did Keats : and those paths are alike. There is no necessary reason why Keats should have been conscious of the similarity.

And yet, of course, there is a necessary reason. Man is conscious, and by virtue of his consciousness, he can leap the bank and shoal of time and hold converse with his similars though they have put off this mortality. It was indeed necessary that Keats should turn to Shakespeare, because there was no one else to whom he could turn. This is plain to me now; but when I began my narrative of Keats' life it was hidden from me. I was amazed when I found that in the critical moments of Keats' life his appeal to Shakespeare was inevitable. When preparing my material, I had copied out passage after passage of Keats' letters with no thought of anything but their bearing upon the hidden workings of Keats' soul : they marked the crises. When I came to read them through in isolation, there, manifest to my eyes, was the golden thread—Shakespeare, Shakespeare, Shakespeare.

I lay stress, even though it be to my own detriment as a critic, upon my unconsciousness of this more intimate relation between Keats and Shakespeare; because it may be thought (from the title of the book) that, having the notion that there was some intimate relation between Keats and Shakespeare other than the purely *poetic* likeness between them, I set about to collect the evidence for it. That is not so; and that is why I have found it necessary to tell the story of the genesis of this book. Originally it was to have been a first sketch of the development of Shakespeare himself: I found it impossible to approach him directly; so I instinctively turned to Keats to bridge the gap between the normal consciousness and the pure, unmediated poetic consciousness of Shakespeare. I found that Keats would not suffer himself to be treated as a means and not as an end: so I confined myself to the study of Keats alone. I continued to conceive the book under the title 'Keats and Shakespeare' simply because I still regarded, and do still regard, this study of Keats primarily as a sort of prolegomena to the study of Shakespeare, in the sense that I believe that a right understanding of Keats is the easiest, and perhaps the only possible, way to a right understanding of Shakespeare.

That it should have turned out that this title 'Keats and Shakespeare' is applicable to these lectures in quite another sense than that which I first intended is not due to me. That is simply the reality asserting itself through the medium of my interpretation. I went out to reveal a relation of one kind between Keats and Shakespeare; Keats himself has revealed, through me, a relation of another kind. That the relation which I had discerned between them demands for its own completeness the relation which I had not discerned has since become clear to me; it has not only strengthened my conviction that I am right in my view of Shakespeare, but it has enabled me to make my grasp of my own view more complete. Through Keats the poet I penetrated more deeply into Shakespeare the poet; and now through Keats the man I have (in my own belief) penetrated more deeply into Shakespeare the man.

I had finished my reconstruction of Keats' life when I was compelled to make a journey to the British Museum for the purpose of confirming certain conjectures made in the course of it. I took advantage of the opportunity to search out what the most eminent of my predecessors had written concerning Keats. It may be said that I should have done this before. That is a matter of opinion: I think it best in criticism to make one's approach to an author as direct as possible. I have read, because I happened to possess, Sir Sidney Colvin's *Life of John Keats*, Professor de Selincourt's edition of his poems, and above all the little Buxton Forman five-volume edition of Keats' Poems and Letters. I hope that I shall not be accused of lacking in courtesy either to Sir Sidney Colvin or to Professor de Selincourt if I say that my chief debt is to the late Mr. Buxton Forman. He arranged the material for any and every one to use. I am not conscious of owing a debt to anyone in the prime matter of interpretation and reconstruction.

But when I came to read my eminent predecessors in *criticism* of Keats it appeared to me that two among them towered high above all others—Dr. Bridges, the Poet Laureate, and Professor A. C. Bradley. Had the scope of this book been other than it is, I am sure that I should have been deeply indebted to them. The Poet Laureate's essay on Keats' poetry (which is, alas, very difficult to procure) and Professor Bradley's lecture on Keats' letters and his little essay on what 'Philosophy' meant for Keats are masterly. For what may be called in the highest sense a 'technical' criticism of Keats' poetry and diction, Dr. Bridges' essay will hardly be surpassed: while it seems only an accident that Professor Bradley did not treat of Keats' letters and poetry together as a kind of preamble to his famous lectures on Shakespeare—in which case, I fear, the best part of my present occupation would be gone. Time and again in his lecture and his essay, Professor Bradley seems to me on the brink of formulating the view and the doctrine I have been driven to expound in this book. Time and again he marshals the evidence, in his masterly fashion, so that the conclusion to which I have been forced appears inevitable: yet for some reason he does not draw it. Perhaps, by reason of his instinctive avoidance of that conclusion, his criticism remains on the safe side of the river of oblivion, whereas mine, by reason of my acceptance of that conclusion, has taken the fatal plunge. I hope it will not prove to be so: but I am conscious of having taken a risk.

But what I wish to emphasize at this moment are the more comfortable conclusions I derived from my reading of what the Poet Laureate and Professor Bradley have written about Keats. These two finely critical minds—in their separate provinces the finest critical minds we have in England to-day—approach Keats' work under two separate aspects. Dr. Bridges considers his poetry in itself, Professor Bradley considers his letters in themselves. Yet both alike declare their conviction of an essential similarity between Keats and Shakespeare—not casually or incidentally, but deliberately, as an article *stantis aut cadentis philosophiæ*. At the end of his essay the Poet Laureate, after specific and detailed criticism of the separate poems, thus continues:

> Many of the main qualities of Keats' poetry have been incidentally brought out; there is one, as yet unmentioned, which

> claims the first place in a general description, and that is the very seal of his poetic birthright, the highest gift of all in poetry, that which sets poetry above the other arts: I mean the power of concentrating all the far-reaching resources of language on one point, so that a single and apparently effortless expression rejoices the æsthetic imagination at the moment when it is most expectant and exacting and at the same time astonishes the intellect with a new aspect of the truth. This is only found in the greatest poets, and is rare in them ; and it is no doubt for the possession of this power that Keats has often been likened to Shakespeare, and very justly, for Shakespeare is of all poets the greatest master of it; the difference between them here is that Keats' intellect does not supply the second factor in the proportion or degree that Shakespeare does: indeed, it is chiefly when he is dealing with material or sensuous objects that his poems afford illustrations; but these are, as far as they go, not only like Shakespeare, but often as good as Shakespeare when he happens to be confining himself to the same limited field.

For my own part, I subscribe to that final limitation with reluctance, though I know that it is inevitable, considering the amount of Keats' poetry and his length of years compared with Shakespeare's. But what is more important is to insist on the real scope of Dr. Bridges's mature and deliberate judgement. Keats' poetry, he says, has the chief excellence of all, an excellence which sets poetry above all the other arts, a quality which is found only in the greatest poets, and is rare even in them; of this quality Shakespeare is of all poets the greatest master. A declaration of an essential likeness between Shakespeare and Keats could hardly be more categorical, above all when we remember that Dr. Bridges's comparison is deliberately restricted to their poetry alone, considered as an independent object of æsthetic analysis, not as the expression of a mind.

On the other hand, in the different but complementary province of Keats' letters considered as the expression of a mind, Professor Bradley, whose familiarity with Shakespeare's mind will not be doubted by any reader of his lectures on Shakespeare, is no less emphatic. ' Keats,' he says, ' was of Shakespeare's tribe. . . . . In quality—and I speak of nothing else—the mind of Shakespeare at three-and-twenty may not have been very different.' The Shakespearean reference is, indeed, the continual undertone of Professor Bradley's lecture on Keats' letters. It is by reason of his essential likeness to Shakespeare that ' while Keats' mind had much general power, he was, more than Wordsworth or Coleridge or Shelley, a poet pure and simple.' And again in regard to Keats' light-hearted and flippant comment on *La Belle Dame sans Merci* (which has the incidental importance of showing that Keats did not make quite so much of this lovely poem as certain enthusiastic Pre-Raphaelites did*), Professor Bradley says: 'This is not very like the comment of Wordsworth on his best poems, but I daresay the author of *Hamlet* made such jests about it.' Indeed, I do not think it would be in any way straining the actual sense or the underlying intention of Professor Bradley's essay to say that he is inclined even in the details of temperament to see a fundamental likeness between the man Keats we actually know and the man Shakespeare whom we conjecture.

This independent corroboration of the æsthetic and ethical judgement, from which this book takes its origin, by the two modern critics for whom I have the deepest regard, is naturally precious to me, the more precious because I was ignorant of it; and it may be profitable to consider for a moment what points there are in common between the Poet Laureate and Professor Bradley. First, in the general award, they are at one with Matthew Arnold when he cries: 'He is: he is with Shakespeare'; but they are more specific than Arnold. Professor Bradley declares that 'Keats, though his mind had much general power,* was, more than Wordsworth or Shelley or Coleridge, a poet pure and simple.' 'A poet pure and simple'—it is almost a double-edged phrase; but Professor Bradley's meaning is single: he means that Keats is a poet pure and simple, as Shakespeare is a poet pure and simple. His poetic gift has little or no admixture of non-poetic elements. And it is precisely in this question of 'pure poetry' that the Poet Laureate is most illuminating, for he claims for Keats the supreme and quintessential poetic gift, and he has the courage to define it. It is 'the power of concentrating all the far-reaching resources of language on one point, so that a single and apparently effortless expression rejoices the æsthetic imagination at the moment when it is most expectant and exacting, and at the same time astonishes the intellect with a new aspect of truth.' That seems to me in itself as fine a definition of pure poetry as any critic has ever given. I am, however, immediately struck with its fidelity to Keats' own dictum at the close of the Ode on a Grecian Urn:

> Beauty is truth, truth beauty—that is all
> Ye know on earth and all ye need to know.

No doubt the echo was unconscious—after all, there can be only one truth in such a matter—but it is at least curious that we should find the Poet Laureate in his definition expanding Keats' own central thought: 'What the imagination seizes as beauty must be truth,' in order to define that supreme quality of 'pure poetry' which Keats possessed in common with Shakespeare.

If, then, we combine the declarations of Dr. Bridges and Professor Bradley something of this kind will emerge. Keats and Shakespeare are alike, because they are both pure poets, and pure poetry consists in the power so to express a perception that it appears at the same time to reveal a new aspect of beauty and a new aspect of truth. Though I claim no finality for the phrasing of that definition, it may suffice for the moment to indicate the scope and aim of the remainder of this book. Essentially it is an attempt to examine the nature of *pure poetry*, to discover what it is, what is its significance, from what kind of human being it is produced, and, as far as possible, the causes which make that kind of human being what he is. Of course, there is a limit to the possibilities of such an inquiry. We cannot search out the means by which the pure poet actually obtains his command over language, much less can we elucidate the causes why he is endowed with a certain gift of ' more than ordinary organic sensibility ' at birth. All that one can hope to have done is to have illuminated some of the inward processes of the pure poet, and by this means to have proved at least one thing, that the pure poet is the highest of all poets, not because he turns his face away from life to devote himself to some abstract and ideal perfection, but precisely because he, more than any other kind of poet, submits himself steadily, persistently and unflinchingly to life. He, more than any other poet, has the capacity to see and to feel what life is. Because of this, the pure poet is the complete man. That, more than any other single thing, is what I hope to have proved in this book.

' The complete man ' is a vague phrase. I hope that by the end of this book a real, if not a definable, significance will have been poured into it, and that I shall have been able to show that the pure poet deserves the name of ' the complete man ' in a special and peculiar sense, that the name belongs really to him pre-eminently among men. Just as I believe that there is a final *human* truth which men can attain, and that the pure poet expresses this truth; so also I believe that there is an actual human completeness which men can attain, and that the pure poet attains this completeness more fully than others. I hope to have shown in what that completeness consists, and why the pure poet is recompensed for his exceeding suffering by the exceeding great reward of achieving this completeness to the uttermost.

These things, and other things closely knit with them, I hope to have shown in the actual case of Keats. If I have been successful, it will not be because they have been demonstrated in the sense of a logical demonstration. Many of these things are, in the exact meaning of the word, mysteries: that is to say, they can be shown, but they cannot be demonstrated. I have the sense of being a pioneer in an unknown country, of having embarked on a voyage of exploration without a map to guide me; I have no conviction that the road I have taken is either the easiest or the best; and I have sometimes had difficulty in clearing a trail at all. Such weaknesses and defects cannot but be obvious. I ask the reader not to bear too hardly upon them, but to remember that I am struggling to express conceptions which I do not fully possess—that, as Keats himself said in a letter which will occupy us deeply, concerning this very mystery with which I am engaged: 'I can scarcely express what I but dimly perceive—and yet I think I perceive it': and I ask this above all of my reader that he will not allow his logical mind to obstruct his more immediate understanding, because the things I am trying to investigate—the nature of pure poetry and the character of the pure poet—are not rational at all.

Finally, though it proved to be utterly impossible to deal with Shakespeare as I planned, the reference to Shakespeare is implicit in every page that I have written. Whatever I may have been able to show to be true in the case of Keats—I speak of movements of the soul, more than of external circumstances—I believe to be true of Shakespeare also. I cannot ask that that statement should be accepted on my bare word at this moment. But if I shall in the end have persuaded the reader that what is said of Keats is substantially true, then perhaps my bare word will have acquired a validity which it does not now possess. It was through an understanding of Keats that I came to understand what I call the reality of Shakespeare; but it was through my understanding of Shakespeare that I came to understand the full reality of Keats. These realities, of course, are simply realities for me: whether they are realities for others the event alone will show. But if I succeed in convincing others in the case of Keats, then there will be, in my own mind at least, no doubt that I should have been able—had I had the opportunity—to convince them also in the case of Shakespeare. That is the reason why, although my original plan has gone by the board, I cling to my original title: 'Keats and Shakespeare.' This book is, in my own mind, still nothing more than an 'Introduction to a Study of Shakespeare.'

CHAPTER II

THE FIRST YEAR: 'SLEEP AND POETRY'

THE whole poetic story of Keats is contained in four years. He died on 23rd February 1821; his fatal hæmorrhage, after which he wrote practically no poetry, occurred in February 1820. Four years before that time he was a medical student in the Borough, who had but just begun to write verses—or perhaps more truly—but just begun to feel himself devoured by the ambition to become a poet. Those four years are the most prodigious four years in the life of genius of which we have record. No one, as far as I know, in any nation or at any time, has travelled so far along the steep road of poetic achievement in such a space of years: certainly no one in England. In four years to have achieved, with no advantages of education and against the dead-weight of a Cockney tradition, the opulent perfection of language, the living depth of poetical thought which is in *Hyperion* and the *Eve of St. Agnes* and the great *Odes*! It is a miracle.

Yet this miracle happened, and we have a record of the process. It appears to us as a quite natural miracle. The more closely we examine it, the less of a problem it presents, except in so far as the creation of every true work of art is an eternal problem. But the mere fact of this natural miracle must be emphasized, for a whole mushroom growth of literature has arisen out of the impossibility for certain minds of admitting a smaller miracle of the same kind for Shakespeare. How (it is asked) could a grammar-school boy from the country, without contact with the university, without experience of the refinements of civilization, have written Shakespeare's plays? The sole and sufficient answer to such a question is that Shakespeare managed to do what he did precisely as Keats managed to do what he did, and that Keats managed to do far more in his four years than Shakespeare managed to do in the same space. Shakespeare could take his time: Keats had the vague foreboding of death unconsciously driving him to pack hours into minutes and years into months. Shakespeare had thirty years, where Keats had four.

At the beginning of his four years in 1816, Keats had written a handful of raw sonnets, from which I doubt whether the most perceptive of critics could have deduced even a moderate harvest to come; and he had written one longer piece—*The Epistle to George Felton Matthew*—which might have given our imaginary critic pause. There is something about it—a blend of fluency and enthusiasm—which might conceivably have impressed him. There is a melody in the rippling movement of the verse: with all its faults of taste and weakness of rhyme, the piece comes naturally. Knowing the after-event, we think of Keats' own words: Poetry must come 'as naturally as the leaves to a tree.' Whether I, or any other of my tribe, would have had the confidence and goodwill to ignore the faults and recognize the quality of effortlessness in thought and diction I cannot say. Probably not. But the quality is there. The thought is the ordinary romantic thought that the cares of the practical world are fetters to hamper men from ascending into the true poetic heaven. In order to hold communion with the true spirit of poetry, Keats declares he must be in

> Some flowery spot, sequester'd, wild, romantic,
> That often must have seen a poet frantic.

There he and his companions would

> Sit, and rhyme and think on Chatterton;
> And that warm-hearted Shakespeare sent to meet him
> Four laurell'd spirits, heavenward to entreat him.
> With reverence would we speak of all the sages
> Who have left streaks of light athwart their ages:
> And thou shouldst moralize on Milton's blindness,
> And mourn the fearful dearth of human kindness
> To those who strove with the bright golden wing
> Of genius, to flap away each sting
> Thrown by the pitiless world. We next could tell
> Of those who in the cause of freedom fell;
> Of our own Alfred, of Helvetian Tell;
> Of him whose name to ev'ry heart's a solace,
> High-minded and unbending William Wallace.
> While to the rugged north our musing turns
> We well might drop a tear for him, and Burns.

That is, I think, a fair example of Keats' poetry at the beginning of the four years—crude and naïve, but spontaneous in feeling and unashamed in phrase, a confession of generous enthusiasm in thought and act, for the poem itself is an act of enthusiasm.

It was written in November 1815, when Keats was just twenty. Within a year from that time he had written the immortal sonnet: *On first looking into Chapman's Homer*. That sonnet was prophetic: it was far in advance of the rest of his work at the moment—secure and masterly throughout, where his other poems were secure and masterly in parts only. But the sonnet itself is a monument more enduring than brass to the excited and thrilling turmoil of his mind during the year in which he entered a circle of men whose interests and enthusiasms, if not their powers, were of the same order as his own. He had, as far as a man of supreme genius can do so in the actual world, come into his own country and among his own friends; he had entered into the companionship of men who were, in the main, moved by the same consuming and unselfish ambition which he felt, to seek out great literature and add to its treasures—to live in great company and be themselves worthy of it.

How many times must Keats have trod on air as he returned from Leigh Hunt's cottage in Hampstead to his lodgings in the Borough or in Cheapside! How deeply he must have thrilled to the sense that he had entered into his birthright! It is difficult for those who have been born into the atmosphere of a liberal education and nurtured at a university to realize precisely what those nightly meetings at Leigh Hunt's cottage meant to Keats. It was as though he had been taken up into a mountain like Moses and looked upon the riches of a promised land—the realms of gold, indeed—and even those who have had the rapture of a like experience, have not possessed what Keats possessed, the secret knowledge that in this golden kingdom he was not a sojourner only, but one of the blood-royal. No wonder then that he was in a fever of noble emulation; no wonder that one night when he came away early from Hunt's he should have written this:

> Give me a golden pen, and let me lean
> On heap'd up flowers, in regions clear, and far;
> Bring me a tablet whiter than a star,
> Or hand of hymning angel, when 'tis seen
> The silver strings of heavenly harp atween:
> And let there glide by many a pearly car,
> Pink robes, and wavy hair, and diamond jar,*
> And half-discovered wings, and glances keen.
> The while let music wander round my ears
> And as it reaches each delicious ending,
> Let me write down a line of glorious tone,
> And full of many wonders of the spheres:
> For what a height my spirit is contending!
> 'Tis not content so soon to be alone.

That is the very ecstasy of youthful power. The voice trembles a little; it is not yet self-controlled and serene: but how splendid is the utterance! To what should we naturally compare it, but to the early music of Shakespeare? Shakespeare also, when he came from remote and placid Stratford to the fervid life of London, must have felt the same thrill of entering his own kingdom and the same dawning consciousness of power.

Through all the poetry of Keats' first volume, poetry for the most part written at the age of twenty-one, we feel this tremulous expectancy, this half-fledged confidence, this boyish enthusiasm. Great things are being done, and he is privileged to have a hand in them. 'Great spirits now on earth are sojourning,' and he has the fortune to be joined to their company.

> Great spirits now on earth are sojourning;
> He of the cloud, the cataract, the lake,
> Who on Helvellyn's summit, wide awake,
> Catches his freshness from Archangel's wing:
> He of the rose, the violet, the spring,
> The social smile, the chain for Freedom's sake:
> And lo !—whose steadfastness would never take
> A meaner sound than Raphael's whispering.
> And other spirits there are standing apart
> Upon the forehead of the age to come;
> These, these will give the world another heart,
> And other pulses. Hear ye not the hum
> Of mighty workings ?—
> Listen awhile, ye nations, and be dumb.

It is impossible not to feel the consciousness of election, and the voice of power in that poem—the more clearly because it is the unselfish proclamation of the genius of others. But how proclaimed ?

> And other spirits there are standing apart
> Upon the forehead of the age to come.

It is the very voice of Shakespeare, compelling language to serve one knows not what spirit of beauty and of truth. What does it matter that of these three 'great spirits' only Wordsworth has been accepted by the after-times as truly great ? Haydon the painter is remembered chiefly for the contrast between his own bombastic achievement and the profound impression he made upon his friends and contemporaries. A man whom the mature Wordsworth and the wise Lamb believed to be of commanding genius could not conceivably have been less to Keats at twenty-one. And as for Leigh Hunt, if he was not great, he has suffered a great injustice in being set so far beneath the level of greatness as he has been: Hunt was a man of great gifts who, when men's vision has cleared a little more, will be seen not only as one of the bravest and most generous men who have suffered for the popular cause, but as one of the most natural critics of poetry England has ever possessed. He had an intuitive understanding of the essence of poetry, of the order and nature of poetic creation, not inferior to that of Coleridge. That he was himself but a second-rate poet, and that in some respects his influence on Keats at this moment may have been harmful, need not be denied. But these things are nothing compared with the fact that more than any other single man Hunt encouraged Keats in his beginnings, and defended and justified him when he was dead.* The dedicatory sonnet to Keats' 1817 volume was a tribute to Hunt that was his due: it was also an exactly fitting acknowledgment, for if it was largely through Hunt that Keats surrendered to the sentimental weakness of the ending, it was largely through Hunt also that he had come so quickly to command the lovely music of its opening lines.

> Glory and loveliness have passed away;
>   For if we wander out in early morn,
>   No wreathed incense do we see upborne
> Into the east, to meet the smiling day:
> No cloud of nymphs soft voic'd and young, and gay,
>   In woven baskets bringing ears of corn,
>   Roses, and pinks, and violets, to adorn
> The shrine of Flora in her early May.
> But there are left delights as high as these,
>   And I shall ever bless my destiny
> That in a time, when under pleasant trees
>   Pan is no longer sought, I feel a free,
> A leafy luxury, seeing I could please
>   With these poor offerings, a man like thee.

'Glory and loveliness have passed away'; 'Great spirits now on earth are sojourning.' These two lines, apparently contradictory, mark the range of Keats' thought during the first tumultuous year of his entry into his poetic birthright. They are not contradictory: the great spirits were great in Keats' eyes because he believed they were bent with all the force of genius to the task of restoring glory and loveliness to the earth. They were vindicating man's freedom to perceive and to create beauty against the orthodoxy and dogmatism that had chilled a century.

In the closing months of this first year Keats wrote two longer poems which more fully reveal this dominant thought. *I stood tip-toe upon a little hill* opens with a beautiful and living description of an early summer's day. Enraptured by it, his mind is filled with pleasant visions of still more beauties of nature, flowers and streams, woodbine and marigolds and minnows, each in his particular and all together calling to the poet to sing them. For the poet is their brother, fellow-child with them of that Nature whom Keats at once invokes:

> O Maker of sweet poets, dear delight
> Of this fair world, and all its gentle livers;
> Spangler of clouds, halo of crystal rivers,

Mingler with leaves, and dew and tumbling streams,
Closer of lovely eyes to lovely dreams,
Lover of loneliness, and wandering,
Of upcast eye, and tender pondering!
  Thee must I praise above all other glories
That smile us on to tell delightful stories.
For what has made the sage or poet write
But that fair paradise of Nature's light?

That is the burden of the poem in all its meanderings. Nature is the perennial source of poetry: all the tales that have enchanted men, tales of Psyche and Narcissus and Endymion, have sprung from the poet's ecstasy of delight in nature.

In *Sleep and Poetry* the thought is developed. Poetry, which is even higher than the great gift of sleep, is the natural song of rejoicing which springs from the heart in response to Nature.

No one who once the glorious sun has seen,
And all the clouds, and felt his bosom clean
For his great Maker's presence, but must know
What 'tis I mean, and feel his being glow.

Nevertheless, as the next invocation shows, Poetry is something more than this to Keats: it is a power, a potency which exists in its own right, and of itself will bring to him 'the fair visions of all places,' and inspire him to set down all beauties seen or remembered or imagined; it will carry him even beyond this:

Then the events of this wide world I'd seize
Like a strong giant, and my spirit teaze
Till at its shoulders it should proudly see
Wings to find out an immortality.

It is hard in a sense to follow Keats' thought, not only because his mind is filled to overflowing, but more because his thought now and henceforward is not of a kind that can be paraphrased. It is, with all its crudities and imperfections, essentially poetic thought, a comprehension by and through the concrete and particular, of which a magnificent and famous example follows immediately in the sudden balancing of one vision of life against another:

Stop and consider! life is but a day;
A fragile dewdrop on its perilous way
From a tree's summit; a poor Indian's sleep
While his boat hastens to the monstrous steep
Of Montmorenci. Why so sad a moan?

Life is the rose's hope while yet unblown;
The reading of an ever-changing tale;
The light uplifting of a maiden's veil;
A pigeon tumbling in clear summer air;
A laughing schoolboy, without grief or care,
Riding the springy branches of an elm.

Put that into the prose of ordinary thought and it means: 'I may not have time—yes, I may.' And that is the bald connection between these lines and the next:

O for ten years, that I may overwhelm
Myself in poesy; so I may do the deed
That my own soul has to itself decreed.

Concerning the nature of this self-decree, Keats is for a second time more explicit. 'First the realm I'll pass of Flora and old Pan.' But into that realm he straightway plunges: he has not been for more than a line a rational mind plotting out the future, he is actually become a denizen of the realm. But at last he drags himself back with the question:

And can I ever bid these joys farewell?

And he replies:

Yes, I must pass them for a nobler life,
Where I may find the agonies, the strife
Of human hearts.

He will put away from himself the romantic indulgence of fancy in visions of a golden age, for the contemplation of human life as it is. And this explicit thought is instantly transmuted into a vision of a splendid chariot and a mighty charioteer:

Most awfully intent
The driver of those steeds is forward bent
And seems to listen. . . .

It is a symbolic vision of Poetry itself, and a vague premonition of some mysterious knowledge which Poetry attains. But the vision fades.

A sense of real things comes doubly strong,
And, like a muddy stream, would bear along
My soul to nothingness: but I will strive
Against all doubtings, and will keep alive
The thought of that same chariot, and the strange
Journey it went.

Then he breaks out into the splendid apostrophe :

> Is there so small a range
> In the present strength of manhood, that the high
> Imagination cannot freely fly
> As she was wont of old ? prepare her steeds,
> Paw up against the light, and do strange deeds
> Upon the clouds ? Has she not shown us all ?
> From the clear space of ether, to the small
> Breath of new buds unfolding ?

It is confused, perhaps, but we do understand it, and it thrills us. By the free and sovereign working of the poetic mind, through imagination, all can be known and revealed: all has been known and revealed—' e'en in this isle ' of England.

But England has been renegade to its great tradition :

> Ah dismal-soul'd !
> The winds of heaven blew, the ocean roll'd
> Its gathering waves—ye felt it not. The blue
> Bared its eternal bosom, and the dew
> Of summer nights collected still to make
> The morning precious : beauty was awake !
> Why were ye not awake ? But ye were dead
> To things ye knew not of,—were closely wed
> To musty laws lined out with wretched rule
> And compass vile: so that ye taught a school
> Of dolts to smooth, inlay, and clip, and fit,
> Till, like the certain wands of Jacob's wit,
> Their verses tallied. Easy was the task:
> A thousand handicraftsmen wore the mask
> Of Poesy. Ill-fated, impious race !
> That blasphemed the bright Lyrist to his face,
> And did not know it,—no, they went about,
> Holding a poor, decrepid standard out
> Mark'd with most flimsy mottos, and in large
> The name of one Boileau !

But the time of dearth is over. ' Fine sounds are floating wild about the earth.' Wordsworth and Coleridge have slain the dragon and snapped the chains which bound the maiden Poetry to the rock.

Nevertheless, Keats is not satisfied. There follow a few lines which have puzzled the editors. Certainly they are not very good poetry, but the thought in them is of some importance. ' These things,' says Keats—meaning the return of true poetry to England —' are doubtless.'

> Yet in truth we've had
> Strange thunders from the potency of song;
> Mingled indeed with what is sweet and strong,
> From majesty: but in clear truth the themes
> Are ugly clubs, the Poets Polyphemes
> Disturbing the grand sea. A drainless shower
> Of light is poesy: 'tis the supreme of power;
> 'Tis might half-slumbering on its own right arm. . . .

Whether the particular reference is to Byron (or, as I think, to Byron and Wordsworth together) the thought of this passage, which has been a stumbling-block to some, is both clear and important. 'Themes'—that is didactic and dogmatic thought—muddy the clear truth of poetry, which is marked by an effortless majesty and an unobtrusive magnificence. Keats goes on to say—and here the reference is probably to Byron alone—that 'Strength alone, though of the Muses born, Is like a fallen angel.' Pure poetry rejects both the assertion of thought and the self-assertion of strength. That is to say, it does not assert, it reveals; it does not bludgeon, it persuades. Keats' perception of the true nature of poetry is rather obscurely expressed; but its substance is unmistakable when it is illuminated by two passages from his later letters. The first is one to Reynolds, in which he criticizes Wordsworth:

> For the sake of a few fine imaginative or domestic passages are we (he asks) to be bullied into a certain Philosophy engendered in the whims of an Egotist? Every man has his speculations, but every man does not brood and peacock over them till he makes a false coinage and deceives himself. Many a man can travel to the very bourne of Heaven, and yet want confidence to put down his half-seeing. . . . We hate poetry that has a palpable design upon us, and, if we do not agree, seems to put its hand into its breeches pocket. Poetry should be great and unobtrusive, a thing which enters into one's soul, and does not startle or amaze it with itself, but with its subject. How beautiful are the retired flowers! how they would lose their beauty were they to throng into the highway, crying out, 'Admire me, I am a violet! Dote upon me, I am a primrose!' (*Letter of 3rd February* 1818.)

And the second is the famous 'axiom' concerning poetry which, at about the same time, he confided to Taylor, his friend and publisher:

> I think poetry should surprise by a fine excess, and not by singularity; it should strike the reader as a wording of his own highest thoughts, and appear almost a remembrance. (*Letter of 27th February* 1818.)

The germ of these maturer thoughts is in the passage of *Sleep and Poetry*, and by their aid we can sense the full implications of the lines with which the passage ends :

> the great end
> Of poesy, that it should be a friend
> To sooth the cares, and lift the thoughts of man.

Taken by itself, the sentiment seems almost pure Wordsworth. But the truth is that in this passage Keats is struggling with an intuition of the nature of poetry, which is wholly his own. He is at once denouncing Byron and dissociating himself with Wordsworth. He is striving to express his vision of poetry as a thing which is in the highest sense of the word *natural;* whose thought and strength are organic to itself, not superimposed or asserted.

This intuition of the nature of poetry is very difficult to apprehend or to express, because it is the most essential. Poetry is a thing-in-itself, unique, and the more truly it is poetry the less possible it is to assimilate the elements which compose it to the things which ordinarily bear the names of those elements. We speak, for instance, of thought in poetry; but if the poetry is pure and uncontaminated, the thought it contains is of a different *kind* from what is ordinarily called thought: it is a perception, not a cogitation, and in the finest kind of poetry it is a perception of the general in the particular. But there again, and quite inevitably, by dragging in these words 'general' and 'particular,' as we are forced to do, we are doing violence to the unique thing. We are, in spite of ourselves, assimilating poetic thought to ordinary thought. We cannot do otherwise: exposition in such a case is necessarily transposition, from one order of reality into another. How then can one convey the truth that poetic apprehension and comprehension are of a totally different kind from the processes we ordinarily understand by those names ? Yet this is a vital point, and unless we have some grasp of it, a real penetration of poetry is impossible; and we shall fall into the error of imagining that poetry which contains the greatest amount of explicit and recognizable thought is the profoundest poetry. It is an error which was propagated by the greatest critic England has had —Matthew Arnold. And he propagated it precisely because he *was* a great critic, because he was convinced that poetry was of the utmost importance to life, that it was, so to speak, a quintessence of human experience. In order to express that truth, he had to employ similitudes; he was forced into saying that poetry was 'a criticism of life.' So it is; but it is a *poetical* criticism of life, not a philosophical one. And Matthew Arnold himself could not maintain the fine but all-important distinction.

In the passage of *Sleep and Poetry*, on which we are trying to throw light, Keats is struggling with his own perception of the nature of poetry. But even so, he was not struggling as a critic must struggle. In *Sleep and Poetry* he was the natural and spontaneous poet, making instinctive use of the very process of perception whose ultimate goal he is trying to discern. He was not at that moment concerned, he was subsequently to be concerned in his letters, with the effort of translating this process of knowledge into terms of another and different process of knowledge; and in a single line he reveals more of the essential nature of poetry than a critic could do in many paragraphs. He says that poetry is

> Might half-slumb'ring on its own right arm.

That is a definition of poetry by poetry; it is the poetic faculty as it were momentarily self-conscious and declaring its own nature, as it must declare it, in an image or metaphor. It is obvious that such a definition has nothing in common with what is ordinarily understood by a definition, and that the process of thought by which it was reached is radically different from what is ordinarily understood by thinking. Yet it *is* a definition; it is a precise definition; and it is a truer definition than Keats' own when he tried to translate it into the words: 'I think poetry should surprise by a fine excess, and not by singularity; it should strike the reader as a wording of his own highest thoughts, and appear almost a remembrance.' Now, though it may at first sight seem a curious assertion, I should say that the whole of that definition, and more, is contained in the single line

> 'Tis might half-slumb'ring on its own right arm.

Strength, ease, majesty, naturalness, a softness as of sleep, a relaxation of all tensions, a passing-beyond all efforts, a sovereignty of instinctive comprehension—one could go on trying to capture all the manifold implications of that line for ever. Strictly for ever, to infinity like a mathematical series, because the order of thought in which we seek an approximation to it is a different order of thought from that in which it was conceived.

Nevertheless, in the passage of *Sleep and Poetry* in which this line occurs, Keats could not maintain himself on the height of his momentary intuition. He also fumbled after his own half-hidden meaning, like any critic, when he declared that poetry

> should be a friend
> To soothe the cares, and lift the thoughts of man.

We can interpret it; but it is in itself not poetry, but prose in verse: the process of thought is not poetic. Nor can we wonder. Here is a boy of twenty-one, but this moment uplifted into an awareness of his own powers, trying to grapple with their inmost secret. The wonder is that he saw so much, not that he could not see wholly and all the time.

After this effort he plunges, with ease and relief, into that ' realm of Flora and old Pan ' beyond which in his prophetic imagination he had already passed. It is a lovely passage of spontaneous melody and exquisite fancy. He conceives that the poetry to be written now—whether his own or Leigh Hunt's we cannot tell, and it does not matter—will be as such a realm to after-generations, and he longs that the time may come in his own life-time when

> they shall be accounted poet-kings
> Who simply tell the most heart-easing things.

In a sense he has descended from the height of his previous vision, because he could not maintain himself there. Though he already had glimpses of a poetic kingdom, clean beyond the realms of Flora and old Pan, and beyond Wordsworth's achievement, at this time the natural habitation of his mind was the kingdom of pure romantic beauty. He had yet to enter, to wander in, and at moments cut his way through the lovely wilderness of *Endymion*. But he already had more than a premonition of what lay beyond.

In the next lines of *Sleep and Poetry* he boldly proclaims his faith in his own prophetic vision. He imagines himself bidden beware of the thunderbolt for his previous presumption. If I hide myself from it, he replies, I shall hide in the secret shrine, the midmost light of Poetry. And he goes on:

> What though I am not wealthy in the dower
> Of spanning wisdom; though I do not know
> The shiftings of the mighty winds that blow
> Hither and thither all the changing thoughts
> Of man; though no great minist'ring reason sorts
> Out the dark mysteries of human souls
> To clear conceiving: yet there ever rolls
> A vast idea before me, and I glean
> Therefrom my liberty: thence too I've seen
> The end and aim of Poesy.

Could the challenge be more direct? Against the charge of presumption he vindicates himself by claiming that his essential knowledge is complete. There are many things he does not know and must know: but the vast idea which he has makes him free and gives him knowledge of the end and aim of poetry.

It is strange that a claim so staggering—Byron, in his anger at it, called Keats 'a tadpole of the Lakes'—a claim, moreover, made with a full consciousness of the charges to which it would lay him open, has not received more attention from the commentators on Keats' work. From the silence with which it is passed over, we may conclude that it is felt by them also to be a piece of bombastic presumption, which is to be deplored in private and hushed up in public. This is a mistake, just as it is a mistake to assimilate *Sleep and Poetry* too closely to *Tintern Abbey*. The poetic mind of Keats was of a higher order than Wordsworth's. It is true that there is a letter of Keats to Reynolds (which shall be quoted in its place) in which he discusses the development of his own mind in relation to Wordsworth's poem in a way that seems to give support to the attempt to read *Sleep and Poetry* as a boy's version of *Tintern Abbey*. But it can be shown that Keats' mind was moving at that time with a vigour and amplitude greater than Wordsworth's towards a goal beyond Wordsworth's. There is overwhelming evidence that Keats had seen Wordsworth's insufficiency as measured by his own perception of the nature of poetry months before he wrote the letter to Reynolds. Moreover, a careful reading of *Sleep and Poetry* itself by anyone who is able to distinguish between poetic and philosophic thought, will convince him that Keats' claim is not the presumption of 'whining boyhood,' but a deliberate assertion of a real knowledge. Keats meant what he said: that he truly had a 'vast idea' from which he derived a certainty of the end and aim of poetry. If others hesitate to admit this, I ask them simply to listen to what he says. It is plain to the understanding: he is not speaking the mysterious language of poetry now.

There ever rolls
A vast idea before me, and I glean
Therefrom my liberty; thence too I've seen
The end and aim of Poesy. 'Tis clear
As anything most true; as that the year
Is made of the four seasons—manifest
As a large cross, some old cathedral's crest,
Lifted to the white clouds. Therefore should I
Be but the essence of deformity,
A coward, did my very eye-lids wink
At speaking out what I have dared to think.
Ah! rather let me like a madman run
Over some precipice: let the hot sun
Melt my Dedalian wings, and drive me down
Convuls'd and headlong! Stay! an inward frown
Of conscience bids me be more calm awhile.
An ocean dim, sprinkled with many an isle,
Spreads awfully before me. How much toil!

How many days! what desperate turmoil!
Ere I can have explored its widenesses.
Ah, what a task! upon my bended knees
I could unsay those—no, impossible!
Impossible!

But once more he turns back: the burden of his own thought is too heavy for him.

For sweet relief I'll dwell
On humbler thoughts, and let this strange assay
Begun in gentleness die so away.

And so it does die away into a memory of his happiness at Hunt's cottage, a recollection of the pictures that hung there, and of the sleepless night that followed, crowded by thought after thought, and among them the strange thought of which *Sleep and Poetry* is the record and the witness.

The integrity of soul manifested in Keats' work and life and letters is such that we should be compelled to take him at his word, even if *Sleep and Poetry* did not contain flashes of pure poetic thought at its maximum intensity. But these are the proof positive of his own claim. We have to believe his own assertion implicitly. He verily had the vast idea, the freedom, and the knowledge: he had the intention and the vision. He was now to conquer the achievement and the expression. The first year of his fated four is now at an end.

But what, it may be asked, *was* this 'vast idea'? Nothing more and nothing less than the conception of poetry as a distinct and separate mode of attaining that final truth which can only be described in language borrowed from Keats himself, as the truth of the soul, which comprehends and reconciles the partial truths of the heart and of the mind. That obscure definition and the obscure terms of which it is composed will become clearer as we follow the process of organic development which was the growth of Keats' soul. It is, however, essential at any given moment in this process not to go further in exposition than Keats could himself have gone. That necessarily involves putting questions off with half-answers, with vague hints and cloudy surmises. I ask that the reader should not be impatient, but wait and see whether more complete and satisfying answers will not emerge.

CHAPTER III

THE SECOND YEAR: *ENDYMION*

SLEEP and Poetry was the confession of faith with which Keats concluded the first of his four years of full poetic life at the end of 1816. 1817 was the year of *Endymion.* His first volume containing work up to and including *Sleep and Poetry* was published in March 1817. In April he had begun *Endymion.* I have no intention of trying to analyse that extraordinary poem, with its immaturities and indecisions, and its exquisite beauties. I do not believe that Keats meant anything particular by a great deal of it. He was driven to make trial of his own powers of imagination and invention, to follow his fancy where it led, to create beauty, which he did abundantly. We may take as final his retrospective judgement of his own work in his letter to Hessey of 9th October 1818, so characteristic of him is its blend of modesty and firmness, in the manifest truth and directness with which he ever judged himself.

> It is as good as I had power to make it—by myself. Had I been nervous about its being a perfect piece, and with that view asked advice, and trembled over every page, it would not have been written; for it is not in my nature to fumble—I will write independently.—I have written independently *without Judgment.* I may write independently, and *with Judgment,* hereafter. The Genius of Poetry must work out its own salvation in a man. It cannot be matured by law and precept, but by sensation and watchfulness in itself. That which is creative must create itself. In *Endymion* I leaped headlong into the sea, and thereby have become better acquainted with the Soundings, the quicksands and the rocks, than if I had stayed upon the green shore, and piped a silly pipe, and took tea and comfortable advice. I was never afraid of failure, for I would rather fail than not be among the greatest. . . .

The writing of *Endymion* was indeed an exploration by Keats of his own powers. He wrote in the original preface: 'Before I began I had no inward feel of being able to finish; and as I proceeded my steps were all uncertain'; and in the published preface that it was a 'feverish attempt, rather than a deed accomplished.'

Though it is a mistake therefore to read a sustained poetic purpose into *Endymion,* it is equally a mistake to suppose that the poetic purpose is not there. It is there; but it is intermittent, continually lost in the proliferation of Keats' fancy. *Endymion* is neither a profound symbolic poem nor a meandering fairy-tale. Certain crucial portions of the story have a plain significance: Endymion's love-sick wanderings in search of the moon-goddess are palpably the wanderings of the soul in search of the ideal, and the metamorphosis of the Indian Maid into the Goddess signifies that the road to this ideal lies through surrender to beauty in the particular. And, again, it is because of Endymion's forgetfulness of his own woes and his pity for another's miseries that Glaucus reveals the long-sought secret to him. Surrender to beauty in the particular, and a heartfelt sympathy with human destinies are the paths to the ultimate goal.

The two paths seem unconnected. Yet it was these same two paths that Keats had seen before him in *Sleep and Poetry;* and in a letter to his friend Bailey, written towards the end of the composition of *Endymion* Keats reasserts their significance together:

> 'I am certain of nothing,' he wrote, 'but of the holiness of the Heart's affections, and the truth of Imagination. What the Imagination seizes as Beauty must be Truth—whether it existed before or not,—for I have the same idea of all our passions as of Love: they are all, in their sublime, creative of essential Beauty. In a Word, you may know my favourite speculation from my first book [that is, of *Endymion*]. . . . The Imagination may be compared to Adam's dream,—he awoke and found it truth:—I am more zealous in this affair, because I have never yet been able to perceive how anything can be known for truth by consecutive reasoning—and yet it must be. Can it be that even the greatest Philosopher ever arrived at his Goal without putting aside numerous objections? However it may be, O for a life of Sensations rather than Thoughts! It is "a Vision in the form of Youth," a shadow of reality to come.' . . . (*Letter of* 22nd *November* 1817.)

That is not easy: Keats' letters are not easy to understand: they have a deceptive spontaneity which invites the mind to pass over them with a delightful smoothness, without pausing to penetrate below the surface. We should be in a better position to understand this letter could we invoke the aid of some that must come later in this narrative. However, for the moment one must be dogmatic. 'The Heart's affections' and 'Imagination' are two kinds of the experiences which Keats calls Sensations, which he contrasts with and prefers to Thoughts. The Heart's affections are the instinctive impulses, Imagination is intuition. Keats, to the frequent consternation of his critics, links them together. Whether he is right or they, the event will show. But this linking of the two kinds of Sensations together is fundamental to Keats' thought; this is the meaning of his words: 'I have the same idea of all our passions as of Love: they are all, in their sublime, creative of essential Beauty.' Follow the instincts, says Keats, and you will reach intuition, and by intuition you will reach the final goal, essential Beauty, which is essential Truth. And then he states quite simply, as a fact of his own nature, that he has never been able to understand how anything can be known for truth by consecutive reasoning. It seems to him that the process of the rational mind in ' even the greatest philosopher ' involves ' putting aside numerous objections.' That is to say, the rational mind is partial, because it excludes everything that is non-rational; it applies a scheme to reality and denies reality to all that will not enter the scheme. Against this method Keats pits his own: of denying truth to nothing that is really experienced and above all not to the instinctive impulses, for they eventually sublimate themselves into Imagination, which seizes truth under the form of beauty.

I do not say this is at all clear ; I do not believe that it was at this moment clear to Keats himself: but that is as exact a re-statement as I can give of Keats' thought. How are those instinctive impulses sublimated—that is the question. Keats gives no answer, because he had at this moment no answer to give. He holds fast to two certainties—the sacredness of the instinctive impulses, and the truth of that which the intuition seizes as beauty—he knows they are connected, but he does not know how. That knowledge and that ignorance are alike fundamental to *Endymion;* they are the sources of its strength and weakness.

He refers Bailey to the first book of *Endymion* for a poetic expression of his thought. The passages in question are, I think, two—the induction to the poem and Endymion's words to Peona towards the end of the book. In the first he tells of the passage of the soul from the instinctive perception and creation of beauty to a consummation. ' A thing of beauty is a joy for ever.' Therefore, the human spirit goes on perceiving and creating beauty as ' a flowery band to bind us to the earth.' Once again, Keats means what he says. This instinctive impulse towards beauty ' binds us to the earth ' ; it is a means to endurance of our mortal destiny. His meaning is indeed beyond doubt, for he goes on :

> Spite of despondence, of the inhuman dearth
> Of noble natures, of the gloomy days,
> Of all the unhealthy and o'er-darkened ways
> Made for our searching : yes, in spite of all,
> Some shape of beauty moves away the pall
> From our dark spirits. . . .

Then, as is his wont, under compulsion from his power of concrete imagination, he gives a sequence of instances of beauty—the sun, the moon, clear rills, the grandeur of the dooms we have imagined for the mighty dead—before continuing:

Nor do we merely feel these essences
For one short hour; no, even as the trees
That whisper round a temple become soon
Dear as the temple's self, so does the moon,
The passion poesy, glories infinite,
Haunt us till they become a cheering light
Unto our souls, and bound to us so fast,
That, whether there be shine, or gloom o'ercast,
They always must be with us, or we die.

The moon—beauty perceived; poetry—beauty created: this perception and creation of beauty is abiding, for it is a contact with a truth which externally exists, and a sense of this eternally existent truth must remain with us, 'or we die.'

That is a re-statement of the mystery, but not a revelation of it. In the second passage, Keats makes another attempt. And this attempt we know from a letter to Taylor his publisher was, though he was conscious of its obscurity, of extreme importance to himself. 'Wherein lies happiness?' Endymion asks Peona, and answers his own question:

In that which becks
Our ready minds to fellowship divine,
A fellowship with essence; till we shine
Full alchemiz'd and free of space. Behold
The clear religion of heaven!

That at least is clear: true happiness lies in communion with essential beauty, which is communion with the divine. Endymion goes on:

Fold
A rose leaf round thy finger's taperness,
And soothe thy lips: hist, when the airy stress
Of music's kiss impregnates the free winds,
And with a sympathetic touch unbinds
Æolian magic from their lucid wombs:
Then old songs waken from enclouded tombs;
Old ditties sigh above their father's grave;
Ghosts of melodious prophecyings rave
Round every spot where trod Apollo's foot;
Bronze clarions awake and faintly bruit,
Where long ago a giant battle was;
And, from the turf, a lullaby doth pass
In every place where infant Orpheus slept.
Feel we these things?—that moment have we stept
Into a sort of oneness, and our state
Is like a floating spirit's.

It is hardly necessary to comment upon this. When we are deeply stirred by some inscrutable harmony of nature or of art, we pass 'into a sort of oneness.' The experience is familiar to many. This experience Keats regards as prophetic of a condition attainable by the human soul:

> But there are
> Richer entanglements, enthralments far
> More self-destroying, leading, by degrees,
> To the chief intensity:* the crown of these
> Is made of love and friendship, and sits high
> Upon the forehead of humanity.
> All its more ponderous and bulky worth
> Is friendship, whence there ever issues forth
> A steady splendour; but at the tip-top
> There hangs by unseen film, an orbed drop
> Of light, and that is love: its influence
> Thrown in our eyes, genders a novel sense,
> At which we start and fret; till in the end,
> Melting into its radiance, we blend,
> Mingle, and so become a part of it,—
> Nor with aught else can our souls interknit
> So wingedly: when we combine therewith
> Life's self is nourished by its proper pith. . . .

That also is, in the main, clear enough. Friendship first, then love: these are richer entanglements than the oneness felt in communion with Nature, richer because they are more 'self-destroying.' In them the surrender of self is more complete and permanent, reaching its pinnacle in love, which is the final 'fellowship with essence.' In that condition, 'Life's self is nourished by its proper pith,' whatever that may mean. So, in the words of his letter to Bailey, 'the passion of love is, in its sublime, creative of essential Beauty.' The thought is not unlike the thought of Plato. But Keats insists more firmly than Plato ever did upon the sensuous reality of love. One might justly say that he here regards the self-surrender in the ecstasy of physical love as the directest road to communion with—with what? That Keats could hardly say: he gives it many names—essential Beauty, essential Truth, oneness—whatever it is, it is the goal of human effort, a mysterious condition wherein 'Life's self is nourished by its proper pith.'*

That such a goal there was and such a condition is the theme of *Endymion:* that it was to be reached by following the sacred impulses of instinct, is also fundamental to *Endymion*. But the road by which these should lead to the goal Keats did not know. The beginning he knew, the end he knew; of what should come between he was ignorant: and that is the reason why *Endymion* is a perplexing poem.

In it also the beginning is clear and the end is clear, but the path between them wanders and is lost.

Of the speech of Endymion to Peona, which we have just been considering, Keats wrote to Taylor (30th January 1818):

> The whole thing must, I think, have appeared to you, who are a consecutive man, as a thing of mere words, but I assure you that, when I wrote it, it was a regular stepping of the Imagination towards a truth. My having written that argument will perhaps be of the greatest service to me of anything I ever did. It set before me the gradations of happiness, even like a kind of pleasure thermometer, and is my first step towards the chief attempt in the drama—the playing of different natures with joy and Sorrow.

That is a remarkable utterance. It shows again that Keats' conception of an argument is very different from other people's. In what sense Endymion's speech is 'a regular stepping of the Imagination towards a truth' may have appeared. But how Endymion's speech could be Keats' 'first step towards the chief attempt in the drama' cannot be made clear now. In one sense, the remainder of this book is an attempt to show that to such a beginning the drama is the inevitable end. The drama is the only complete expression of that 'vast idea' of which Keats had had so thrilling a glimpse in *Sleep and Poetry*, which he had striven in vain to express in *Endymion*. And what was to follow of Keats' life and work was a further realization, a 'proving upon his pulses' of the idea of which he already had intuitive possession. He lived, thought, felt, imagined and wrote himself into it more fully, but it was already his.

And, truly, it was a vast idea, even in the form in which Keats already apprehended it: that the rational faculty was impotent to achieve truth, that intuitive apprehension was the sole faculty by which an ultimate truth could be known, that this truth could be recognized for what it was only by its beauty, that perceptions of beauty were premonitions of a final reality, that the way towards intuitive knowledge of this reality lay through a reverence for the instinctive impulses, and that somehow in this final knowledge all discords would be reconciled. And the discords were already serious to Keats. Already we find him writing to Reynolds: 'Lord! a man should have the fine point of his soul taken off to become fit for this world!' But that fine point of his soul was precisely the instrument with which Keats had made the discovery and was to pursue it.

CHAPTER IV

THE INFLUENCE OF SHAKESPEARE: THE POETIC CHARACTER

ENDYMION was finished in December 1817. Throughout the months in which that poem was composed, Keats had been drinking deep of Shakespeare; during some of them one might fairly say he had been drunk with Shakespeare. There are but three of all the letters which Keats wrote between April 1817, when he began *Endymion*, and December 1817, when he ended it, which do not contain palpable evidence of this saturation: and of these three letters, one was written to his little sister Fanny, and the other two from Oxford in September when Keats was momentarily under the influence of his Wordsworthian friend, Bailey.

The mere statement might be sufficient, were it not that the effect of Shakespeare upon Keats was of a peculiar, subtle, and far-reaching kind. Those who would understand its nature must submit to a relation which may seem tedious, yet cannot be wholly avoided; for the thread of the Shakespearean influence runs so close to the centre of Keats' being that we can, with patience, watch it gradually merge into the very substance of his soul.

In the middle of April 1817 Keats left London for the Isle of Wight in order to work undisturbed upon *Endymion*. He had no sooner reached Southampton than he wrote to his brothers: 'I felt rather lonely this Morning at Breakfast so I went and unboxed a Shakespeare. "There's my comfort."' Two days later he had found lodgings in Carisbrooke, in a house with a portrait of Shakespeare in the passage.*

> In the passage (he wrote to Reynolds) I found a head of Shakespeare, which I had not before seen. It is most likely the same that George spoke so well of, for I like it extremely. Well—this head I have hung over my books . . . having first discarded a French Ambassador—now this alone is a good morning's work.

One suspects that it was the portrait of Shakespeare which decided Keats' choice for Mrs. Cook's house. The auspices were good, Mrs. Cook was indeed a kindly soul; for when, barely a week later, Keats fled precipitately from her house and the Isle of Wight, she insisted on his taking the portrait of Shakespeare with him as a parting present.

Though Keats was busy settling in when he wrote to Reynolds, he was already unsettled and excited. He had spent the previous day in walking to Shanklin, and he had been so enchanted by the place that he had hesitated for a moment between it and Carisbrooke.

> Shanklin is a most beautiful place (he told Reynolds); sloping wood and meadow ground reach round the Chine, which is a cleft between the Cliffs of the depth of nearly 300 feet at least. This cleft is filled with trees and bushes in the narrow part, and as it widens becomes bare, if it were not for primroses on one side, which spread to the very verge of the Sea, and some fishermen's huts on the other, perched midway in the Balustrades of beautiful green Hedges along their steps down to the sand. But the sea, Jack, the sea. . . .

'But the sea, Jack, the sea. . . .' This, more than any other enchantment, accompanied him back from his walk, and it remained with him through a sleepless night. A little later in the same letter he told Reynolds: 'From want of regular rest, I have been rather *narvus*, and the passage in *Lear*—"Do you not hear the Sea?" has haunted me intensely.' Without another word he abruptly copies this sonnet on *The Sea*:

> It keeps eternal whisperings around
> Desolate shores, and with its mighty swell
> Gluts twice ten thousand caverns, till the spell
> Of Hecate leaves them their old shadowy sound.
> Often 'tis in such gentle temper found
> That scarcely will the very smallest shell
> Be moved for days from where it sometime fell,
> When last the winds of heaven were unbound.
> O ye! who have your eye-balls vex'd and tired,
> Feast them upon the wideness of the Sea;
> O ye! whose ears are dinn'd with uproar rude
> Or fed too much with cloying melody,—
> Sit ye near some old cavern's mouth, and brood
> Until ye start, as if the sea-nymphs quired.

To penetrate the connection between the 'intense haunting' of Keats' mind by the phrase from Shakespeare which inspired the sonnet, and the 'eternal whispering' of the sea itself, we need to have before our eyes the passage from the play.

> *Edg.* Hark! do you hear the sea?
> *Glo.* No, truly.
> *Edg.* Why, then your other senses grow imperfect
> By your eyes' anguish.
> *Glo.* So may it be indeed. . . .

Edg. Come on, sir ; here's the place : stand still.
How fearful
And dizzy 'tis to cast one's eyes so low !
The crows and choughs that wing the midway air
Show scarce so gross as beetles ; half way down
Hangs one that gathers samphire, dreadful trade !
Methinks he seems no bigger than his head.
The fishermen that walk upon the beach
Appear like mice, and yond tall anchoring bark
Diminished to a cock, her cock a buoy
Almost too small for sight. The murmuring surge,
That on the unnumbered idle pebbles chafes,
Cannot be heard so high. I'll look no more,
Lest my brain turn, and the deficient sight
Topple down headlong.

The most striking fact that emerges from a comparison of the Shakespeare with Keats' sonnet is that the only visible connection between them is the strange use of the word ' eye-balls ' in the sonnet. That surely comes from a memory of Gloucester's torture, of which Edgar speaks. The Shakespearian use of Hecate also derives from the first act of *Lear*. But that is the sum-total of the direct and visible connections between Shakespeare's play and Keats' poem.

Yet, as we shall see, the whole passage from *Lear* was running verbatim in his mind. Its intense haunting, the sea's eternal whispering, Keats' unsleeping night-thoughts of ' the end and aim of poetry ' and his brooding on Shakespeare as his mighty forerunner, composed one tumultuous and scarcely separable whole. At this moment of intense creative excitement Shakespeare, poetry and sea became knit together in a single thought and feeling. Each worked upon the other, till the ferment of his inward excitement became unbearable and Keats fled to the company of his brother Tom at Margate.

I went to the Isle of Wight (he wrote to Hunt on 10th May), thought so much about poetry, so long together, that I could not get to sleep at night ; and, moreover, I know not how it was, I could not get wholesome food. By this means, in a week or so, I became not over-capable in my upper stories, and set off pell-mell for Margate, at least a hundred and fifty miles, because, forsooth, I fancied I should like my old lodging here, and could contrive to do without trees. Another thing, I was too much in solitude, and consequently was obliged to be in continual burning of thought, as an only resource. However, Tom is with me at present.

It is not to be supposed that a landlady so kind as Mrs. Cook, who gave her picture of Shakespeare to her hurriedly departing lodger, did not feed Keats well. His nervousness, not his food, played havoc with his stomach; and in this nervousness we can trace three elements: the murmur of the sea, the thought of Shakespeare, and the thought of poetry. The arduous nature of Keats' night-thoughts upon poetry has already been revealed by *Sleep and Poetry*.

The condition had no doubt quietened a little by the time he wrote to Hunt and Haydon from Margate. But the complex yet single thought was still beating in his brain. For with Hunt he discusses Shakespeare's religion and concludes that he was neither for nor against Christianity, and says:

> I have asked myself so often why I should be a poet more than other men, seeing how great a thing it is,—how great things are to be gained by it, what a thing to be in the mouth of Fame,—that at last the idea has grown so monstrously beyond any seeming power of attainment, that the other day I nearly consented with myself to drop into a Phaeton.

The backward reference of this mood and thought to *Sleep and Poetry* is evident; but his confession of it to Haydon, to whom at this moment in his life Keats could most freely speak his heart, shows more strikingly the place held by Shakespeare in his alternately depressed and excited mind.

> Truth is I have been in such a state of Mind as to read over my Lines and hate them. I am one that 'gathers Samphire, dreadful trade'—the Cliff of Poesy towers above me—yet when Tom who meets with some of Pope's Homer in Plutarch's Lives reads some of those to me they seem like Mice to mine. I read and write about eight hours a day. There is an old saying 'well begun is half done'—'tis a bad one. I would use instead, 'Not begun at all till half done'; so according to that I have not begun my Poem and consequently (à priori) can say nothing about it. Thank God! I do begin arduously where I leave off, notwithstanding occasional depressions; and I hope for the support of a High Power while I climb this little eminence, and especially in my years of more momentous Labor. I remember your saying that you had notions of a good Genius presiding over you. I have of late had the same thought, for things which I do half at Random are afterwards confirmed by my judgement in a dozen features of Propriety. Is it too daring to fancy Shakespeare this Presider? When in the Isle of Wight I met with a Shakespeare in the Passage of the House at which I lodged—it comes nearer to my idea of him than any I have seen—I was but there a Week, yet the old woman made me take it with me though I went off in a hurry. Do you not think this is ominous of good?*

And then in the same letter, before a long sequence of quotations from *Antony and Cleopatra* which he was then reading, Keats says to Haydon:

> I know no one but you who can be fully sensible of the turmoil and anxiety, the sacrifice of all what is called comfort, the readiness to measure time by what is done, and to die in six hours could plans be brought to conclusions—the looking upon the Sun, the Moon, the Stars, the Earth and its contents, as materials to form greater things—that is to say ethereal things—but here I am talking like a Madman,—greater things than our Creator himself made ! !
>
> . . . I never quite despair and I read Shakespeare—indeed I think I shall never read any other Book much. Now this might lead me into a long Confab but I desist. I am very near agreeing with Hazlitt that Shakespeare is enough for us.

From these letters we gain a curious glimpse into the excited working of Keats' mind while he began *Endymion.* The thought of poetry, the murmur of the sea, and Shakespeare became ever more inextricably blent together. The passage from *Lear* which had first supplied the words in which the sound of the sea is concentred, supplies the vivid image of his impossible climb towards the summit of the towering cliff of Poetry, and the picture of Shakespeare, which his landlady so significantly had given him, becomes the portrait of a presiding genius smiling encouragement upon his desperate endeavour.

How long-lasting was the effect of this strange, yet strangely natural, condition of thought and emotion, is oddly revealed by a letter written to Jane Reynolds from Oxford fully four months later (14th September). Jane was on holiday at Littlehampton :

> Now (Keats wrote) let us turn to the sea-shore. Believe me, my dear Jane, it is a great happiness to see that you are, in this finest part of the year, winning a little enjoyment from the hard world. In truth, the great Elements we know of, are no mean comforters: the open sky sits on our senses like a sapphire crown—the Air is our robe of state—the Earth is our Throne and the Sea a mighty minstrel playing before it—able, like David's harp, to make such a one as you forget almost the tempest cares of life. I have found in the ocean's music,—varying (tho' self-same) more than the passion of Timotheus, an enjoyment not to be put into words; and, though 'inland far I be,' I now hear the voice most audibly while pleasing myself in the idea of your sensations . . . Which is the best of Shakespeare's plays ? I mean in what mood and with what accompaniment do you like the sea best ? *

The obvious riddle in that letter is almost automatically solved by what has gone before. To ask which is the best of Shakespeare's plays is certainly a strange way of asking in what mood and with what accompaniment someone best likes the sea. But the sea and Shakespeare had become, at a moment of intense receptivity, part of the same thought for Keats; the sea's ' eternal whispering ' was for him identical with the words of *Lear*.

So far we have been unravelling in its varieties and repercussions the content of Keats' mind during the few intolerably excited days in which he began *Endymion*. The living centre of his thought and feeling, into which his deepest speculations on the nature of poetry and his most intimate sensations were inseparably merged, was Shakespeare; and those who are curious in these things may pick out the clues of Shakespearean word and phrase in his letters of these months: they are legion. But the conscious working of this deep and inscrutable influence is for a moment suspended in this month of September. In this same letter to Jane Reynolds he quotes from Wordsworth's ' Immortal Ode.'

Keats was at this moment staying at Oxford in vacation with Bailey, an ardent Wordsworthian, whose admiration for that great poet, like the admiration of many others, was an admiration of the pietist rather than the poet. Keats' next few letters reveal accordingly less a preoccupation with Shakespeare than a reaction against an excessive and indiscriminate admiration of Wordsworth.* Writing from Oxford, Keats unburdens himself to Reynolds: ' Wordsworth sometimes, though in a fine way, gives us sentences in the style of school exercises.—For instance :

> The lake doth glitter,
> The bird doth twitter, etc.'

And he finds relief in describing Oxford by an amusing parody of the manner:

> The Gothic looks solemn,
> The plain Doric column
> Supports an old Bishop and Crosier. . . .

When he had left Oxford and returned to Hampstead, he finds the courage to criticize a poem by Bailey's idol (*The Gipsies*) in a letter to Bailey himself:

> It is a bold thing to say (he wrote in November)—and I would not say it in print—but it seems to me that if Wordsworth had thought a little deeper at that moment, he would not have written the poem at all. I should judge it to have been written in one of the most comfortable moods of his life—it is a kind of sketchy intellectual landscape, not a search after truth. . . .

The criticism flies like an arrow to the heart of the poem: a harsher critic and a more unjust, would say it was written in one of the most condescending moods of Wordsworth's life; but 'comfortable'—that is the word. There is in *The Gipsies* indeed no 'search after truth.' Wordsworth was not intensely contemplating that band of gipsies for what they were; they were to him merely appropriate adjuncts to a landscape of which he was the complacent patentee and proprietor.

This dissociation of himself from Wordsworth, whom within limits he sincerely admired, was continuous during the next few months; and it was a consequence and corollary of his deeper identification of himself with Shakespeare. When he left Hampstead at the end of November, to give himself up to the last book of *Endymion* in solitude and seclusion at Burford Bridge, the tide of the Shakespearean influence came flooding in again. He wrote to Reynolds on 22nd November.

One of the three books I have with me is Shakespeare's Poems: I never found so many beauties in the Sonnets—they seem to be full of fine things said unintentionally—in the intensity of working out conceits. Is this to be borne? Hark ye!

> When lofty trees I see barren of leaves
> Which erst from heat did canopy the herd
> And Summer's green all girded up in sheaves,
> Borne on the bier with white and bristly beard.

He has left nothing to say about nothing or anything: for look at snails—you know what he says about Snails—you know when he talks about 'cockled Snails'—well, in one of these sonnets he says—the chap slips into—no! I lie! this is in the *Venus and Adonis:* the simile brought it to my Mind.

> As the snail, whose tender horns being hit,
> Shrinks backwards in his shelly cave with pain
> And there, all smothered up, in shade doth sit,
> Long after fearing to put forth again;
> So, at his bloody view, her eyes are fled
> Into the deep dark cabins of her head.

He overwhelms a genuine Lover of poesy with all manner of abuse, talking about

> a poet's rage
> And stretched metre of an antique song.

which, by the by, will be a capital motto for my poem, won't it? He speaks too of 'Time's antique pen'—and 'April's first-born flowers'—and 'Death's eternal cold.'

On the same day he wrote to Bailey the letter in which he announced his conviction that 'what the Imagination seizes as Beauty must be Truth.' He is deferential to his friend; he contrasts his own simple mind avid of 'Sensations rather than Thoughts,' to his own disadvantage, with a complex mind, 'one that is imaginative and at the same time careful of its fruits,—who would exist partly on Sensation, partly on thought—to whom it is necessary that 'years should bring the philosophic Mind.' Such a one,' he generously adds, 'I consider yours.' But for all his deference, Keats is making distinctions; and as he here distinguishes between the poetic and philosophic minds, so elsewhere in his letter he makes his first approach to a cardinal distinction between the poetic and the philosophic characters.

> To a Man of your nature such a letter as Haydon's must have been extremely cutting. What occasions the greater part of the world's quarrels? Simply this—two Minds meet, and do not understand each other time enough to prevent any shock or surprise at the conduct of either party. As soon as I had known Haydon three days, I got enough of his Character not to have been surprised at such a Letter as he has hurt you with. Nor, when I knew it, was it a principle with me to drop his acquaintance; although with you it would have been an imperious feeling. I wish you knew all that I think about Genius and the Heart—and yet I think that you are acquainted with my innermost breast in that respect, or you could not have known me even thus long, and still hold me worthy to be your dear Friend. In passing, however, I must say one thing that has pressed upon me lately, and increased my Humility and capability of submission—and that is this truth—Men of Genius are great as certain ethereal Chemicals operating on the Mass of neutral intellect—but they have not any individuality, any determined Character—I would call the top and head of those who have a proper self, Men of Power.

Here we touch, almost at its birth, one of Keats' fundamental conceptions, one which is most intimately connected with his understanding of Shakespeare. It might be described as the conception (though it is far more instinctive and intuitive than any conception) of Shakespeare as the ideal of human character. With his usual modesty, Keats puts it forward to Bailey in the form that the ideal poetic character is to be without any determined character. But we have only to read between the lines with a very moderate amount of subtlety to see that he is really imputing to Bailey a *rigidity* of character, from which he dissociates himself and the man of Genius.

This gradual identification of himself with the Shakespearean character was perhaps the deepest effect produced in Keats by his continual converse with Shakespeare during this year. It was a seed of deep knowledge out of which were to grow, ' as naturally as the leaves to a tree,' many of Keats' most piercing discoveries of life. This knowledge is essential Keats, and it can be observed in the process of becoming quintessential. At this moment it is a consciousness of a contrast between the Wordsworthian character (with which he rightly identifies Bailey) and the Shakespearean (with which he, yet more rightly, identifies himself). At the moment of his letter to Bailey (22nd November) the contrast is not yet consciously formulated in those terms; that was apparently the work of the next few days of undisturbed work and thinking at Burford Bridge; but by the end of this year 1817 Keats is in full and secure possession of his intuition. This opposition between Wordsworth and Shakespeare is in some ways more important, as it was more continual, than the opposition between Milton and Shakespeare about which Keats' supreme poetic struggle was subsequently to be waged. His most intimate history could be written in terms of his rejection first of Wordsworth, then of Milton, in favour of a deeper and unchanging loyalty to Shakespeare.

The last letter of this year 1817, written to his brothers on 28th December, is so emphatic and revealing a conclusion to the story of the influence of Shakespeare upon Keats since the beginning of *Endymion* that it must be quoted in full. If any single piece of evidence can make palpable the intimate nature of the relation by now established between Keats and Shakespeare, it is this letter in this place.

My dear Brothers,

I must crave your pardon for not having written ere this. . . . I saw Kean return to the public in *Richard III*, and finely he did it, and, at the request of Reynolds, I went to criticize his Duke in Richard. The critique is in to-day's *Champion*, which I send you, with the *Examiner*, in which you will find very proper lamentation on the obsoletion of Christmas Gambols and pastimes: but it was mixed up with so much egotism of that drivelling nature that one's pleasure is entirely lost. Hone, the publisher's trial, you must find very amusing, and, as Englishmen, very encouraging: his *Not Guilty* is a thing, which not to have been, would have dulled still more Liberty's Emblazoning. Lord Ellenborough has been paid in his own coin. Wooler and Hone have done us an essential service.

I have had two very pleasant evenings with Dilke, yesterday and to-day, and am at this moment just come from him, and feel in the humour to go on with this, begun in the morning, and from which he came to fetch me. I spent Friday evening with Wells, and went next morning to see ' Death on the Pale Horse.' It is a wonderful picture, when West's age is considered; but there is nothing to be intense upon, no women one feels mad to kiss, no face swelling into reality. The excellence of every art is its intensity, capable of making all disagreeables evaporate from their being in close relationship with Beauty and Truth. Examine *King Lear*, and you will find this exemplified throughout: but in this picture we have unpleasantness without any momentous depth of speculation excited, in which to bury its repulsiveness. The picture is larger than 'Christ rejected.'

I dined with Haydon the Sunday after you left, and had a most pleasant day. I dined too (for I have been out too much lately) with Horace Smith, and met his two brothers, with Hill and Kingston, and one Du Bois. They only served to convince me how superior humour is to wit, in respect to enjoyment. These men say things which make one start, without making one feel; they are all alike; their manners are alike; they all know fashionables; they have all a mannerism in their very eating and drinking, in their mere handling a decanter. They talked of Kean and his low company. 'Would I were in that company instead of yours,' said I to myself! I know such like acquaintance will never do for me, and yet I am going to Reynolds on Wednesday.

Brown and Dilke walked with me and back to the Christmas pantomime. I had not a dispute, but a disquisition, with Dilke upon various subjects; several things dovetailed in my mind, and at once it struck me what quality went to form a man of achievement, especially in literature, and which Shakespeare possessed so enormously—I mean *Negative Capability*, that is, when a man is capable of being in uncertainties, mysteries, doubts, without any irritable reaching after fact and reason. Coleridge, for instance, would let go by a fine isolated verisimilitude caught from the Penetralium of mystery, from being incapable of remaining content with half-knowledge. This, being pursued through volumes, would perhaps take us no further than this, that with a great poet the sense of Beauty overcomes every other consideration, or rather obliterates all consideration.

Two of the clues to the thought behind this letter are manifest to the eye. First, Shakespeare's *King Lear* is the ideal of poetic excellence because it has that *intensity* which causes 'all disagreeables to evaporate from their being in close relationship with beauty and truth.' Secondly, Shakespeare's character is the ideal of human character, because of its Negative Capability. And, thirdly, these two qualities are somehow intimately connected, because this conception of Negative Capability (which is a quality of the man and not of his work) would, 'if pursued through many volumes, perhaps take us no further than this, that with a great poet the sense of Beauty . . . obliterates all consideration.'

Keats has a sense of some mysterious and simple relation between the character and the works of Shakespeare, which he cannot articulate. In the work there is an *intensity* which makes all disagreeables evaporate from the closeness of their relationship with Beauty and Truth; in the man there is a Negative Capability which enables the sense of Beauty to obliterate all consideration, which is only another word for 'all irritable reaching after fact and reason.'

That, one might say, was the main result of Keats' submission to Shakespeare during the year which had ended. But the letter contains other and less manifest clues to a deeper thought. Keats dines out with some of the 'literary fashionables,' and is convinced, by personal contact, how superior humour is to wit in respect of enjoyment. The literary fashionables are witty, and as dully and lifelessly alike as any two buttons stamped out by the same machine. They have no warm and living individuality; they have no spontaneity. These mechanical wits deplore Kean's frequenting of low company. Keats longs to be in Kean's company rather than theirs.

The criticisms of Kean which, as Keats tells his brothers, he had just been writing, should throw some further light on the thoughts which were now beginning to form in Keats' mind. The illumination they give is very pertinent. In his paper in *The Champion* for 21st December, on Kean's reappearance in *Richard III*, we find the following:

> A melodious passage of poetry is full of pleasures both sensual and spiritual. The spiritual is felt when the very letters and points of charactered language show like the hieroglyphics of beauty; the mysterious signs of our immortal freemasonry. 'A thing to dream of, not to tell!' The sensual life of verse springs warm from the lips of Kean, and to one learned in Shakespearian hieroglyphics—learned in the spiritual portion of those lines to which Kean adds a sensual grandeur, his tongue must seem to have robbed the Hybla bees and left them honeyless! There is an indescribable *gusto* in his voice, by which we feel that the utterer is thinking of the past and future while speaking of the instant.

Kean and Shakespeare are evidently part of a single reality for Keats; or rather Kean is the complete and fitting sensuous vehicle of Shakespeare. In his next article, on Kean's performance in an abridgment of the three *Henry VIs*, Keats discusses Shakespeare in general and makes a distinction which was to be prophetic of himself.

> The poetry of *Romeo and Juliet*, of *Hamlet*, of *Macbeth* is the poetry of Shakespeare's soul—full of love and divine romance. It knows no stop in its delight, but 'goeth where it listeth'—remaining, however, in all men's hearts a perpetual and golden

> dream. The poetry of *Lear*, *Othello*, *Cymbeline*, etc., is the poetry of human passions and affections, made almost ethereal by the power of the poet. . . .

Keats was to readjust his actual ascription of Shakespeare's plays to these two classes; the distinction was to abide and to be realized even in his own brief work.

But we are immediately concerned rather with the relation between Kean and Shakespeare which Keats felt to exist. It was a relation almost of identity.

> Kean always 'dies as erring men do die.' The bodily functions wither up, and the mental faculties hold out till they crack. It is an extinguishment, not a decay; the lip trembles with the last breath, as we see the autumn leaf thrill in the cold wind of evening. The very eyelid dies. The acting of Kean is Shakespearian—he will fully understand what we mean.

Kean may well have done, if Keats was right about him. But ordinary mortals may be perplexed by this insinuation of a secret understanding between Kean and Shakespeare and Keats himself. It creeps out again in the final lines of this second paper.

> One thing we are convinced of on looking over the three parts of *Henry*, from which this play is gleaned; which is that Shakespeare was the only lonely and perfectly happy creature whom God ever formed. He could never have a mate—being most unmatchable.

Keats was to change his mind completely, not about the loneliness but about the perfect happiness of Shakespeare.

But in order to understand the insinuation of a secret understanding between Kean and Shakespeare, we need to return to the first paper.

> Other actors are continually thinking of their sum-total effect throughout a play. Kean delivers himself up to the instant feeling, without a shadow of a thought about anything else. He feels his being as deeply as Wordsworth, or any other of our intellectual monopolists. . . .

Here, in this submission of Kean's to the instant feeling, and the deep sense of his own being he thereby attains, we come perhaps as near as we can to an understanding of what Keats implied by his curious words: 'Kean's acting is Shakespearian—he will fully understand what we mean.' Kean and Keats knew that this natural posture of the being was Shakespeare's secret, and the knowledge of that secret they shared between themselves—that is what Keats was saying.

This explains what seems at first sight the gratuitous sneer at Wordsworth. Wordsworth's name appears to be dragged in simply for the sake of calling him ' an intellectual monopolist.' Actors cannot in general be profitably compared to poets. The cause of the trouble is that Keats' thought is so deep and intuitive that he cannot clearly articulate it. The real contrast is between Shakespeare and Wordsworth, and the point of the contrast depends upon that conception of loyalty to the instinctive impulses which Keats had lately proclaimed to Bailey as ' the holiness of the Heart's affections ' and which he had tried to reveal in *Endymion* as necessary to the full perfection of man. Shakespeare, in Keats' view, had this loyalty; and Keats believed that Kean also had it: that is why his acting was Shakespearian. This loyalty Wordsworth had betrayed. Kean, in consequence, felt his own being as deeply as (Keats meant, of course, more deeply than) Wordsworth. In other words, Kean had a natural and spontaneous self-awareness, while Wordsworth's had become an intellectual self-consciousness. These are very different things.

Keats is thus at one and the same moment completing that reassertion of his integral and spontaneous self against the Wordsworthian influence—a reassertion which began in his letters to Bailey of November—and identifying himself through Kean with Shakespeare. It is the same contrast which he was to make far more explicitly a year later in a letter to Woodhouse (22nd October 1818), the contrast ' between that sort of poetical character of which, if I am anything, I am a member: that sort as distinguished from the Wordsworthian or egotistical sublime.' Wordsworth always was to Keats essentially an ' egotist,' because he had denied his own instinctive impulses and imposed upon himself an intellectual self-consciousness, instead of achieving within himself that organic unity which was (in Keats' view) the condition of a true self-awareness. This attitude towards Wordsworth is expressed more fully in the letter to Reynolds of 3rd February 1818. ' For the sake of a few fine domestic and imaginative passages are we to be bullied into a certain philosophy engendered in the whims of an egotist ? ' And in that letter he makes the real contrast, of Wordsworth against Shakespeare himself, and not merely the greatest actor of Shakespeare. ' Why with Wordsworth's " Matthew with a bough of wilding in his hand " when we can have Jacques " under an oak " ? '

Nevertheless, though the real contrast was one between Shakespeare and Wordsworth, the contrast between Kean and Wordsworth was a true one, for Keats was thinking rather of the poetic nature than the works of poets. In his thought they could never be really separated. Poetry was for Keats always an organic function of the human being who produced it, or it fell short of true poetry.

And this identification of himself with Kean, as a means to a further identification of himself with Shakespeare, receives an unexpected emphasis from the description of Keats as a boy by Charles Cowden Clarke, one of the few men who, at any period of Keats' life, could justly claim to have known him well. Cowden Clarke speaks of 'his highly pugnacious disposition which, when roused, was one of the most picturesque exhibitions—off the stage—I ever saw. One of the transports of that marvellous actor, Edmund Kean . . . was its nearest resemblance; and the two were not very dissimilar in face and figure.' Moreover, Keats certainly regarded Kean as the counterpart, in the art of acting, of himself or what he hoped to be in the art of poetry. Some eighteen months later we shall find him writing to Bailey (5th August 1819) that his ambition is 'to make as great a revolution in modern dramatic writing as Kean has done in acting.' And in that letter to Bailey is revealed the fundamental thought which underlay all these thoughts of Shakespeare, of Kean, of Wordsworth and himself: 'I am convinced more and more every day that a fine writer is the most genuine being in the world.'

It is desirable that the chronological sequence of the story should in this instance be anticipated, in order to show more clearly the scope and ultimate consequences of Shakespeare's influence upon Keats during the year 1817. We may take the sentence which has just been quoted from the letter to Bailey as the key. 'I am convinced more and more every day that a fine writer is the *most genuine being* in the world.' The italics are not Keats'; they have been added to draw attention to the emphatic and arresting nature of a phrase which, like so many of Keats' emphatic and arresting phrases, seems to have passed unnoticed. The reason for this neglect, here and elsewhere, is that it is too exacting to assume that Keats meant what he said; it is easier to imagine that he was using words in the slipshod, falsely emphatic manner of ordinary conversation. This presumption is surely ill-advised in the case of a natural master of language like Keats. Not only is it unwarrantable on this obvious ground; but in almost every case it interposes between ourselves and Keats' real movement of soul a veil which, by force of reduplication, finally becomes impenetrable.

The conception of the fine writer as the 'most genuine being in the world' lies at the core of Keats' inward life. Not only was his gradual understanding of that obscure and difficult truth the most essential process in his mental growth; but it necessarily had a profound influence upon his actual life. This was not an abstract truth, but one which Keats 'proved upon his pulses'; he lived himself into an apprehension of it, and his life could be faithfully described as the gradual and instinctive discovery that 'genuineness of being' is the inescapable condition of that kind of 'fine writing' to which he had completely devoted himself. That is to say, if we read the story of Keats loyally, we come into possession of a truth such that the old and vexing conflicts between art and morality, between literature and life, cease to exist for us. Pure poetry (which, it need scarcely be said, has no inseparable connection with the form of verse) is revealed to us as the natural utterance of the finest and completest living. It is no longer a bewildering accident or a troublesome excrescence in a rational scheme of things, it is the most perfect flower on the tree of life. To know that such a statement, however inadequate it may be, is not a rhetorical metaphor, but a sober statement of the truth, is to touch the fringe of a certitude before which the burden of the mystery dissolves away. We should hold it in our grasp if we could know by what means the pure poet, the exemplar of complete humanity, attains to that 'genuineness of being' of which his work is the natural utterance.

We have seen how the conception of Shakespeare's 'genuineness of being' originated in Keats' mind. We have watched him groping towards this conception, after months spent in absorbing Shakespeare so deeply that on 27th February 1818 he could write to Taylor: 'Thank God I can read, and perhaps understand Shakespeare to his very depths.' His first attempt to give the conception shape is in the letter to Bailey of 22nd November 1817, wherein he explains that he himself would not have been surprised by Haydon's behaviour, as Bailey is surprised by it, nor felt himself bound by principle to drop Haydon's acquaintance, as Bailey feels himself bound by principle to do. And he explains (though, modestly, he does not insist on it *as* an explanation) this difference between them by saying that 'Men of Genius have not any individuality, any determined Character.' Keats' hand is stayed by his own modesty, and for the moment he may seem to be far from the conception of the man of genius as 'the most genuine being in the world.' But the discrepancy is superficial. The Man of Genius is, indeed, not a Man of Principle, or a Man of Character, in the sense that Bailey was a man of principle and character. There is something more flexible and tolerant in his attitude to his fellowmen. So far Keats, identifying himself with the man of genius, has merely disclaimed the possession of 'a determined character' such as Bailey possessed.

In his next letter, as we have seen, he makes a further advance towards his own conception. This time the counter-irritant away from which Keats reacted towards a fuller knowledge of his own nature and affinities was not the pietistic sensualist, Bailey,* but Dilke, the 'Godwin Methodist.'

> I had not a dispute, but a disquisition with Dilke upon various subjects; several things dovetailed in my mind and at once it struck me what quality went to form a man of achievement, especially in literature, and which Shakespeare possessed so

> enormously—I mean *Negative Capability*, that is, when a man is capable of being in uncertainties, mysteries, doubts, without any irritable reaching after fact and reason.

The words are repeated in order that an essential step may not be missing from the fuller development we are now following. The intimate connection between this Negative Capability of Shakespeare and the 'lack of determined character' in the man of genius is palpable; it is no less palpable that this Negative Capability is in fact a very positive capability, and further that in Keats' eyes it is the highest of all capabilities. The mere fact that 'Shakespeare possessed it so enormously' is proof enough of this. We may fairly say also that 'the lack of determined character,' as Keats meant the words, is a very positive character; it corresponds in the moral realm of direct relations between human beings to what in a higher and more purely spiritual realm Keats has now grasped as Negative Capability. For this supreme quality there is no familiar name: few people save Keats have even suspected its existence. For the moral quality we can find a word; it is more than tolerance, it is forgiveness. It is that quality which Christ pre-eminently possessed. But for this other kind of forgiveness, a forgiveness which forgives not only men, but life itself, not only the pains which men inflict, but the pains which are knit up in the very nature of existence, we have no word.* We have, as yet, scarcely even a sense of the quality itself. Let it be called, though the word cannot fail to be misunderstood, Acceptance.

Towards the end of September 1819, at a moment when Keats had fought and won the greatest battle of his life and returned finally and for ever to the Shakespearean ideal, in the letter in which he announced that victory to his brother George he described the character of Dilke in these words:

> Brown complained very much in his letter to me of yesterday of the great alteration the disposition of Dilke has undergone. He thinks of nothing but political justice and his boy. Now the first political duty a man ought to have a mind to is the happiness of his friends. I wrote Brown a comment on the subject, wherein I explained what I thought of Dilke's character, which resolved itself into this conclusion, that Dilke is a man who cannot feel he has a personal identity unless he has made up his mind about everything. The only means of strengthening one's intellect is to make up one's mind about nothing—to let the mind be a thoroughfare for all thoughts, not a select party. The genus is not scarce in population; all the stubborn arguers you meet are of the same brood. They never begin upon a subject they have not pre-resolved on. They want to hammer their nail into you, and if you turn the point, still they think you wrong. Dilke will never come at a truth

so long as he lives, because he is always trying it. He is a Godwin Methodist.

Here Keats is reasserting the ideal of Negative Capability as a necessary means to the description of Dilke's character. It is obviously no coincidence that it was in the course of ' a disquisition ' with this same Dilke that Keats first came to grasp his own conception. That act of the mind was the flowering into consciousness of a profound reaction of Keats' being from Dilke's nature, just as the first groping towards a formulation of it was the echo in his consciousness of a reaction from Bailey's. No doubt by September 1819 Keats had completely forgotten that Dilke was the original occasion of his own first fully grasping the reality of Shakespeare and his own identity with the Shakespearean character. A year and a half later the same irritant produces the same reaction—a reassertion of the Shakespearean ideal; but Shakespeare is not now mentioned by name. ' The only means of strengthening one's intellect is to make up one's mind about nothing—to let the mind be a thoroughfare for all thoughts, not a select party.' That is, in terms, identical with the Negative Capability Keats had discerned in Shakespeare; the only difference is that Keats now instinctively propounds it as the absolute ideal, as the most vital quality of a kind of man to which he himself belongs.

It is significant of much that had happened to Keats in the pregnant twenty months between that he now speaks of Dilke as ' one who cannot feel he has *a personal identity* until he has made up his mind about everything.' Since the letter to Bailey concerning Haydon Keats' whole conception of the sense of personal identity has changed. Negative Capability is become the only road to a true personal identity as it is to truth itself. Whereas in his letter to Bailey he had allowed that the Man of Genius ' had not any individuality, any determined character,' and he would call ' the head and top of those who have a proper self, Men of Power,' now, on the contrary, the head and top of those who have a proper self are Men of Genius; and true individuality is achieved through the achievement of Negative Capability.

This profound change in Keats' conception of personality seems at first sight almost a *volte face*. Provided we are aware that the process by which it was reached was gradual and organic, there is no harm, but rather much good, in considering it as a complete reversal of attitude on the most urgent of all ethical problems—the achievement of true personality. To conceive the change in this absolute and schematic fashion has at least the advantage of emphasizing the striking nature of the change itself, and fixing attention upon that aspect of Keats' genius which has yet to be fully recognized—the depth and significance of his thought upon the nature of man. Nevertheless, to conceive the change so rigidly is to conceive it falsely.

The germ of his future knowledge of the nature of personality was present in his mind almost at a moment when he was making a present of ' individuality ' and ' a proper self ' to Bailey's Man of Character. Very few days after that he was writing of Kean, that is, of the Shakespearean character as distinguished from the Wordsworthian: ' Kean delivers himself up to the instant feeling, without a shadow of a thought about anything else. He feels his being as deeply as Wordsworth, or any other of our intellectual monopolists.' That is a precise anticipation of the distinction he was to draw in September 1819 concerning Dilke. Dilke was ' an intellectual monopolist ' ; Dilke laboured under the error that he could not have a personal identity except by intellectual monopolism. No more exact description of what he meant by ' personal identity ' was ready to Keats' hand in December 1817 than the phrase ' to feel one's being deeply.'

What we are confronted with is an example—one of many, and perhaps the most important—of the working of what can only be called Keats' ' prophetic intuition.' In reality, he knew in December 1817 the true nature of personality, just as in December 1816 in *Sleep and Poetry* he knew the nature of pure poetry : but in the one case as in the other, the knowledge was intuitive and momentary. It had not yet become a secure possession of his highest consciousness; it had not yet become—to anticipate a later phraseology—an integral part of his soul-knowledge. The process by which Keats made it a part of his soul-knowledge can, I believe, be followed ; I have, at least, made the attempt to follow it. The moment when he did so can, I believe, be fixed ; I have, at least, made the attempt to fix it. Up to that moment of secure possession, the knowledge might waver. As such a moment of wavering we may, if we are so inclined, regard his letter to Woodhouse of 27th October 1818.

> The best answer I can give you (he writes to Woodhouse) is in a clerk-like manner to make some observations on two principal points which seem to point like indices into the midst of the whole pro and con about genius, and views, and achievements, and ambition, et cætera. 1st. As to the poetic character itself (I mean that sort, of which, if I am anything, I am a member; that sort distinguished from the Wordsworthian, or egotistical Sublime ; which is a thing *per se*, and stands alone), it is not itself—it has no self—It is everything and nothing—It has no character—it enjoys light and shade; it lives in gusto, be it foul or fair, high or low, rich or poor, mean or elevated. It has as much delight in conceiving an Iago as an Imogen. What shocks the virtuous philosopher delights the chameleon poet. It does no harm from its relish of the dark side of things, any more than from its taste for the bright one, because they both end in speculation.* A poet is

the most unpoetical of anything in existence, because he has no Identity—he is continually in for and filling some other body. The Sun,—the Moon,—the Sea, and men and women, who are creatures of impulse, are poetical, and have about them an unchanging attribute, the poet has none, no identity—he is certainly the most unpoetical of God's creatures.—If then he has no self, and if I am a poet, where is the wonder that I should say I would write no more ? Might I not at that very instant have been cogitating on the Characters of Saturn and Ops ? It is a wretched thing to confess, but it is a very fact, that not one word I ever utter can be taken for granted as an opinion growing out of my identical Nature—how can it, when I have no Nature ? When I am in a room with people, if I ever am free from speculating on creations of my own brain, then, not myself goes home to myself, but the identity of everyone in the room begins to press upon me, so that I am in a very little time annihilated—not only among men, it would be the same in a nursery of Children. I know not whether I make myself understood. . . .

That letter was written at a moment when Keats was passing through an extreme of suffering. He was living all his days at the bedside of his dearly loved and dying brother Tom.* His mood, and the effects of his mood upon his life and poetry are described in a later chapter. He was taking refuge from the anguish of life in the abstract images of *Hyperion*; he was making an agonized effort to detach himself from a suffering which, he felt, was gnawing at his own life. For the moment, however, it is interesting to follow the clue offered by the singular phrase : '*the identity of every one in the room begins to press upon me* so that I am in a very little time annihilated.' This striking phrase, with its potent suggestion of an almost physical suffocation, occurs three times in all in Keats' letters. The other two occasions belong to this same period—the late autumn of 1818. It first occurs in a letter to Dilke of 21st September 1818; second, in this letter to Woodhouse; and third, in a letter to his brother George of about the same time (October 1818). It does not occur again.* Evidently it is a phrase that is running in Keats' head; a phrase that corresponds to some recurrent quality of his experience at this moment and no other. To follow it home may yield an insight into Keats' condition of being. The full context is necessary to the understanding of it on its first appearance:

Reynolds, by what I hear, is almost over-happy (Keats wrote to Dilke), and Rice is in town. I have not seen him, nor shall I for some time, as my throat has become worse after getting well, and I am determined to stop at home till I am quite well. I was going to Town to-morrow with Mrs. D[ilke] but I thought it best to ask her excuse this morning. I wish I could say Tom was any better. *His identity presses upon me so all day* that I am obliged to go out—and although I intended to have given some time to study alone, I am obliged to write and plunge into abstract images to ease myself of his countenance, his voice, and feebleness—so that I live now in a continual fever. It must be poisonous to life, although I feel well. Imagine ' the hateful siege of contraries '—if I think of fame, of poetry, it seems a crime to me, and yet I must do so or suffer. . . .

To complete the picture we must add a few lines of the letter written to the ' over-happy ' Reynolds on the same day. Reynolds was engaged to be married. ' Think of nothing but pleasure,' Keats adjures him :

I pity you as much that it cannot last for ever, as I do myself now drinking bitters. . . . I never was in love—yet the voice and shape of a Woman has haunted me these two days—at such a time, when the relief, the feverous relief of Poetry seems a much less crime. This morning Poetry has conquered—I have relapsed into these abstractions which are my only life—I feel escaped from a new and threatening sorrow—and I am thankful for it. There is an awful warmth about my heart like a load of immortality. Poor Tom—that woman—and Poetry were ringing changes in my senses. . . .

There follows the letter to Woodhouse on the poetic character which has been already quoted. The next letter, to his brother and sister-in-law in America, also contains the revealing phrase:

Your content in each other is a delight to me which I cannot express—the Moon is now shining full and brilliant—she is the same to me in Matter, what you are to me in Spirit. If you were here my dear Sister I could not pronounce the words which I can write to you from a distance: I have a tenderness for you and an admiration which I feel to be as great and more chaste than I can have for any woman in the World. You will mention Fanny —her character is not formed, *her identity does not press upon me* as yours does. I hope from all my heart that I may one day feel as much for her as I do for you. . . .

It would be possible to take the phrase, in these three instances, as a vague expression taking its colour from the context. But surely it is the very opposite of a vague expression, and its occurrence in Keats' letters at this moment alone is extremely significant. Keats is in a condition receptive to the point of agony. Every nerve is tingling with awareness. And the condition has been created in him by his suffering from Tom's desperate illness—a suffering made still more acute by his own ill-health. No wonder that, when every contact threatens to annihilate him, he should stress his lack of personal identity in his letter to Woodhouse. Keats means what he says. One chance contact with a woman sets his whole being quivering for days. The only escape he can find is in the abstract images of *Hyperion*, in a world of imagination where he is partly himself and partly free. The moment he leaves it he is in jeopardy of annihilation once more.

This state of extreme and agonizing receptivity, this passive sensitiveness of the being, underlies the whole of his letter to Woodhouse on the poetic character. It is a condition which recurs continually in Keats' life, though perhaps but once again with such an accompaniment of pain; it is a condition essential to the nature of the pure poet. This is that moment in the unceasing process of the pure poet's being when he absorbs to his utmost capacity the material of 'sensation' out of which he creates both himself and his work. It is the 'negative' movement of which the 'positive' and inseparable counterpart is a more complete sense of identity and a richer poetic creation. The inward movement of the pure poet towards self-achievement is twofold. Keats is not really wavering in his belief as to the nature of the self; he is plunged into the depths of the 'negative' movement. When he emerged from it he emerged with a full knowledge of the necessity of this self-annihilation as a means to self-achievement. This is a form of that 'dying into life' through which he was afterwards to compel Apollo, and, in his revised *Hyperion*, the poet himself, to pass into possession of themselves.

In this excursion the chronological sequence of the story has been deliberately overrun in order that one deep effect of Shakespeare's influence upon Keats should be apparent in some of its manifold ramifications. It is beyond my power to hold all the threads of Keats' life together in an orderly chronological story without overburdening it beyond endurance. My hope is that this anticipation will enable the reader to respond to certain implications in the subsequent narrative which I cannot pause to emphasize. The real cause of these difficulties is not far to seek. It lies in the peculiar nature of Keats: he is organic and spontaneous; his being is not divided. His thoughts, his acts, his sufferings are all implicit in each other, so that the arbitrary detachment of a single thread is impossible without violence.

CHAPTER V

'PURGATORY BLIND'

WE are back at the beginning of 1818, on the threshold of the third year of Keats' poetic life. It opened ominously with an agonizing premonition of the shortness of his span, uttered in the sonnet:

> When I have fears that I may cease to be
> Before my pen has gleaned my teeming brain . . .;

and with the first symptoms of an unending heart-ache for the pains of humanity. 'One saying of yours I shall never forget,' he wrote to Bailey on 23rd January, 'merely you said, "Why should woman suffer"? Aye, why should she? . . . These things are, and he, who feels how incompetent the most skyey Knight-errantry is to heal this bruised fairness, is like a sensitive leaf in the hot hand of thought,' and he goes on to deplore a quarrel between Haydon and Reynolds in words filled with the humane and generous wisdom which seems to have been his birthright.

> Men should bear with each other: there lives not the Man who may not be cut up, aye Lashed to pieces on his weakest side. The best of men have but a portion of good in them—a kind of spiritual yeast in their frames, which creates the ferment of existence—by which a Man is propelled to act, and strive, and buffet with Circumstance. The sure way, Bailey, is first to know a Man's faults, and then be passive—if after that he insensibly draws you towards him then you have no power to break the link.

These opening utterances reveal the undertone of Keats' thought during the coming year. It is, to use the phrase of Wordsworth, which was dear to Keats, the year of 'the burden of the mystery' of human suffering and the pain of the world; to use his own more passionate phrase, it was the year of 'purgatory blind.' And Keats' sense of the pain of the world was no mere intellectual speculation upon 'the problem of evil': it was the knowledge of real experience. Tom Keats, his brother—of whom the third brother, George, declared that no one understood John as he did—was dying of consumption. Keats spent half the year at his side, in the spring at Teignmouth, in the winter at Hampstead, where he watched and tended him while he lingered towards inevitable death. Even to an ordinary man such an experience is terrible and crucial; it can change the pattern of a man's soul, because it alters the background of life from which the soul takes form. How much more then was this crucial for the soul of Keats, with his far greater share of that 'organic sensibility' which is the foundation of poetic genius, and his tormenting premonition that a like fate awaited him.

To give him courage to look fearlessly into the darkness and to bear unflinching the burden of the mystery, what had he? First and foremost, the secret vitality of his own genius, which enabled him to turn his face towards his own knowledge. Man's instinct is to turn away; but the chosen spirits are driven to look steadily upon the pain of the world. To comprehend this pain, they instinctively feel, is their duty and their privilege; by their honesty in striving to admit this to their souls their greatness and their truth will be measured. First and foremost then, as we shall see more clearly hereafter, Keats was maintained by the sense of his own poetic destiny. And, secondly, he had the example of Shakespeare, who had gone this way before him. He had learned from his great forerunner the secret of 'Negative Capability'—that the supreme poet is he who can accept the fact that the mystery must be, and wait for the moment when he can comprehend it by the faculty of poetic intuition, instead of impatiently turning for aid to faculties less potent than his own. That the example and inspiration of Shakespeare were of deep comfort to Keats in the opening months of this year we might have guessed, knowing what they had been to him before: but the evidence is there.

On 22nd January he is re-reading with passionate absorption *King Lear*—that example of the intensity of contemplation which 'makes all disagreeables evaporate from their being in close relationship with Beauty and Truth'—and re-reading it in such a ferment of the mind that, as he confesses, he is compelled to write a sonnet before opening the volume. It is an experience from which he shrinks and for which he has to prepare himself. He bids farewell to Romance and his delightful visions of beauty unalloyed and undisturbed.

> O golden-tongued Romance with serene lute!
> Fair plumed Syren! Queen of far away!
> Leave melodizing on this wintry day,
> Shut up thine olden pages, and be mute:
> Adieu! for once again the fierce dispute
> Betwixt damnation and impassion'd clay
> Must I burn through; once more humbly assay
> The bitter-sweet of this Shakespearian fruit.

Great poets mean what they say. It is easy to regard them as mere creators of beauty and to allow their strange words to slip pleasantly over the superficies of our minds: but the beauty of great poetry is not of this amiable and unexacting kind. It is a beauty that is truth. And the only way to understand it is to approach it with the conviction that the great poet, speaking deliberately, means what he says. That, in the simplest words, is the deep distinction between the great poet and the little one. The little poet does not mean what he says. But when Keats says: 'I must *burn* through the fierce dispute betwixt damnation and imprisoned clay,' he means it. He is about to endure an agony; he is going to be burned in the flames of suffering. And, in the closing lines of his sonnet, he also means what he says:

> Chief Poet! and ye clouds of Albion,
>   Begetters of our deep eternal theme,
> When through the old oak forest I am gone,
>   Let me not wander in a barren dream,
> But when I am consumed in the fire,
> Give me new Phœnix wings to fly at my desire.

This fire that he is to burn through will quite consume his soul. He asks that he shall not be left soulless and barren, but that a new soul shall be born in him: that he may have the strength to clasp the bitter knowledge that is in *King Lear* to his inmost self, and rise beyond it.

Perhaps the words which he wrote to Bailey on 13th March will stand as evidence that the importance of Shakespeare to Keats at this time is no invention. He tells Bailey that he is 'sometimes so very sceptical as to think Poetry itself a mere Jack o' Lantern to amuse whoever may chance to be struck by its brilliance.' In such a mood he thinks:

> Probably every mental pursuit takes its reality and worth from the ardour of the pursuer—being in itself a Nothing. Ethereal things may at least be thus real, divided under three heads—Things real, things semi-real, and nothings. Things real, such as existences of Sun, moon and Stars—and passages of Shakespeare. Things semi-real, such as love, the Clouds, etc., which require a greeting of the Spirit to make them wholly exist—and Nothings, which are made great and dignified by an ardent pursuit.

Keats is not altogether serious; he is in a curious and curiously attractive mood that we shall meet again during these months. But it is a very much more serious mood than the unwary observer would imagine. It could be described as a mood in which he is disinclined to make the effort to translate his poetic thought into the language of discourse; and it seems always to have followed a moment when his poetic thought had been intensely active. He goes on:

> I have written a sonnet here of a somewhat collateral nature—so don’t imagine it an ‘ apropos des bottes ’

That is an indication of Keats’ own awareness that the connection between his expressed thought and his true poetic thought is so occult that Bailey will be baffled; and also an assertion that the connection is nevertheless intimate. Here is the sonnet:

> Four Seasons fill the measure of the year;
> There are four seasons in the mind of Man:
> He hath his lusty Spring, when Fancy clear
> Takes in all beauty with an easy span:
> He has his Summer, when luxuriously
> He chews the honied cud of fair Spring thoughts,
> Till in his Soul, dissolv’d, they come to be
> Part of himself: He hath his Autumn Ports
> And havens of repose when his tired wings
> Are folded up and he content to look
> On Mists in idleness—to let fair things
> Pass by unheeded as a threshold brook.
> He has his Winter too of Pale misfeature
> Or else he would forego his mortal nature.

The relation between that lovely sonnet (which is intimately connected with the first sonnet *On Fame* and the *Ode to Autumn*) and the thought which preceded it is far from obvious. Yet Keats declares that the relation exists. We may have a glimmering of it if we understand that the sonnet expresses an acceptance of mortal destiny. The burden of the mystery, and the actual pain of the world, are natural to man. A part, and not the least part, of Keats’ share of that burden (as was to be made terribly plain in the second *Hyperion*) was a scepticism concerning the ultimate value of poetry as he himself practised it. That particular agony is also natural to man. And at this moment, filled with the mood of his sonnet, he can accept it and be light-hearted about it, but in the same moment of smiling acceptance he also declares his faith that ‘ passages of Shakespeare ’ belong with Sun, Moon and Stars to the highest and wholly real order of spiritual things.

That is no more than a crude outline of a simple and complex relation. It is given merely as finger-post to a reality that cannot be fully expressed. And Keats himself laughingly gives up all attempt to make the relation explicit:

> Now, my dear fellow (he says to Bailey), I must once for all tell you I have not one idea of the truth of any of my speculations—I shall never be a reasoner, because I care not to be in the right, when retired from bickering and in a proper philosophical temper.

But even that is an odd statement. When Keats is in the true philosophical temper he does not care to be in the right. That is to say, his philosophy is the very reverse of what is ordinarily understood by philosophy. And that is the key to the little *aperçu* on Wordsworth in a letter to his brothers three weeks before (21st February). He says that he is sorry that Wordsworth has left a bad impression wherever he visited in Town by his egotism, vanity and bigotry. ‘Yet he is a great poet, if not a philosopher.’ What Keats holds to be true philosophy abstains from all dogmatism, from all self-assertion, from all ‘irritable reaching after fact and reason.’ True philosophy is precisely that Negative Capability that was so supremely manifested in Shakespeare. It proceeds from a natural submission of the self to all experience.

What that natural submission is, how it can be achieved, and to what it leads will concern us hereafter. But for the moment we must be content to imagine these two thoughts of ‘naturalness’ and of Shakespeare as dominant and intimately related in Keats’ mind. Shakespeare is the ideal embodiment of the quality of ‘naturalness.’ The closeness of the connection is plainly visible in a letter to Taylor his publisher, written on 27th February to thank him for an alteration which he has made in the proofs of *Endymion*. (How different was Keats from the irritable race of bards is beautifully apparent in his modest and frank acceptance of the alteration as ‘a great improvement’.)

> In *Endymion* (he continues) I have most likely but moved into the go-cart from the leading-strings. In poetry I have a few axioms, and you will see how far I am from their centre.
>
> 1st. I think poetry should surprise by a fine excess, and not by singularity; it should strike the reader as a wording of his own thoughts, and appear almost a remembrance.
>
> 2nd. Its touches of beauty should never be half-way, thereby making the reader breathless, instead of content. The rise, the progress, the setting of Imagery should, like the sun, come natural to him, shine over him, and set soberly, although in magnificence, leaving him in the luxury of twilight. But it is easier to think what poetry is, than to write it. And this leads me to
>
> Another axiom—That if poetry comes not as naturally as the leaves to a tree, it had better not come at all.

It is not in any way forcing the sense of those axioms to say that they are wholly based on some idea in Keats’ mind of the ‘naturalness’ of poetry. Poetry should come naturally from the poet, it should come naturally to the reader. This word ‘natural’ is vague, and has been the parent of innumerable misunderstandings from the Greek Sophists onwards. But to Keats the word ‘natural’ obviously has nothing to do with what has been called 'the state of nature.' What comes naturally to the reader is not his everyday speech, but his 'own highest thoughts.' These thoughts which are his, and naturally his, though the reader could not utter them, are uttered by the poet; and this utterance should come naturally to the poet.*

We cannot at this moment make any further advance towards a comprehension of what Keats means by 'natural'. Fundamentals are involved, for what we understand by 'natural to man' depends immediately upon our conception of the nature of man and of the human soul. We shall not avoid this encounter with fundamentals: the chief purpose of this book is to show that it is inevitable. But for the moment we must be content with whatever hints we may glean from that connection between 'naturalness' and Shakespeare, which was dominant in Keats' mind, and with noting how different is Keats' conception of naturalness in poetry from that of a Wordsworth or a Leigh Hunt, intent on 'the real language of real people.' On 23rd January he wrote to his brothers that he had shown the first book of *Endymion* to Hunt:

> He allows it not much merit on the whole; says it is unnatural and made ten objections to it in the mere skimming over. He says the conversation is unnatural and too high-flown for Brother and Sister—says it should be simple, forgetting do ye mind that they are both overshadowed by a supernatural Power, and of force could not speak like Francesca in the *Rimini*. He must first prove that Caliban's poetry is unnatural. This with me completely overturns his objections.

That makes it clear that Keats' ideal of naturalness in poetry is the naturalness of Shakespeare. But the connection is still more strikingly revealed in the continuation of the letter to Taylor. 'However it may be with me,' he goes on after enouncing his third axiom, 'I cannot help looking into new countries with an 'O for a muse of Fire to ascend'!

> If *Endymion* serves me as a pioneer, perhaps I ought to be content—I have great reason to be content, for thank God I can read, and perhaps understand Shakespeare to his depths; and I have I am sure many friends who, if I fail, will attribute any change in my life and temper to humbleness rather than pride—to a cowering under the wings of great poets rather than to a bitterness that I am not appreciated.

The underlying thought throughout that passage and throughout this period is intimately connected with Shakespeare. It is no accident that Keats’ temper should be expressed in that beautiful and wholly Shakespearean sonnet: ‘Four Seasons fill the measure of the year.’ It is his understanding of Shakespeare which brings him not only a knowledge of what true poetry is, but content and humility, though it may bring him also a change of life and temper which may be misunderstood except by his intimates. His winter of pale misfeature is at hand.

Throughout this year and to the end of his life, Keats intermittently felt the need of withdrawal and retirement, in which he could acquire the depths of knowledge which would fit him for the heights of poetry he dreamed. Two months later, writing again to Taylor (24th April), he more definitely utters what is in his mind:

> I find earlier days are gone by—I find that I can have no enjoyment in the world but continual drinking of knowledge. I find that there is no worthy pursuit but the idea of doing some good to the world. Some do it with their society—some with their wit—some with their benevolence—some with a sort of power of conferring pleasure and good humour on all they meet—and in a thousand ways, all dutiful to the command of great Nature—there is but one way for me. The road lies through application, study, and thought. I will pursue it; and for that end purpose retiring for some years. I have been hovering for some time between an exquisite sense of the luxurious, and a love for philosophy—were I calculated for the former, I should be glad. But as I am not, I shall turn all my soul to the latter. . . .

There is no need to insist further that the word Philosophy in Keats’ writings does not mean the technical subject which bears that name. What it means is a comprehension (and a comprehension of a peculiar kind) of the mystery of human life. To acquire this comprehension is necessary for Keats if he is to achieve his purpose of doing some good in the world by poetry. The thought, what good to humanity is done or may be done by poetry, was never far from Keats’ mind henceforward. He had his moments of doubt, which later became agonizing: but even in the supreme struggle which is marked by the re-cast of *Hyperion*, he conquered his doubts. Unshakable convictions and inviolable principles do not fall to the lot of the men of genius who are the epitomes of the life of humanity at its most intense; they are the prerogatives of another kind of men. Still, provided that we retain a sense of the kind of man of whom we are saying it, we may say that Keats never really wavered in his belief that the highest kind of poetry was the vehicle of the highest kind of truth, and as such the supreme benefit that could be conferred upon humanity at large. This highest kind of poetry, Keats felt, called for great sacrifice and demanded great suffering. It is only half with exhilaration, and half with foreboding, that he decides upon his self-dedication to the inexorable god of poetic truth. Were he calculated for a life of exquisite delight in beauty, he would be glad. But he is not, he is driven to another destiny.

Poetic genius is a thing of organic life: it cannot be wholly comprehended in its own definitions of itself, or confined into its own declarations of its purposes, for those definitions and declarations cannot in the nature of things be more than partial. In trying to grasp its essential reality, we also, like the poet himself, are dependent on our powers of intuition, for intuition alone will enable us to apprehend the essence that lies behind all partial formulations. We must be prepared at any moment to reconcile apparent contradictions, and to reconcile them not by an arbitrary and enforced accommodation of one to the other, but by a deeper perception which can reach to the living reality which evades direct expression. It has already been emphasized that the Philosophy to which Keats proposed to dedicate himself was quite different from the philosophy of the schools: a further passage from his letters at this time will show that the whole process of acquiring knowledge which he had in mind was one which would hardly be given that name by the man of common sense. On 18th February he wrote to Reynolds on the virtues of 'delicious, diligent Indolence.' 'Diligent Indolence'—it is a happy phrase; let us see what it meant.

> I had an idea (he wrote) that a Man might pass a very pleasant life in this manner—let him on a certain day read a certain Page of full Poesy or distilled Prose, and let him wander with it, and muse upon it, and reflect upon it, and prophesy upon it, and dream upon it, until it becomes stale—but when will it do so? Never! . . . Nor will this sparing touch of noble Books be any irreverence to their Writers—for perhaps the honours paid by Man to Man are trifles in comparison to the Benefit done by great Works to the 'Spirit and pulse' of good by their mere passive existence. Memory should not be called Knowledge.

'Memory should not be called Knowledge.' The mere remembering of great works is not knowledge of them: knowledge of them arises out of a passive saturation, and for this saturation and the subsequent creative activity of the spirit but little is necessary. A dozen lines of 'full poesy' are enough. Then he goes on:

> Man should not dispute or assert but whisper results to his neighbour and thus by every germ of spirit sucking the sap from mould ethereal every human might become great, and Humanity instead of being a wide heath of Furze and Briars, with here and there a remote Oak or Pine, would become a grand democracy of Forest Trees. . . .

It is a restatement, from a different angle, with a different vista beyond, of his ideal of Negative Capability and his renunciation of all irritable reaching after fact and reason. The results of this ‘diligent indolence,’ this quiet receptivity of the soul, are not to be asserted but whispered. If men would allow themselves such natural and effortless expansion, Humanity would be no longer a vast and indistinguishable aggregate but a company of individual souls. ‘Let us not therefore’ (he continues) ‘go hurrying about and collecting honey, bee-like buzzing here and there impatiently from a knowledge of what is to be aimed at,* but let us open our leaves like a flower and be passive and receptive.’ And then he makes Reynolds a regal present of the lines which the thrush sang to him :

> O thou whose face hath felt the Winter's wind,
> Whose eye has seen the snow-clouds hung in mist,
> And the black elm-tops 'mong the freezing stars,
> To thee the Spring will be a harvest time.
> O thou, whose only book has been the light
> Of supreme darkness which thou feddest on
> Night after night when Phoebus was away,
> To thee the Spring shall be a triple morn.
> O fret not after knowledge—I have none,
> And yet my song comes native with the warmth.
> O fret not after knowledge—I have none,
> And yet the Evening listens. He who saddens
> At thought of idleness cannot be idle,
> And he's awake who thinks himself asleep.

In a sense Keats is not quite serious. He is in a mood that we have met before. He admits it. ‘I am sensible’ (he says) ‘all this is a mere sophistication (however it may neighbour to any truths), to excuse my own indolence.’ But the neighbouring truth is there. The knowledge he seeks cannot be gained by intellectual determination and clenched teeth; like poetry itself it has to come as naturally as the leaves to a tree. It is born of a brooding over real experience, not over intellectual abstractions. It is the knowledge not of the philosopher, but of the poet.

We must have the meaning of these three conceptions—of Negative Capability, of diligent Indolence, of Knowledge as an instinctive faculty of the complete man—present continually to our minds whenever Keats is talking of knowledge or philosophy, and in particular while we examine the magnificent letter which he wrote to Reynolds on 3rd May. We must remember always that philosophy for Keats is intuitive, and knowledge is organic; and by this word ‘organic’ is meant that it is not a knowledge that can be *added* to oneself. Memory is not knowledge. This knowledge is essentially self-engendered; it is the self's creation of itself out of experience; it is a shaping of the soul by a true contact with reality;—and this dark saying may be added, that it is a thing which cannot be uttered directly, but only by the language of metaphor and parable, which is poetry. This was the knowledge after which Keats fretted, not ' a knowledge of what is to be aimed at ';—a consolidation into a permanent possession of his scattered intuitions—a knowledge which should partake as much of the nature of being as of the nature of knowing.

> An extensive knowledge (he wrote to Reynolds) is needful to thinking people—it takes away the heat and fever; and helps, by widening speculation, to ease the Burden of the Mystery, a thing which I begin to understand a little, and which weighed upon you in the most gloomy and true sentence in your letter. The difference of high Sensations with and without knowledge appears to me this: in the latter case we are falling continually ten thousand fathoms deep and being blown up again, without wings, and with all the horror of a bare-shouldered creature—in the former case, our shoulders are fledged, and we go through the same air and space without fear. This is running one's rigs on the score of abstracted benefit. [That is to say, the intellectual knowledge of which he is mainly speaking so far is abstract, not proven and made concrete by experience.] When we come to human Life and the affections, it is impossible to know how a parallel of breast and head can be drawn . . . it is impossible to know how far knowledge will console us for the death of a friend, and the ill ' that flesh is heir to.' . . . You may perhaps be anxious to know for fact to what sentence in your Letter I allude. You say: ' I fear there is little chance of anything else in this life ' [than pain, probably] —you seem by that to have been going through with a more painful and acute zest the same labyrinth that I have—I have come to the same conclusion thus far. My Branchings out therefrom have been numerous: one of them is the consideration of Wordsworth's genius and as a help, in the manner of gold being the meridian Line of worldly wealth, how he differs from Milton. And here I have nothing but surmises, from an uncertainty whether Milton's apparently less anxiety for Humanity proceeds from his seeing further or not than Wordsworth: and whether Wordsworth has in truth epic passion, and martyrs himself to the human heart, the main region of his song. In regard to his genius alone—we find what he says true as far as we have experienced, and we can judge no further but by larger experience—for axioms in philosophy are not axioms till they are proved upon our pulses. We read fine things, but never feel them to the full until we have

> gone the same steps as the author. I know this is not plain: you will know exactly my meaning when I say that now I shall relish *Hamlet* more than I ever have done. . . .

At this point Keats takes a long plunge into fun. He laughs at himself and his letter, breaks off for dinner, and returns to the question of Wordsworth—' whether or no he has an extended vision or a circumscribed grandeur—whether he is an eagle in his nest or on the wing.'

> And to be more explicit and to show you how tall I stand by the giant, I will put down a simile of human life as I now perceive it; that is, to the point to which I say we both have arrived at. Well—I compare human life to a large Mansion of many apartments, two of which I can only describe, the doors of the rest being as yet shut upon me. The first we step into we call the Infant, or Thoughtless Chamber, in which we remain so long as we do not think. We remain there a long while, and notwithstanding the doors of the second Chamber remain wide open, showing a bright appearance, we care not to hasten to it; but are at length imperceptibly impelled by the awakening of the thinking principle within us—we no sooner get into the second Chamber, which I shall call the Chamber of Maiden-Thought, than we become intoxicated with the light and the atmosphere, we see nothing but pleasant wonders, and think of delaying there for ever in delight. However among the effects this breathing is father of is that tremendous one of sharpening one's vision into the heart and nature of Man—of convincing one's nerves [not one's mind] that the World is full of Misery and Heartbreak, Pain, Sickness and oppression—whereby this Chamber of Maiden-Thought becomes gradually darkened, and at the same time, on all sides of it, many doors are set open—but all dark—all leading to dark passages. We see not the balance of good and evil [that is, the harmony of good and evil]; we are in a mist, *we* are now in that state, we feel the 'Burden of the Mystery.' To this point was Wordsworth come, as far as I can conceive, when he wrote *Tintern Abbey*, and it seems to me that his genius is explorative of those dark Passages. Now if we live, and go on thinking, we too shall explore them. . . .

Towards the end of the letter occur a few lines which reveal by a sudden flash how Keats' philosophy was being 'proved upon his pulses,' and how resolutely he was facing the ordeal:

> After all there is certainly something real in the world—Moore's present to Hazlitt is real—I like that Moore, and am glad I saw him at the Theatre just before I left town. Tom has spit a *leetle* blood this afternoon, and that is rather a damper—but I know—the truth is, there is something real in the World.

In this last sentence, if we read it in the full illumination of its context, is expressed the nature of the struggle that was occupying Keats' soul. He was proving upon his pulses, being convinced in his nerves that life was a contradiction—on the one hand its beauty, on the other its pain. The discord was naked and unresolved; and yet he had a deep instinctive conviction that it could be resolved. This agonizing contradiction, he felt now dimly, now clearly, was in some sort an appearance. Real, yes; torturingly real, but real as the outward and necessary manifestation of a mystery, not as the inward core of the mystery itself. This is the faith which he proclaims in the sentence: 'Tom has spit a leetle blood this afternoon and that is rather a damper—but I *know*—the truth is, there is something real in the world.' It is the critical moment: the burden of the mystery is full upon him. It was never to leave him, and he was never to be crushed beneath it.

At about this time Keats had sent an epistle in verse to Reynolds (25th March 1818), in which he gives more fully perhaps than in his letters, the whole turmoil of his soul, its doubts and surmises. He says that he has been lying awake with a throng of disjointed and disturbing phantasms, which must fall to the lot of all men save the happy few whose dreams are of beauty only:

> Some Titian colours touch'd into real life,—
> The sacrifice goes on; the pontiff knife
> Gleams in the Sun, the milk-white heifer lows,
> The pipes go shrilly, the libation flows:
> A white sail shows above the green-head cliff,
> Moves round the point, and throws her anchor stiff;
> The mariners join hymn with those on land.

Quite casually thrown off, the picture is bright with the serene of beauty, and shines with the radiance of a golden age. Keats turns aside into a romantic mediaeval vision, based on a picture by Claude: then he breaks off, and cries:

> O that our dreamings all, of sleep or wake,
> Would all their colours from the sunset take:
> From something of material sublime,
> Rather than shadow our own soul's day-time
> In the dark void of night. For in the world
> We jostle,——

He does not end the thought. He is not mature, he says, he dares not yet philosophize:

> Oh, never will the prize,
> High reason, and the love of good and ill,
> Be my award!

The words are striking: let us understand them clearly. The prize, which he despairs of obtaining, is ‘ High reason, and the *love* of good and ill.’* It is the same goal as that announced in the letter to Reynolds. ‘ We see not the balance of good and evil.’ There is a point of vision to be attained whence the chaos and contradiction of the world can be seen as a harmony, and loved as a harmony. That is what Keats means by ‘ the love of good and ill.’ This final harmony he surmises but cannot see. How shall he attain to the sight of it? He goes on:

> Things cannot to the will
> Be settled, but they tease us out of thought.

Intellectual comprehension is impotent: thought breaks like a reed in one's hands.

> Or is it that Imagination brought
> Beyond its proper bound, yet still confin'd,
> Lost in a sort of Purgatory blind,
> Cannot refer to any standard law
> Of either earth or heaven? It is a flaw
> In happiness, to see beyond our bourn,—
> It forces us in summer skies to mourn,
> It spoils the singing of the Nightingale.

How, and to what recompense of eternal truth the singing of the nightingale was spoiled for Keats, the *Ode to a Nightingale* is witness. That bird-voice was to become immeasurably richer and more magical, for having blent with it the pain of mystery in the poet's soul.

> Dear Reynolds! I have a mysterious tale
> And cannot speak it: the first page I read
> Upon a Lampit rock of green sea-weed
> Among the breakers; 'twas a quiet eve,
> The rocks were silent, the wide sea did weave
> An untumultuous fringe of silver foam
> Along the flat brown sand; I was at home
> And should have been most happy,—but I saw
> Too far into the sea, where every maw
> The greater or the less feeds evermore.—
> But I saw too distinct into the core
> Of an eternal fierce destruction,
> And so from happiness I far was gone.
> Still am I sick of it, and tho', to-day,
> I've gather'd young spring-leaves and flowers gay
> Of periwinkle and wild strawberry,
> Still do I that most fierce destruction see,—

The Shark at savage prey,—the Hawk at pounce,—
The gentle Robin, like a Pard or Ounce,
Ravening a worm. . . .

The vision should be remembered, for it was to revisit Keats in a changed light. For the present it stands as the vision of the pain and evil of the world irremediably opposed to the vision of the beautiful and the good; yet not quite irremediably, for Keats has a surmise of a condition of soul, although he despairs of attaining it, in which the good and evil of the world will be perceived as a harmony and loved as a harmony.

CHAPTER VI

'BEAUTY IN ALL THINGS'

IN the early summer of 1818, Keats left England for an arduous and exhausting walking-tour in Scotland, which lowered his vital powers of resistance to the seeds of disease which he had inherited. Throughout the spring he had been with his invalid brother Tom at Teignmouth, and he had felt the overpowering and desperate desire of a man who had been watching and watching over the illness of a loved one to be free for a space of the devouring agony of helpless sympathy, which gnaws at the heart and nerves. But such a respite is not to be had: Keats did not find it on his Scottish tour. The effect was like that of a drug which fails to work: he was not taken out of himself, and he was exhausted bodily. He returned with an obstinate 'sore-throat' that never left him. The undertone of the mood in which he left England may be gathered from a letter to Bailey written on 10th June:

> Were it in my choice, I would reject a Petrarchal coronation—on account of my dying day, and because women have cancers. . . . Now I am never alone without rejoicing that there is such a thing as death, without placing my ultimate in the glory of dying for a great human purpose.

The great human purpose, which was henceforward for ever in Keats' mind, was the writing of great poetry: and poetry to be great, had to comprehend and be adequate to the pain and suffering of the world, to be informed by that 'high reason and the love of good and ill,' which he knew, by his own intuition and Shakespeare's example, might be achieved. The poetry of *King Lear*, which by its intensity was 'capable of making all disagreeables evaporate from their being in close relationship with Beauty and Truth,' was the ideal. And perhaps, if we know how the seeds of the dread disease from which he suffered bring with them to the mind of genius an almost prophetic clarity of knowledge, we shall not think it fanciful to suppose that Keats had already a presentiment that he would be required to die for his great human purpose.

For the moment it was inevitable that Keats' vision of the ideal should be beyond his accomplishment. His chief works of this year were *Isabella, or the Pot of Basil* in the spring; and the greater part of the first *Hyperion* in the winter, when he had returned from Scotland, himself ill, to take up his place by the side of his dying brother. *Isabella* is the least mature of all his complete long poems after *Endymion.* It is a poem with many beauties and many weaknesses; and I am completely unable to understand the process of mind of those critics who place it at the head and front of Keats' long poems. I can understand the attitude of a mind which on principle places a complete poem before an incomplete one, though the attitude is not my own. But if Keats' complete long poems are to be considered apart from *Hyperion,* then surely *Isabella* is the least of the three in true poetic power. One may prefer *The Eve of St. Agnes* to *Lamia* for its sheer opulence of imaginative realization, or *Lamia* to *The Eve of St. Agnes* for its dramatic intensity: that is a matter partly of taste, partly of one's views concerning the highest form of poetry. But that both these poems are superior to *Isabella* seems to me not a question of taste at all.

The greatest of all Keats' long poems is to me undoubtedly *Hyperion,* whether we consider it in its original and familiar form, as it appeared in the 1820 volume, or in the revised form as *The Fall of Hyperion: a Dream.* But in neither form is *Hyperion* as perfect as the *Odes.* They have the same deep sufficiency of inspiration and the same wealth of profound experience as *Hyperion,* and they have a perfection of form which *Hyperion* has not. Still, *Hyperion* is the greater achievement. It was begun in the autumn of this year 1818, when Keats had returned ill from his Scottish tour and was spending painful days at the bedside of his dying brother, dying of the same disease of which Keats' obstinate sore-throat was a premonitory symptom.

Hyperion differs from all Keats' other poems in one important respect. Its composition was frequently interrupted and abandoned and resumed. *Endymion, Isabella, The Eve of St. Agnes, Lamia* were all written straight ahead. The *Odes*—so far as we can tell—were each written in one piece. But *Hyperion* was composed quite differently. It is impossible to say with the certainty of external evidence when many parts of it were written. We know that it was begun in the September of 1818, that it was taken up again in January and the early spring of 1819, that a complete recast of the poem was begun in the summer, and finally that the poem was abandoned altogether in both forms in September 1819. In this book the attempt is made to prove by internal evidence that the first two books of *Hyperion* were written before the end of 1819; but that the main portion of the third book belongs to a different and later period of Keats' development.

A consideration of the causes why *Hyperion* was abandoned does not belong to this year 1818, but only a consideration of the causes why it was begun. We may say that Keats had fallen under the spell of Milton: and, if we remember the nature of the man of whom we are speaking, the phrase will pass. But few of those who use the phrase do remember the nature of the man of whom they use it, and therefore they forget that the kind of spell which Milton had for Keats was in the nature of things limited and circumscribed. We need only to remember the letter to Reynolds, in which Keats compares Milton with Wordsworth, and decides that Wordsworth 'thinks deeper into the human heart' to see that Milton could not finally satisfy Keats, and to understand the nature of the spell which Milton exerted upon him. It was the spell of a great technique and a prodigious art; and, more potent than this, it was the spell of a verse which could be constructed by a man of genius in abstraction from the torment of experience. Milton held for Keats the promise of a release from the pain of life, of a world of abstractions into which he could enter and be free, where his poetic genius would be nobly occupied and his overstrained nerves relaxed. Towards the end of September, when the work on *Hyperion* was well begun, he wrote to Reynolds, who was about to be married:

> I conjure you to think at present of nothing but pleasure. . . . I pity you as much that it cannot last for ever, as I do myself now drinking bitters. . . . This morning Poetry has conquered—I have relapsed into those abstractions which are my only life. . . .

On the same day he wrote to Dilke:

> I wish I could say Tom was any better. His identity presses on me so all day that I am obliged to go out—and although I intended to have given some time to study alone, I am obliged to plunge into abstract images to ease myself of his countenance, his voice, and feebleness.

Hyperion and Miltonics were a refuge of abstractions that Keats was building for himself to shut out the concrete world. But the hiding place which an architect of genius builds for himself is a palace. I am not, as I hope to prove abundantly, trying to diminish by a single scruple the sublime beauty of *Hyperion*. For me, taken together with its recast induction, it is the pinnacle of Keats' actual achievement; but because I wish to show that Keats was greater, far greater, than his actual achievement, because I wish to present him as the perfect type of the great poet, as a poetic genius second only to Shakespeare in our literature, and of the same pattern as Shakespeare, I am concerned at this moment to show that *Hyperion* was not central to Keats' poetic purposes. Those purposes were persistent, and I have tried to show their inward nature. They had a definite outward embodiment also. Keats' purpose was not to write epics, or even odes, but to write plays; all the poems he wrote from *Endymion* onwards were but a step towards his 'chief attempt in the drama'; he desired to reveal the truth of human life, not through abstractions, but in a mirrored reflection of life itself. The drama as the supreme height of literature was a necessary part of Keats' 'vast idea'; it was in the hierarchy of literary forms that alone which permitted the identification of the poet with every manifestation of the human universe, which as he had told Woodhouse in a letter of this time (27th October) was fundamental to the poetical character:

> As to the poetical character itself (he wrote)—I mean that sort, of which, if I am anything, I am a member; that sort distinguished from the Wordsworthian or egotistical Sublime— . . . it is not itself—it has no self.—It is everything and nothing.—It has no character—it enjoys light and shade; it lives in gusto, be it foul or fair, high or low, rich or poor, mean or elevated. It has as much delight in conceiving an Iago as an Imogen. What shocks the virtuous philosopher delights the chameleon poet. . . A poet is the most unpoetical of any thing in existence, because he has no Identity—he is continually in for and filling some other body.

Keats saw truly into the nature of his own genius. It was, as we say nowadays, objective; it was concrete; it moved not in a world of philosophic thought and abstraction, but in a world of imaginative realizations. It was purely and truly poetic; and it turned towards the drama as the form which offered the most complete fulfilment of its own nature. At the beginning of this year (30th January) he had written to Taylor, his publisher, concerning the passage of *Endymion*, beginning 'Wherein lies happiness, Peona,' that his having written that argument would perhaps be of the greatest service to him of anything he ever did.

> It set before me the gradations of happiness, even like a kind of pleasure thermometer, and is my first step towards the chief attempt in the drama. The playing of different natures with joy and Sorrow.

The drama, then, as the necessary form of 'the vast idea', was already an essential part of Keats' intention; and perhaps we have gained some perception of what was to be embodied in it—the apprehension of Beauty as Truth, the high reason which brings with it 'the love of good and ill,' the acceptance of the burden of the mystery as a thing not to be dissipated by some trick of the intellect, or by some self-delusion imposed by 'an irritable reaching after fact and reason.' But we shall find no deeper, nor any more transparent, phrase for the content of Keats' ideal poetry than his own familiar words: 'the principle of beauty in all things.'

This phrase is usually and rightly remembered in the form in which Keats wrote it to Fanny Brawne soon after the haemorrhage which told him of his inevitable end. 'If I should die, said I to myself, I have left no immortal work behind me, nothing to make my friends proud of my memory, but I have loved the principle of beauty in all things, and if I had had time, I would have made myself remembered.' It seems almost a sacrilege to anatomize words so poignant, so lovely. They are locked up in men's hearts for ever, as the voice of one of the bravest and wisest and most beautiful spirits this England has been privileged to engender—the voice of one who is passed beyond pride and beyond humility. But because they are so precious and so haunting, it is our duty to know what they mean.

The meaning of the words 'I have loved the principle of beauty in all things' is not obvious. Of course, if they are taken vaguely as meaning 'I have loved beauty,' there is no difficulty; and since I have never seen an admission that a difficulty exists, I suppose that this vague sense is the one that is usually given to them. It seems clear to me that they mean more than this; but when we try to extract the further meaning from them, by giving each word its full weight the difficulty begins. For we can read them in two ways, thus: 'I have loved the principle of beauty—in all things,' or, 'I have loved the principle—of beauty in all things.' Between these two interpretations there is a vital difference. In the first case 'principle' means 'element': it is the old *principium* of the scholastic philosophers which survives in such a phrase as 'the vital principle': and Keats' sentence will run 'I have loved the element of beauty—in all things.' And, again, even this is not quite clear: he may be saying that he has loved this element of beauty, in whatsoever things he has found it, or he may be saying that he has loved this element of beauty, and he has found it in all things. Even there the difference is important: but whichever of these interpretations we choose, the underlying thought is the famous thought of Plato: that there is an ideal and perfect Beauty which is partially manifested, as a shadow is a manifestation of the object which casts it, in the beautiful things of earth. 'This ideal beauty,' Keats will then be saying, 'I have loved'; and there is no means of telling whether he is saying further that he has loved it in whatsoever thing he has found it, or that he has found it in everything.

This may appear a singularly abstruse sort of quibbling. I ask those who shrink from it to remember that we are dealing with Keats' central thought, and that the central thought of a poetic genius such as his is not likely to be simple to understand; I ask them also to realize that there is all the difference in the world between the statement 'I have loved beauty, and beauty is in all things' and the statement 'I have loved all beautiful things.' The one implies acceptance, the other, rejection. With a sense of that difference in our minds, and a sense also of the importance of deciding which was Keats' belief, let us read the sentence as I believe it should be read, not as 'I have loved the principle of beauty—in all things,' but as 'I have loved the principle—of beauty in all things.' 'Principle' now does not mean 'element,' it means 'idea'; and Keats is saying 'I have loved the idea, that there is beauty in all things.' Now, I admit that if I had that single sentence alone to interpret: 'I have loved the principle of beauty in all things,' I should hesitate to read it 'I have loved the principle—of beauty in all things,' even though I am convinced that Keats meant by his sentence not that he had loved all beautiful things; but that he had loved beauty and beauty is in all things.

But the sentence does not stand alone. The phrase 'the principle of Beauty' occurs elsewhere in Keats' letters; so does the phrase 'Beauty in all things.' In the spring of this year, 1818, he had written to Reynolds (9th April): 'I have not the slightest feel of humility towards the public—or to anything in existence—but the eternal Being, the principle of Beauty, and the Memory of great Men.' That absolute use of the phrase would settle the question, were it not that six months later (October 1818) we find him writing to his brother George, then in America: 'The mighty abstract Idea I have of Beauty in all things stifles the more divided and minute domestic happiness.'

Those two sentences, in their sequence, the first in the spring, the second in the autumn of this year of 'purgatory blind,' are of cardinal importance. They establish the real meaning of 'I have loved the principle—of Beauty in all things': that love is essentially the same as 'the love of good and ill' for which he had striven. They reveal the intimate connection between 'the principle—of Beauty in all things' and 'the vast idea' which came to Keats in *Sleep and Poetry*; it was 'the mighty abstract idea of Beauty in all things.' And above all they reveal, in the history of a single phrase, the secret movement of Keats' mind. The 'vast idea' of *Sleep and Poetry* had involved the poet's passing beyond 'the realm of Flora and old Pan,' that is away from the realm of beautiful things. He had asked

> And can I ever bid these joys farewell?

And he had answered:

> Yes, I must pass them for a nobler life
> Where I may find the agonies, the strife
> Of human hearts.

He had thus, in that prophetic poem, seen beyond the principle of beauty to the principle of beauty in all things. But in *Endymion*, for all his efforts, he had remained almost wholly within 'the realm of

Flora and old Pan.' The principle of beauty had triumphed over the principle of beauty in all things. For many reasons, but for one in chief: Keats was a truly natural poet who could not write save out of that which he had proved upon his pulses: 'The agonies, the strife of human hearts' had not yet touched him directly. Ecstatic contemplation of beauty, the being thrown 'into a sort of oneness'—that he knew by direct experience; but the pain of life he did not know. He knew that he had to triumph over pain, but the pain had not yet come, and he was not one to invoke it intellectually. A merely intellectual reality was no reality at all to him; even 'a proverb was no proverb to him until his life had illustrated it.' And so in April 1818, when he is writing to Reynolds with *Endymion* in his mind, regarding the preface to *Endymion*, it is simply 'the principle of beauty' of which he speaks. He has just been putting his loyalty to the principle again to the proof by writing *Isabella*, which is pre-eminently a romantic tale in the sense of being devoid of all substance of actual life-experience.

At this very moment, when he was proclaiming the principle of beauty thus absolutely, pain had approached him: he was condemned to watch his brother die. He knew that in his actual life he was to be called upon to bid a long farewell to the principle of beauty. It was then that he was convinced upon his nerves of the pain and misery and heartbreak in the world, and confessed his despair of attaining to the love of good *and* ill. It was then that he told Taylor (24th April) that he 'had been hovering for some time between an exquisite sense of the luxurious and a love for philosophy.' The exquisite sense of the luxurious is the homage to the principle of beauty; philosophy is to Keats the apprehension of the principle of beauty in *all* things. Now he is caught midway between the two: he has lost hold of the one, he has not laid hold of the other. This is the condition he describes in the *Epistle to Reynolds:*

> Or is it that Imagination brought
> Beyond its proper bound, yet still confin'd,
> Lost in a sort of Purgatory blind
> Cannot refer to any standard law
> Of either earth or heaven? It is a flaw
> In happiness to see beyond our bourn.

This 'purgatory blind' is the condition which lies between allegiance to the principle of beauty and discovery of the principle of beauty in all things. This year 1818 had been a year of such a purgatory. After *Isabella* Keats wrote nothing until he began *Hyperion*, and in that poem the principle of beauty changes to the principle of beauty in all things. It is, as he tells his brother George, still a mighty *abstract* idea; he speaks, as ever, truly, for in *Hyperion* the 'vast idea' *is* abstract; but it is there—and the remainder of Keats' life was to be burned away in the process of its becoming concrete in and through pain.

'Beauty in all things.' This was Keats' great poetic intuition, and the revelation of this beauty the great human purpose to which he dedicated himself and for which he was prepared to die. It sounds simple; it is tremendous. It involves a profound acceptance of life as it is, a passing beyond all rebellion, not into the apathy of stoic resignation, but into a condition of soul to which the sum of things —'foul or fair, high or low, rich or poor'—is revealed as necessary and true and beautiful: and for the creative genius of the poet it means not only to have this vision, not only to have attained 'high reason, and the love of good and ill,' but to have the purpose and the power to reveal to men that good and ill are to be loved; not only the faculty to see that the sum of things is supremely beautiful, but the faculty to show to other men that it is supremely beautiful.

Such an achievement, Keats knew, was possible only in the form in which Shakespeare had achieved it, in the drama, in the poetry of representation, which in the hands of great genius, does perform this manifest miracle of revealing the secret harmony and high design which lie behind all human discomfiture. This consummate poetry which represents and reveals was, as Keats had already confessed to Taylor, and as he was to confess to him more fully hereafter, his poetic goal: it was one which he never attained. It was in the despairing vision of this unattained ideal that, when he wrote to Fanny Brawne, all his glorious poetic achievement dissolved away and he said that he had left no immortal work behind him, but if he had had time he would have made himself remembered. He is remembered; he will never be forgotten: but he is remembered, too often, and even by those who have devoted themselves to his memory, as something of a weakling, as a boy of genius in whose soul there was an element of sickness and sickliness, as someone who can be patronized, and be told that he was wrong to love with a passion so devouring, misguided to reject the influence of Milton, peevish and morbid to spoil his beautiful *Hyperion* by adding to it an opening in a different tone and manner.

That Keats should be remembered in this way fills me with passionate indignation. It is wrong, utterly wrong. There is no man living, and no man has lived, who has the right to pass judgement upon Keats. It is an act of terrible presumption. When I read in a Life of Keats that 'there was a great spiritual flaw in his nature,' I am first amazed, then indignant. By what standard, by what right is Keats thus judged? What spiritual flaw was in him that was not in Shakespeare? And if we do not dare to say that Shakespeare was morbid and sickly, let us have at least the generosity to hold our peace about Keats. With the genius of the pure poet, as Keats' was, you cannot make conditions: you cannot say you will accept this and reject that, approve of this and disapprove of that. You must accept the whole; you must understand that the elements of which you disapprove are the foundation of the achievement which you do approve, and therefore in addition to rank ingratitude you lay yourself open to the charge of not truly understanding what you profess to admire. Shakespeare without some of *The Sonnets* and *Measure for Measure* and *Troilus* would be a much more pleasant and gentlemanly Shakespeare, no doubt, but he would not be Shakespeare. By the same stroke by which you deprive him of *Measure for Measure* and *Troilus*, you would deprive him also of *Hamlet* and *Lear*. The same 'spiritual flaw' in Keats' nature which made of his love for Fanny Brawne a consuming and mortal passion, gave the intolerable beauty to the music of his *Ode to a Nightingale*. And the odds are great that if you cannot bear to look upon the one, you will not be able to hear the other.

Not only have we not the right to judge Keats, but there is no occasion to judge him. Keats judged himself by standards far higher than any that are in our possession. He judged himself and his work by his own ideal, which was a thing of a different kind from any of our own commonplace notions of good taste and good breeding. By that standard, and by no other, he failed, and he failed for one cause and no other—because he had not time. If any poet was ever assured of supreme achievement, it was Keats: what he has left behind contains not merely the promise of supreme poetry to come, but the assurance of it. And he had no doubt of his own powers. The same letter to his brother, in which he spoke of 'the mighty abstract idea of beauty in all things,' contains this further passage:

> The only thing that can ever affect me personally for more than one short passing day, is any doubt about my powers for poetry—I seldom have any, and I look with hope to the nighing time when I shall have none. I am as happy as a *Man* can be—that is, in myself I should be happy, if Tom was well, and I knew you were passing pleasant days. Then I should be most enviable—with the yearning passion I have for the beautiful, connected and made one with the ambition of my intellect.

There, in yet another form, is the central conception—of beauty made profound and comprehensive by depth of thought, not discursive thought,* but the poetic thought that lies beneath 'the mighty abstract idea of Beauty in all things.'

By his vision of the fulfilment of this idea in the drama, Keats judged himself, and decided that he had left no immortal work behind him. Posterity has decided otherwise. Ordinary mortals cannot use the standards of the immortals. But it is their duty also to try to understand what the standards of the immortals are, and what they mean; it is not right to dismiss Keats' judgement of himself as the outcome of 'a mood of fierce injustice to his own achievement,' any more than it is right to impute 'a great spiritual flaw' to the nature which produced the achievement you are jealous to vindicate. It is the old trick of average humanity when it is confronted with genius; it takes from it what it can comfortably accommodate, and throws the rest away as nothing worth. So, when a justly famous editor of Keats comes in his introductory essay to the beautiful *Ode to Autumn*, which he very properly admires, he exclaims: 'How gladly would we sacrifice even the re-cast of *Hyperion* and the superb last sonnet if this poem could have indeed been Keats' swan-song, as it is assuredly his last work of full and conscious power. . . .' We shall consider that re-cast of *Hyperion* in its place and see whether we would gladly sacrifice it in order that the swan-song should be undisturbed. It is a strange thing, this desire that the man of genius should make his quietus comfortably and fade away to slow music. It is less disinterested than it appears; we desire not to make him comfortable, but ourselves, and in order to do that we would gladly sacrifice the words of genius when it trembles on the verge of the unutterable.

Let us have done with this attitude. It is time. Let us make up our minds that we will accept genius as a whole, whatever effort and whatever pain it may cost us. Let us say to ourselves that it cost Keats infinitely more effort and more pain to suffer what he suffered and discover what he discovered than it can possibly cost us to accept him wholly. Let us take upon ourselves the duty of understanding Keats as a whole as an act of gratitude to him for having been what he was. Let us give up once and for all our polite deprecations, our head-waggings and our deplorings; let us make a glad sacrifice of our glad sacrifices. Not for the sake of genius, but for our own sake; for unless we give up these things we shall never learn what genius has to tell.

I am not saying that we should accept Keats' judgement of himself, in the sense that we also should declare that he left no immortal work behind him, because he had not satisfied his own ideal. I am saying simply that we should cease to dismiss his judgement of himself as the petulance of a sick man, but consider it and revere it and use it as a means to a knowledge of what he was. If we would see Keats truly, for what he was and what he would have been, we must see him in his own perspective. In that perspective neither his great *Odes*, nor *The Eve of St. Agnes*, nor *Isabella*, nor *Lamia*, nor the original, nor the revised, *Hyperion* were worth publishing, and they would not have been published but for the sake of money. We are in no danger of making such a perspective our own: we can scarcely breathe the atmosphere that surrounds the pinnacle of poetry from which that view was taken. But Keats breathed that air as his native element. When we have tried to breathe it for a moment we may descend. We shall have had a sight of many things; we shall have learned many things, the chiefest of all being these: we shall have learned to admire his wonderful poetry more than we do, because we shall understand it more. We shall reverence it more than we do, because we shall know that the spirit which shaped it was such that it seemed to him of small account beside the poetry he dreamed. And finally we shall be no longer tempted to deprecate and deplore and gladly sacrifice, because we shall know that the man was such that what he suffered and endured and wrought and dreamed is clean beyond our jurisdiction.

On the first of December in this year 1818 Keats' brother Tom died. Shortly afterwards he met Fanny Brawne. It was a climacteric moment, as it had been a climacteric year, in Keats' life.

CHAPTER VII

THE FIRST *HYPERION*

THE first hint of the future *Hyperion* occurs in the last book of *Endymion* (iv, 770-4), where Keats apostrophizes his hero and commiserates with him on his never-ending wanderings. He should have been

> Ensky'd ere this, but truly that I deem
> Truth the best music in a first-born song.
> Thy lute-voiced brother will I sing ere long,
> And thou shalt aid. . . .

Probably Keats was, by this time, a little impatient of his work on *Endymion*; though it was now nearing the end, he was already distracted by the thought of his next poem. *Endymion* was finished at the end of 1817. On 23rd January 1818, Keats wrote to Haydon in terms which show that it was common property between them that *Hyperion* was to be the next long poem. Keats' publisher had suggested that Haydon should paint a picture taken from the poem for a frontispiece to *Endymion*. Haydon, who was a slow worker, had proposed that the picture should be taken from the next poem.

> I have (Keats wrote) a complete fellow-feeling with you in this business—so much so that it would be as well to wait for a choice out of *Hyperion*—when that poem is done there will be a wide range for you—in *Endymion* I think you may have many bits of the deep and sentimental cast—the nature of *Hyperion* will lead me to treat it in a more naked and grecian Manner—and the march of passion and endeavour will be undeviating—and one great contrast between them will be—that the Hero of the written tale being mortal is led on, like Bonaparte, by circumstance; whereas the Apollo in *Hyperion* being a fore-seeing God will shape his actions like one. But I am counting, etc.

That is of importance, because it shows that even at this early stage in the conception of the poem, Apollo and not Hyperion himself was the chief character in it. Had the letter been made public before, it would have enabled critics to see (what is fairly obvious from *Hyperion* itself) that the fate of the poem hangs upon the fate of Apollo. Whether the poem could go on depended directly upon whether Apollo could go on.

For what was Apollo? The god of Poetry, the immortal poet. It needs no large effort of the imagination to see that the embodiment of such an ideal must have been governed absolutely by Keats' own knowledge of the poetic nature. Whenever he began *Hyperion*, the reality of the chief figure in it would inevitably be shaped according to the pattern of what he, John Keats, was at that moment. Here, far more rigorously than in the case of Endymion, who was not a poet, Keats would have his own nature and his own nature alone to draw upon for his material. The legend of the Titans was vague enough; but of the inward reality of Apollo there was no legend at all. Keats had no choice. *Hyperion* was to be the story of Apollo, in the same sense that *Endymion* was the story of Endymion. There was nothing for it but to present the ideal poet, and the ideal poet was Keats himself. That was not conceit; it was simple honesty. All that Keats truly knew, he knew, as he said over and over again, from his own experience. Even a proverb was not a proverb to him till his life had illustrated it. And had Keats been a much lesser poet than he was, the compulsion would have been essentially the same: being what he was, it was inexorable. Apollo, mere circumstance apart, must be himself.

No wonder then that after that high-spirited and confident letter to Haydon, which makes us feel he is going to begin *Hyperion* to-morrow, or at any rate the day after the last proof of *Endymion* is done with, it should have taken him months to begin. During a year of 'purgatory blind,' when every day his conception of poetry and his knowledge of the function and destiny of the poet changed, and his own instant knowledge of the mystery the poet had to comprehend was deepened, he became reluctant to begin this poem beyond all others. 'Purgatory blind' was no condition for such an attempt; no wonder then that he should have avoided it, and, while his vision of the principle of beauty was overclouded and out of the chaos painfully emerged his knowledge of the principle of 'beauty in all things,' he should have turned aside to write a fanciful tale in verse from Bocaccio—which some strangely believe to have been Keats' masterpiece, whereas it is both in itself and for these reasons the least important of all Keats' long poems whatsoever. No wonder that he should have seized at the opportunity to take a desperate and exhausting walking tour in Scotland, of which the truest thing he said was: 'On the whole I am happier than when I have time to be glum.' The climax of that deliberate and despairing digression was the climbing of Ben Nevis; when Keats reached the top of that mountain he had reached a pinnacle of physical exhaustion and depression of soul. On the top of it he wrote one of the best of the few good poems he wrote during the miserable journey:

> Read me a lesson, Muse, and speak it loud
>   Upon the top of Nevis, blind in mist!
> I look into the chasms, and a shroud

> Vaporous doth hide them,—just so much I wist
> Mankind do know of hell; I look o'er head
> And there is sullen mist—even so much
> Mankind can tell of heaven; mist is spread
> Before the earth, beneath me—even such,
> Even so vague is man's sight of himself!
> Here are the craggy stones beneath my feet—
> Thus much I know that, a poor witless elf,
> I tread on them,—that all my eye doth meet
> Is mist and crag, not only on this height,
> But in the world of thought and mental might.

Was Apollo to know no more than that? No wonder that when finally Keats did begin his poem in September 1818, he began it not only in deep melancholy but as a deliberate escape from the pain of contemplating the suffering of his dying brother. And above all it is no wonder that when he did begin *Hyperion* he kept Apollo out of it as long as he could, or that when Apollo did enter it the poem abruptly ceased.

That is, in essentials, the history of what I shall call the first *Hyperion*, the version of the poem which is most familiar. That poem was finished by the end of April 1819. The first two books were substantially written at his brother's bedside and before his brother's death on 1st December 1818. The third book, which deals with Apollo and consists only of 136 lines, was written at intervals between January and April 1819. By the end of April a fair copy of the the whole was in the hands of his friend Woodhouse. In composing his poem Keats had to struggle against difficulty, against reluctance and at last against downright impossibility. He gave up finally, I think, sometime about the beginning of April: yet he did not give up, for the poem, as I have said, was finished.

I will try to show as clearly as I can from the internal evidence of the poem itself that it was finished: that in the third book of the first *Hyperion*, as we have it, Keats had said all that he could possibly say at that point of time concerning the poetic nature, and therefore concerning Apollo. But there is, fortunately, clear and indisputable evidence that Keats himself regarded the poem as finished. A legend —one among many legends concerning Keats—has grown up of an unfinished *Hyperion*. The sources of this legend are three: first, the note of the publishers in the 1820 volume—a note which may possibly have been inspired by Woodhouse—saying that 'the poem was intended to have been of equal length with *Endymion*, but the reception given to that work discouraged the author from proceeding.' This was a palpable lie. First, because it is diametrically opposed to Keats' character; secondly, because the last of the hostile reviews of *Endymion* appeared in September 1818, at the very moment when

Keats *began* his poem, so that so far from *Hyperion* being abandoned because of the hostile reception of *Endymion*, it is more likely that those hostile reviews gave him the final push towards a new poem which he was immensely reluctant to begin; and, finally, we have Keats' own peremptory words written in a copy of the 1820 volume against the publishers' advertisement. 'I had no part in this: I was ill at the time. . . . This is a lie.' The second source of the legend is that the poem was entitled 'Hyperion: a Fragment,' and ends abruptly:

> At length
> Apollo shrieked; and lo! from all his limbs
> Celestial * * * * * * * * *
> * * * * * * * * * * *

As a matter of fact we know from the manuscript that the poem ended perfectly with the line:

> Apollo shrieked: and lo! he was a god.*

The first *Hyperion* was a 'fragment,' but it was a finished fragment. Keats did not intend it to be continued. Nevertheless, since its fragmentary character is an essential part of its conception, and since by its own nature it could not be more complete than it was, Keats very rightly emphasized its fragmentary character to the outward eye by ending it abruptly and vaguely with a chain of stars. The third source of the legend is Keats' own statement on 22nd September 1819, that he had 'abandoned *Hyperion*.' But he was not speaking of the first *Hyperion*. Ever since his letter to Woodhouse of 22nd September 1819 was made public, it has been demonstrably evident that what he abandoned was not the first but the second or 'recast' *Hyperion*.

These facts dispose completely of the legend that the first *Hyperion* was unfinished It was finished, and it was finished by the end of April 1819. A fair copy was made and sent to Woodhouse. In July, however, Keats took up the poem again. He began that process which he described in his letter to Bailey of 15th August 1819: 'I have been rewriting parts of my *Hyperion*.' This rewriting consisted, as the phrase itself would suggest, not in a continuation of, nor of any attempt to continue, the first *Hyperion*, but in the amplification of the already finished poem. Keats had decided to try to cast the complete and finished first *Hyperion* into the form of a dream. This was not an idle and mistaken artistic experiment, but a feverish and agonized endeavour to cleanse his bosom of much perilous stuff which had accumulated since the completion of the first *Hyperion*.

For the first *Hyperion* was, as I have said, essentially the poem of Apollo, the poem in which Keats was to reveal the secret of the poetic nature. When he finished it he had told all he knew of that nature, which was his own; he could tell no more, because he knew no more. Three months later he did know more, because his own life had taught him more; and he was impelled to add that knowledge to his poem.

But why, it may be asked, did he not *continue* the first *Hyperion?* The answer to that question is contained in the words of the second *Hyperion*, which will be considered in their place. But in a rough outline the answer is simply this: that perhaps the most important part of all his new knowledge concerning the poetic nature was that to the pure poet such an abstract and symbolical poem as the first *Hyperion* was a dream, and not a reality. ' Not here, O Apollo, are haunts meet for thee! ' Because that was so, he cast the first and complete *Hyperion* deliberately into the form of a poet's dream; it became *The Fall of Hyperion: A Dream.* And he brought the dreaming poet into the great hall of judgement, to declare his faith and be tried at the bar of eternity. Therein he restated his knowledge of the poetic nature, and showed the reason why Apollo could go no further on his previous path. In other words, in the second *Hyperion* Apollo re-enters the poem; but he re-enters it, having put off his dream-garment of divinity, as the poet Keats himself. Therefore he re-enters it at the beginning.

The first *Hyperion* is a complete poem. It can be understood wholly in and for itself. But it may be necessary for those who are unaccustomed to read the speech of poetry to use the second *Hyperion* as an approach to the first, in order to understand its scope and significance. But, having done so, they must return to the knowledge that the first *Hyperion* belongs to an earlier period than the second. The first *Hyperion* was completed by April 1819, the second *Hyperion* begun in July 1819. Three months is a short time to regard as a period in a poet's life; but when they happen to be three months in the most crucial year of a poet whose whole poetic life is contained in four years, the necessity of so regarding them is plain.

I have already given some account of the mood in which Keats began the composition of *Hyperion.* He was seeking an asylum of refuge from the pains of life in a world of abstract poetic creation. The greatest of those pains, the most immediate and intense, was the continual watching of his brother's lingering death. All through his year of ' purgatory blind ' this had been preying upon him. In the letter to Bailey, written on the eve of his setting out for his Scottish journey (10th June 1818), he had written:

> Were it my choice, I would reject a Petrarchal coronation—on account of my dying day, and because women have cancers. . . . I should not by rights speak in this tone to you. . . . Yet I am not old enough or magnanimous enough to annihilate self. . . .

> Now I am never alone without rejoicing that there is such a thing as death without placing my ultimate in the glory of dying for a great human purpose. Perhaps if my affairs were in a different state, I should not have written the above—you shall judge: I have two brothers; one is driven by the ' burden of Society ' to America; the other, with an exquisite love of life, is in a lingering state. My love for my Brothers, from the early loss of our parents, and even from earlier misfortunes, has grown into an affection ' passing the love of women.' I have been ill-tempered with them—I have vexed them—but the thought of them has always stifled the impression that any woman might otherwise have made upon me. I have a sister, too, and may not follow them either to America or to the grave. Life must be undergone, and I certainly derive some consolation from the thought of writing one or two more poems before it ceases.

But to watch Tom, ' with his exquisite love of life,' lingering towards death was not merely an anguish to Keats' most loving heart; it was an icy warning of his own end. Keats had returned from that hapless expedition to Scotland with the beginnings of consumption in himself. He returned also to find *Endymion* (of which the first book at least is, in the soberest judgement, the most beautiful and authentic English poetry ever written by a boy of twenty-one) spat upon by the hooligan-critics. Keats was, indeed, the last person to have his life ' snuffed out by an article,' and there has been a just critical reaction against the sentimental conception of him as an ineffectual angel with his heart pierced by the poisoned arrows of *Blackwood.* But one may go too far in this reaction. Keats knew what he had put into *Endymion* better than we know it to-day, and the brutal mudslinging at his poem must have had its effect. He said no word directly about it in his letters, and the very silence is ominous. The depth of his suppressed feeling breaks out in his fierce and bitter saying that being an apothecary is no worse than writing poems and ' hanging them up to be fly-blown on the review-shambles.' That is the speech of a smouldering passion of indignation.

Tom's dying, the chance of his own death, his sense of unmerited failure—these were enough and more than enough to turn him away from life. And there was another cause, perhaps still deeper than these. It shall not be considered here, save briefly. The desire for love, for passionate and devoted love, for that support and reinvigoration which a man can receive from a woman, was also smouldering within him. Keats spoke the exact truth when he said that his profound love for his brothers had always stifled the impression that any woman might have made upon him. But now his brothers were torn away from him and the road was clear for a woman to make her way into his heart. Keats longed for love, and he feared it. For he knew what love would be when it came to him—a devouring passion, an absolute loyalty. He would be plunged headlong into an unknown. It would be no polite *amour de convenance* with him; he would desire to possess body and soul. And that, when he thought of it, and he thought of it incessantly, seemed to him a crime when his brother was dying. He strove with all his might to put the importunate longing out of his heart.

Where was he to escape these pains, but in a world of the imagination? So he embarked upon *Hyperion,* whose abstract images should be a comfort and distraction to him. He embarked upon it reluctantly, because he knew that concerning the character and destiny of the poet-Apollo he was still in the condition of ' purgatory blind.' Nevertheless, one day in September, he began:

> Deep in the shady sadness of a vale
> Far sunken from the healthy breath of morn,
> Far from the fiery noon and eve's one star,
> Sat gray-haired Saturn, quiet as a stone,
> Still as the silence round about his lair. . . .

There is no sadder poem in English than *Hyperion*; but its sadness is not the icy chill of intellectual despair, but the warm, rich, still sadness of a suffering heart determined to control its pain. It throbs, for all that its figures are giant and immortal, with ' the still, sad music of humanity.' Of humanity, indeed, for these divine figures are lovely and human, their sufferings and anger are human and their wisdom is humane.

Keats could not help it: he was writing from his heart, of what he knew. The life of these Titans was the life in which he himself was involved. That is why, although his story, for its own conduct, demanded that the defeated Titans should be inferior to the victorious Olympians, yet no Olympian could be wiser and kinder and more beautiful than Saturn. Saturn is a Lear without his folly. That he should be overthrown by other gods, as he was overthrown, is but a defeat of the wise and kind and beautiful by the wise and kind and beautiful; that he should reconquer his throne from the usurpers would be but another victory of good over good. Tom, ' with his exquisite love of life,' was fading out. For what cause? To what end? To make room for a Tom more beautiful? But let Oceanus speak his noble faith—his ' eternal truth.'

> Now comes the pain of truth, to whom 'tis pain;
> O folly! for to bear all naked truths
> And to envisage circumstance, all calm,
> That is the top of sovereignty. Mark well!
> As Heaven and Earth are fairer, fairer far

> Than Chaos and blank Darkness, though once chiefs;
> And as we show beyond that Heaven and Earth
> In form and shape compact and beautiful,
> In will, in action free, companionship,
> And thousand other signs of purer life;
> So on our heels a fresh perfection treads,
> A power more strong in beauty, born of us
> And fated to excel us, as we pass
> In glory that old Darkness: nor are we
> Thereby more conquered than by us the rule
> Of shapeless chaos.

And yet, noble as is the faith and beautiful the utterance, it is belied by the poem itself. Than Saturn and Rhea, than Oceanus who speaks, than Mnemosyne and Clymene, what power could be more strong in beauty? Could the new kings of heaven be more majestic than Saturn or wiser than the god of the sea?

The only one of the Olympians who appears to us is Apollo, of whom the poem should have been the story. And he perhaps is more beautiful than the dethroned Titans; but he has had no hand in their defeat. He is a poet, a divine singer, and the Titans had no singer save child-like and unconscious Clymene. Is it that Keats really meant that the only 'power more strong in beauty' to excel the Titans was the power of the true poet? Whatever he may, at one time or another, have entertained for his deliberate plan, this is indeed the meaning of what he wrote. In this Keats was like a prophet who can speak only the words which the Lord puts into his mouth. He could not go beyond what he truly knew. Just as the pain of the Titans is the pain of life itself, inflicted without cause and suffered without demerit, so all that can be added to the sufferers is first a comprehension of that pain, and then an utterance of that comprehension. Oceanus comprehends it, but he comprehends it only in part; that 'fresh perfection' which he glimpses will not be what he imagines it—a nobler Jove than Saturn, a wiser Neptune than Oceanus. These things cannot be. There is but one 'fresh perfection' that may come: and that is the perfection of a completer knowledge than his own. Yet even that perfection Mnemosyne already possessed.

But Mnemosyne, like Apollo himself, does not enter into the poem until the third book. She is an entirely new conception, just as the one hundred and thirty-six lines of the third book are an entirely new phase of the poem. The first two books belong together; they were written substantially before Tom's death. The thought of Apollo was warded off in them: we know no more of him than that Clymene has heard the calling of the golden singer's name. I do not think it has occurred to anyone to ask why it is that Apollo should be heard calling his own name.

> A voice came sweeter, sweeter than all tune
> And still it cried, 'Apollo! young Apollo!
> The morning-bright Apollo! young Apollo!'
> I fled, it follow'd me, and cried 'Apollo!'

It is Apollo's own voice, crying his own name. He is drunk with his own lovely destiny. And that golden voice, borne in to them by Clymene, echoes amid the Titans and their cave. Apollo is no more than a golden voice for the first two books of *Hyperion.* Till Tom was dead he could be no more. What Keats was to know and to be could not be decided till after that death; and Apollo could know only what Keats knew, and be only what Keats was.

The opening lines of the third book touch directly on Tom's death:

> O leave them, Muse! O leave them to their woes;
> A solitary sorrow best befits
> Thy lips, and antheming a lonely grief.

The ordeal is over; the gates of life are flung wide for Keats. And for the moment there is a burst of new confidence. With the death of his brother, Keats breathed a full breath once more. That will sound callous only to hypocrisy. Keats had suffered for his brother's suffering as very few human beings are capable of suffering; he had cramped his heart and shut life out in his devotion to Tom. Now, after the final shock, his heart expanded and life poured in again. One has only to read the opening of the journal-letter to his brother after Tom's death to see how swiftly the aching sorrow was over. The sentimentalist will call this unfeeling; the truth is that only such natures do deeply feel.

Keats had starved himself of life for his brother's sake: now life passed into him again, and for a moment into his poem:

> Meantime touch piously the Delphic harp, . . .
> For lo! 'tis for the Father of all verse.
> Flush everything that hath a vermeil hue,
> Let the rose glow intense and warm the air,
> And let the clouds of even and of morn
> Float in voluptuous fleeces o'er the hills;
> Let the red wine within the goblet boil,
> Cold as a bubbling well; let faint-lipp'd shells
> On sands, or in great deeps, vermilion turn
> Through all their labyrinths; and let the maid
> Blush keenly, as with some warm kiss surpris'd.
> Chief isle of the embowered Cyclades,
> Rejoice, O Delos, with thine olives green,
> And poplars, and lawn-shading palms, and beech,

In which the Zephyr breathes the loudest song,
And hazels thick, dark-stemm'd beneath the shade:
Apollo is once more the golden theme!

Can one fail to feel the inrush of new and intoxicating life? What could be more gaily confident a prelude to the coming of Apollo? Yet within ten lines of this, Apollo appears weeping, not for joy, but in an agony of pain:

He listened and he wept, and his bright tears
Went trickling down the golden bow he held.

Nor were those tears such that any immortal could wipe them away —not even Mnemosyne.

What had happened to Keats and to his poem? Simply this. His brother had died: he had entered into life again: and he had fallen in love. There had really been the moment of triumphant confidence. He had begun to pour it into *Hyperion:* but for a moment only. That poem could not contain what was in his heart. There was no place for the ecstasy of new-born love in it. He turned aside and wrote *The Eve of St. Agnes*, which imperishably contains his rapture. When he returned to *Hyperion*, the rapture had faded away; he was torn by a new suffering—the knowledge that his devouring love was also an impossible love. The burden of the mystery had descended upon him more terribly than ever. Morning-bright Apollo's fleeting moment of radiance was over; therefore he wept.

To the weeping Apollo comes a stern comforter:

While from beneath some cumbrous boughs hard by
With solemn step an awful Goddess came,
And there was purport in her looks for him,
Which he with eager guess began to read
Perplex'd. . . .

Mnemosyne has been guarding him, unseen and unknown. But Apollo has seen, or felt rather than seen, traces of her great presence; and now, as she stands before him, he cries to her:

'Goddess! I have beheld those eyes before
And their eternal calm, and all that face,
Or I have dreamed.'
'Yes,' said the supreme shape,
'Thou hast dream'd of me; and awaking up
Did'st find a lyre all golden by thy side,
Whose strings touch'd by thy fingers, all the vast
Unwearied ear of the whole universe

Listen'd in pain and pleasure at the birth
Of such new tuneful wonder.' Is 't not strange
That thou shouldst weep, so gifted? Tell me, youth,
What sorrow thou canst feel . . .
Show thy heart's secret to an ancient Power
Who hath forsaken old and sacred thrones
For prophecies of thee, and for the sake
Of loveliness new born.'

Who and what is this Mnemosyne who has forsaken the old order for the new, of whose face the young Apollo dreamed, and woke into possession of the power of song? For a complete answer to that question we must wait until the second *Hyperion*, where the face of which the young Apollo dreamed, is dreamed by the poet Keats himself, and not merely dreamed of but described in language of miraculous beauty. But let us mark these simple facts. The young Apollo has dreamt of her face, and waked from his dream into possession of the power of poetry. He sees that same face with his waking eyes, and he dies and is reborn. Keats the poet, in the second *Hyperion*, sees her face still more directly; and from that sight, in his reconstruction of the poem, the vision of the whole of the first *Hyperion* is born. There are three phases in the poet's knowledge of Mnemosyne: the first is Apollo's dream of her, by which he becomes a poet; the second is Apollo's waking sight of her, by which his whole being is convulsed and changed by ' knowledge enormous ' and he becomes a God; and the third is the poet Keats' sight of her in the new beginning to *Hyperion*, by which

there grew
A power within him of enormous ken
To see as a God sees.

Whether that will be to others as clear a proof as it is to me that Apollo and Keats himself are essentially the same, I do not know. For me it is conclusive.

But who and what is Mnemosyne? It is better that we should for the moment leave it to the poem itself to tell us. Mnemosyne means Memory; and she has forsaken the old Gods to guard the new-born loveliness of Apollo. Now Apollo sees her before him, and he cries in answer to her question of his sorrow:

Mnemosyne!
Thy name is on my tongue, I know not how;
Why should I tell thee what thou so well seest?
Why should I strive to show what from thy lips
Would come no mystery? For me, dark, dark,
And painful vile oblivion seals my eyes.

He knows mysteriously Mnemosyne's name; and she knows, what is hidden from him, the cause and secret of his sorrow. But to the end of the poem Mnemosyne speaks no word again: she is a silent presence. Apollo cries to her:

> Goddess benign, point forth some unknown thing!
> Are there not other regions than this isle?
> What are the stars? There is the sun, the sun!
> And the most patient brilliance of the moon!
> And stars by thousands! Point me out the way
> To any one particular beauteous star,
> And I will flit into it with my lyre,
> And make its silvery splendour pant with bliss.
> I have heard the cloudy thunder: Where is power?
> Whose hand, whose essence, what divinity
> Makes this alarum in the elements,
> While I here idle listen on the shores
> In fearless yet in aching ignorance?
> O tell me, lonely Goddess, by thy harp
> That waileth every morn and eventide,
> Tell me why thus I rave about these groves!

This is no appeal of an immortal: Apollo is no God. He is none other than the mortal Keats; and he is the mortal Keats at one period of his life and no other. This 'isle' that he longs to flee from is this earth of ours; his agonized appeal is but a premonitory echo of the agonized appeal in the *Ode to a Nightingale*.

> That I might drink, and leave the world unseen,
> And with thee fade away into the forest dim:
> Fade far away, dissolve and quite forget
> What thou among the leaves hast never known,
> The weariness, the fever, and the fret
> Here, where men sit and hear each other groan;
> Where palsy shakes a few, sad, last gray hairs,
> Where youth grows pale, and spectre-thin, and dies;
> Where but to think is to be full of sorrow
> And leaden-eyed despairs,
> Where Beauty cannot keep her lustrous eyes,
> Or new Love pine at them beyond to-morrow.

And the 'aching ignorance' of Apollo is that of Keats in his sonnet *Why did I laugh to-night?* which was written 'with no Agony but that of ignorance.'

I believe that this portion of *Hyperion* can be quite definitely assigned to the moment when that sonnet was written, on or about

19th March 1819. The full story of what was happening to Keats at that moment comes later in this narrative. The sonnet *Why did I laugh to-night?* is given in the journal-letter to his brother George under the date 19th March. Six days before, on 13th March, Keats had written: 'I know not why Poetry and I have been so distant lately.' After 19th March there is a gap of almost a month in the letter. He takes it up again on 15th April, and says: 'I am still at a standstill in versifying—I cannot do it yet with any pleasure—I mean however to look round on my resources and means—and see what I can do without poetry.' In that month of silence, I believe, *Hyperion* was finished. It came to a standstill. A new death and a birth had come to pass in Keats' soul. The record of that new and painful birth is in the concluding lines of *Hyperion.*

To Apollo's appeal in aching ignorance Mnemosyne makes no reply. Apollo looks into her face, and the secret is revealed to him.

> Mute thou remainest—mute! yet I can read
> A wondrous lesson in thy silent face:
> Knowledge enormous makes a God of me.
> Names, deeds, gray legends, dire events, rebellions,
> Majesties, sovran voices, agonies,
> Creations and destroyings, all at once
> Pour into the wide hollows of my brain,
> And deify me, as if some blithe wine
> Or bright elixir peerless I had drunk,
> And so become immortal.

Apollo was already a god: Keats was not.

> Thus the God,
> While his enkindled eyes, with level glance
> Beneath his white soft temples, stedfast kept
> Trembling with light upon Mnemosyne.
> Soon wild commotions shook him, and made flush
> All the immortal fairness of his limbs;
> Most like the struggle at the gate of death;
> Or liker still to one who should take leave
> Of pale immortal death and with a pang
> As hot as death's is chill, with fierce convulse
> Die into life: so young Apollo anguish'd:
> His very hair, his golden tresses famed
> Kept undulation round his eager neck.
> During the pain Mnemosyne upheld
> Her arms as one who prophesied.—At length
> Apollo shriek'd:—and lo! from all his limbs
> Celestial. . . .

The dream of Mnemosyne had made the boy a poet, a lovely and unconscious singer. Beholding her face to face had made him—what?

The true answer is the simplest: a great poet. Apollo is Keats, none other. Now in the pain of his death into life, brought upon him by what he sees in the face of Mnemosyne, he had conquered that which he sought through the year of ' purgatory blind '—' the love of good and ill.' For Mnemosyne's face contains all life, past, present and to come. She is the eternal existence of the universe, as it were Being itself, made conscious. She belongs to the old order and the new, for she is immanent and everlasting; she is but a pure mirror of what is—' agonies, creations and destroyings '—and in that reflection what is revealed is what must be, in all the beauty of its own necessity.

And of her the boy Keats *had* dreamed. She was ' the vast idea ' that had come to him that night as he slept on Leigh Hunt's sofa. From that dream he had awakened to find ' a lyre all golden by his side,' and he had sounded it to ' a new tuneful wonder ' in *Sleep and Poetry*. She had become ' the mighty abstract idea of beauty in all things '; and Keats had struggled through ' purgatory blind ' for a vision of her, face to face. Now he had achieved what he sought, and ' knowledge enormous made a God of him,' through the pain of a death in life and a second birth.

And so the first *Hyperion* ends. There it must end. There is no going on from that point in that path. The poet has become a great poet. Nothing remains for him but to *be* a great poet, to reveal the beauty in all things that he has seen. The pure poet is not a mystic: contemplation of the mystery is no end in itself for him. He is a doer, a maker, a revealer, a creator. The continuation of *Hyperion* is all Keats' later poems, the few that were written, the many that were never to be written. Those that were written are among the very loveliest and profoundest poems in the English language, poems that haunt men's minds and acquire a dominion over their souls, of which they can render no account to themselves—all the great *Odes*, *Lamia*, the second *Hyperion*. And they were only a beginning, and in Keats' eyes a beginning so small that they seemed of no account to him, and not worth publishing save for the sake of the money they might bring.

Even if others cannot admit that complete identification of Keats with Apollo which is so necessary and palpable to me, they may be able to admit that a continuation of the first *Hyperion* was impossible on purely objective grounds, though a purely objective criticism applied to the third book of the poem leads straight to unanswerable questions. Why should Apollo who was already a god, endure such agony in order to become what he already was? And if what he saw in the eyes of Mnemosyne gave him ' knowledge enormous ' that he had not before, then surely this new knowledge has a meaning. It is not all idle words. And if it has a meaning, then it can have a meaning only as some truth concerning the growth of the poetic nature.

In fact, there can be no such thing as a ' purely objective criticism ' of the third book of *Hyperion*. Either it means nothing at all, or it has a direct application to the nature of the poet; and if its application is to the nature of the poet, then it is to the nature of the poet Keats. It is the history of his own soul that is being unfolded. Whence was a poet like Keats, who his whole life long recognized no truths but those which his own experience had had brought to him, to derive so crucial a knowledge of the throes of poetic birth, but from himself?

It was this utter fidelity of Keats to his own experience that brought the first *Hyperion* to an end. Apollo, who was the central figure of the poem, could enter it either as the unconscious singer or as something more. Even as he began to conceive the poem, Keats was no longer the unconscious singer; he delayed beginning it because he had not yet become the something more; even when he did begin he began it as a refuge of abstractions and he delayed to introduce Apollo because he himself was not yet the something more, and he knew that were he to face the reality of his own poetic nature and truly conceive Apollo, there would be an end to his abstract poem and his refuge. When the need of that refuge was over, he let Apollo enter; in order to embody him he faced the reality of himself. He uttered that reality and the poem came to an end.

Keats wrote no more ' abstract ' poems. The second *Hyperion* is not abstract, in the sense that the first *Hyperion* is abstract. Keats tells the story of his own soul, its agonies, its death into life, in his own person; and he did it chiefly in order that it should be impossible for anyone to read the first *Hyperion* without understanding its meaning. If it has taken many years for people to understand its meaning, that is chiefly because the two *Hyperions* have been separated.

The second *Hyperion* Keats did actually abandon, because, after all, it was still too abstract. The poet in it was not fulfilling his function of creating and revealing: he was confessing: he was not facing life and reflecting it, he was again turning away. Keats' turning away is not as other men's. In the second *Hyperion* he searches the depths of his own heart with a pitiless courage of which the like cannot be found in English literature. Nevertheless, it was still to him a turning away. So he abandoned his poem, and turned to life again. He obeyed life, and his own destiny.

CHAPTER VIII

KEATS' LOVE

THE third book of the first *Hyperion* is in essentials the record of the revolution in Keats' mind and being which was the prelude to the great year 1819, the 'annus mirabilis' of his poetic life. During this year were written *The Eve of St. Agnes* and the fragment of *The Eve of St. Mark* in January, the third book of *Hyperion* between January and the middle of April, *La Belle Dame sans Merci*, the sonnet *Bright Star*, and the great *Odes* between the middle of April and the end of May, *Lamia* in June and July, the second *Hyperion* in July and August, and the *Ode to Autumn*, in September. A whole period of Keats' poetic production ends with the *Ode to Autumn*. He wrote four or five poems afterwards, and these poems are of importance, but they belong to a different kind from the sequence of great poems which culminates in the *Ode to Autumn*. These mark the pinnacle of Keats' actual achievement as a poet; the few that followed are purely personal and belong to a period of transition that ended in the poet's death.

This 'annus mirabilis' must receive all the attention we have it in us to bestow. There will be many threads to hold together if we are to apprehend the warm and living reality of Keats' life during this year; but one is dominant. With the beginning of this year begins also Keats' love for Fanny Brawne.

To understand the nature and quality of this love, we need to return to the middle of June 1818, to the letter which Keats wrote to Bailey on the eve of his departure for his tour in Scotland, and in which he explained his mood of depression in these words:

> I have two brothers; one is driven, by 'the burden of Society,' to America; the other, with an exquisite love of life, is in a lingering state. My love for my Brothers, from the early loss of our parents, and even from earlier misfortunes, has grown into an affection 'passing the love of women.' I have been ill-tempered with them—I have vexed them—but the thought of them has always stifled the impression that any woman might have made upon me.

That was the exact truth. The thought of his brothers had stifled, because it had been used to stifle, the impression any woman might have made upon Keats. While his brothers were with him, he had contrived to find in them that intimate affection for which he hungered. But now, at the moment that he wrote, George had departed and Tom was dying. When Tom was dead it was inevitable that the hunger for love which Keats felt, a hunger which only a woman could fully satisfy, but which Keats, having his brother, had not been compelled to look for a woman to satisfy, should demand instantly to be appeased.

Keats idealised women. He felt for them in the abstract a passionate tenderness; and his own diminutive stature—it is always hard to remember that he was but a shade over five feet high—made difficult a nearer approach to them which might have reduced his abstract idealism to more reasonable proportions. He could scarcely have avoided being self-conscious in their presence and diffident of closer contact with them; he must have been acutely sensitive of the touch of almost contemptuous surprise which his keen eyes could not fail to notice in the attitude of any woman introduced to a man of five feet and half an inch. Therefore he was inclined to withdraw from contact with women to the warm affection which he gave to and received from his brothers. Had Keats been six inches taller, the history of English literature in the nineteenth century might have been different.

For, although Keats was speaking the truth when he said that the thought of his brothers stifled the impression any woman might have made upon him, that was the account given by his conscious mind of a process not altogether under its surveyance and control. Had he been more at his ease with women, he would not have clung to his brothers so closely. Because he could not make contact with women, he exalted, and sincerely exalted, the hold of his love for his brothers upon him. That contact with women was difficult for him we could guess without his word; but we have his word. 'I know not how it is,' he wrote to George in October 1818, 'but I have never made any acquaintance [with women] of my own—nearly all through your medium, my dear Brother.' And it is strange and pathetic to think that of all the women whose acquaintance Keats made through George, the girl whom George married, Georgiana Wylie, was the dearest to him. Keats knew her personally only a little while; but he conceived an immediate affection for her which only deepened with time. The charming, beautiful, loyal, unselfish Georgiana Wylie, is by far the loveliest of the women who appear in Keats' letters. She possessed the two qualities for which Keats most deeply longed—physical beauty and utter loyalty. Keats' letters to her are the most delightfully human and tender outpourings of his instinctive self. 'George minor' was his ideal of a woman, and one cannot help speculating what the event might have been had he possessed the height of his tall brother, and so been the first to meet her.

For, in spite of his resolute determination to make of his brothers' affection a love 'passing the love of women,' Keats was hungry for a woman's love. His diffidence and the difficulty of making contact with women made him frequently speak slightingly of them. But no one was more aware than he that these outbursts—' rhodomontades' was his own technical name for them—were but a disguise for his real feelings; no one was more honest to confess it. In July 1818, on hearing that Reynolds had become engaged, he said:

> I have spoken to you against Marriage, but it was general—the Prospect in those matters has been to me so blank, that I have been not unwilling to die. . . . My sensations are sometimes deadened for weeks together—but believe me I have more than once yearned for the time of your happiness to come as much as I could for myself after the lips of Juliet. From the tenor of my occasional rhodomontade in chit-chat, you might have been deceived concerning me in these points . . . one of the first pleasures I look to is your happy Marriage—the more, since I have felt the pleasure of loving a sister in Law. I did not think it possible to become so much attached in so short a time. Things like these, and they are real, have made me resolve to have a care of my health.

'The prospect in those matters has been to me so blank that I have been not unwilling to die.' Those are strong words, but to those who appreciate the deep sensuousness of *Endymion* they are the evident truth. Keats was hungry and ripe for the sensuous fulfilment of passionate love, and he was starved without it. Those strong words were written almost at the same time as his words to Bailey concerning the effect of his love for his brothers on any love he might have felt for a woman. There is no contradiction between them, save to a superficial reading. Keats' despair of gaining the love of a woman drove him to idealize his affection for his brothers, and to use that affection as a means to stifle his own hunger for a woman's love.

And it was inevitable that his discovery that his diminutive size counted for more with them than his real worth, his honesty, his capacity for love, his genius, should have given him a certain contempt for women, which was by no means wholly the contempt that is the instinctive compensation for a sense of physical inferiority: it was in the main a just and motived contempt. When Bailey, in July 1818, reproached him with not continuing his visits to his friends the Reynolds in Little Britain, where Bailey was paying court to one of the two daughters, Keats replied:

> I am certain I have not a right feeling towards women—at this moment I am striving to be just to them, but I cannot. Is it because they fall so far beneath my boyish Imagination? When I was a schoolboy I thought a fair woman a pure Goddess; my mind was a soft nest in which some one of them slept, though she knew it not. I have no right to expect more than their reality—I thought

them ethereal above men—I find them perhaps equal—great by comparison is very small. Insult may be inflicted in more ways than by word or action. One who is tender of being insulted does not like to think an insult against another. I do not like to think insults in a lady's company—I commit a crime with her which absence would not have known. Is it not extraordinary?—when among men I have no evil thoughts, no malice, no spleen—I feel free to speak or be silent—I can listen, and from every one I can learn—my hands are in my pockets, I am free from all suspicion and comfortable. When I am among women, I have evil thoughts, malice, spleen—I cannot speak, or be silent—I am full of suspicions, and therefore listen to nothing—I am in a hurry to be gone. You must be charitable and put all this perversity to my being disappointed since my boyhood. Yet with such feelings I am happier alone among crowds of men, by myself, or with a friend or two. . . . I must absolutely get over this—but how? the only way is to find the root of the evil, and so cure it ' with backward mutters of dissevering power '—that is a difficult thing; for an obstinate Prejudice can seldom be produced but from a gordian complication of feelings, which must take time to unravel, and care to keep unravelled. I could say a good deal about this, but I will leave it, in hopes of better and more worthy dispositions—and also content that I am wronging no one, for after all I do think better of womankind than to suppose they care whether Mister John Keats five feet high likes them or not.

Keats ' could say a good deal about this '—a good deal more, and more to the point than the most advanced psycho-analyst.* Keats knew the nature of his ' gordian complication of feelings,' which is a better if longer phrase than the jargon ' complex.' But he was not going to uncover his nakedness before Bailey, ' the man of character.' However much it may have had its origin in a sense of physical inferiority, Keats' animus against the generality of women was justified. And the irony of his closing sentence, which was surely not altogether unconscious, is at once biting and scrupulously fair. ' I do think better of womankind than to suppose they care whether Mister John Keats five feet high likes them or not.'

But it is clear that the moment the woman arrived who did care whether Mister John Keats liked her or not, he would be in jeopardy of his life. A passionate desire so strong as one of his rich and sensuous nature must have felt, and so suppressed as it must have been in one of his physical stature, might well be devastating when occasion gave it release. On 23rd July 1818 he wrote to his brother Tom: ' With respect to Women, I think I shall be able to conquer my passions hereafter better than I have yet done.' The precise reference of the phrase is not clear; but I think it simply meant that Keats felt at least a momentary confidence that his devotion to Tom would enable him to stifle still more completely the passionate longing that he felt.

So indeed it was. When Keats returned from his Scottish tour he devoted himself to his dying brother, and did with a deliberate effort of the will stifle his desire for a woman's love. But this effort of the will, as was inevitable, only made the desire itself more intense. It is impossible to read his letters during the closing months of 1818 without feeling that their incessant undertone is a suppressed yet devouring desire for a woman's love. It had become more devouring because of the circumstances in which he was caught. Nothing more powerfully prepares a man's instinctive and unconscious nature for passionate love than continual contact with hopeless illness in a loved intimate. The deep unconscious being reacts away from the presence of death and the aching pain of beholding it. The consciousness may strive to suppress this motion as callous and heartless, but the motion persists. The instinctive man turns away from physical death and longs to be renewed by plunging into the instinctive life of which passionate love is the consummation, and longs for this most desperately in the extremity of his own suffering for the dying one. Keats' suffering at Tom's bedside was the origin of his passion for Fanny Brawne.

Throughout those closing months of 1818 he was haunted by the desire for the love of a woman. It is this desire which gives the yearning tenderness to his letter to George and Georgiana: in a letter he can speak his heart, or part of it.

> Your content in each other is a delight to me which I cannot express—the Moon is now shining full and brilliant—she is the same to me in Matter, what you are to me in Spirit. If you were here my dear Sister I could not pronounce the words which I can write to you from a distance: I have a tenderness for you and an admiration which I feel to be as great and more chaste than I can have for any woman in the world. You will mention Fanny—her character is not formed, her identity does not press upon me as yours does. I hope from the bottom of my heart that I may one day feel as much for her as I do for you—I know not how it is, but I have never made any acquaintance of my own—nearly all through your medium, my dear Brother—through you I now know not only a Sister but a glorious human being.

It has already been shown that in the phrase, 'her identity does not press upon me,' we have a key to Keats' condition of extreme suffering at this moment. But the condition is directly revealed in his letter to Reynolds of 22nd September:

> Believe me I have rather rejoiced at your happiness than fretted at your silence. Indeed I am grieved on your account that I am

not at the same time happy. But I conjure you to think at the moment of nothing but pleasure. 'Gather the rose, &c.'—gorge the honey of life. I pity you as much that it cannot last for ever, as I do myself now drinking bitters. Give yourself up to it—you cannot help it—and I have a consolation in thinking so. I never was in love—yet the voice and shape of a Woman has haunted me these two days—at such a time when the relief, the feverous relief of Poetry, seems a much less crime. This morning Poetry has conquered—I have relapsed into those abstractions which are my only life—I feel escaped from a new and threatening sorrow—and I am thankful for it. There is an awful warmth about my heart like a load of Immortality. Poor Tom—that woman—and Poetry were ringing changes in my senses. . . . .

'Poor Tom—that woman—and Poetry were ringing changes in my senses.' Gathered into that single sentence is the whole truth of Keats' condition. The poetry (which was the 'abstract images' of the first *Hyperion*) was the refuge of his conscious mind from Tom's suffering and his suffering for Tom: 'that woman' was the refuge of his unconscious and instinctive being. Shall we wonder that in one for whom poetry was pre-eminently the spontaneous utterance of the complete self, to whom poetry 'must come as naturally as the leaves to a tree, or it had better not come at all,' this suppression of himself into the first two books of *Hyperion* should have created something which, however noble and beautiful and profound, is not intimately his own? Or that, once the necessity for this suppression had passed, he could not continue this torturing discipline of abstraction? When Keats' being was divided against itself, Milton became his ideal; that noble poet who, for some cause to be discovered, could not submit himself to life, became Keats' hero and pattern when he also could not submit himself to life. And thus he strove with genius to erect for his spirit a habitation not his own.

Nearest him
Asia, born of most enormous Caf,
Who cost her mother Tellus keener pangs,
Though feminine, than any of her sons:
More thought than woe was in her dusky face,
For she was prophesying of her glory;
And in her wide imagination stood
Palm-shaded temples, and high rival fanes,
By Oxus or in Ganges' sacred isles.
Even as Hope upon her anchor leans,
So leant she, not so fair, upon a tusk
Shed from the broadest of her elephants.

That is splendid, that is noble, that is beautiful; but it is not essential Keats. It *is* Milton: not an imitation of Milton, but veritable Milton. And if we desire to understand how Milton came to write like that, we have to understand Keats' condition of soul when it was to him also the only possible utterance.

The writing of Miltonic poetry was the refuge in which Keats hid himself from Tom's death. The other refuge, into which he could not flee, was 'that woman.' 'That woman' was not Fanny Brawne. She was a Miss Jane Cox whom Keats had met at the Reynolds'. He describes her in his October letter to George; and we can learn from his description of her the kind of woman towards whom, in this moment of extremity, his instinctive being turned:

> She is not a Cleopatra, but she is at least a Charmian. She has a rich eastern look; she has fine eyes and fine manners. When she comes into a room she makes an impression the same as the Beauty of a Leopardess. She is too fine and conscious of herself to repulse any Man who may address her—from habit she thinks that nothing *particular*. I always find myself more at ease with such a woman; the picture before me always gives me a life and animation which I cannot possibly feel with anything inferior. I am at such times too much occupied in admiring to be awkward or on a tremble. I forget myself entirely because I live in her. You will by this time think I am in love with her; so before I go any further I will tell you I am not—she kept me awake one Night as a tune of Mozart's might do. I speak of the thing as a pastime and an amusement than which I can feel none deeper than a conversation with an imperial woman the very 'yes' and 'no' of whose Lips is to me a Banquet. I don't cry to take the Moon home with me in my Pocket nor do I fret to leave her behind me. I like her and her like because one has no *sensations*—what we both are is taken for granted. You will suppose I have by this had much talk with her —no such thing—there are the Miss Reynoldses on the look out. They think I don't admire her because I did not stare at her. They call her a flirt to me. What a want of knowledge! She walks across a room in such a Manner that a Man is drawn towards her with a magnetic Power. This they call flirting! they do not know things. They do not know what a Woman is. I believe tho' she has faults —the same as Charmian and Cleopatra might have had. Yet she is a fine thing speaking in a worldly way: for there are two distinct tempers of mind in which we judge of things—the worldly, theatrical and pantomimical; and the unearthly, spiritual and ethereal—in the former Buonaparte, Lord Byron and this Charmian hold the first place in our minds; in the latter, John Howard, Bishop Hooker rocking his child's cradle, and you my dear Sister are the conquering feelings. As a Man in the world I love the rich

> talk of a Charmian; as an eternal being I love the thought of you. I should like her to ruin me; and I should like you to save me.*

It is the natural, instinctive, unconscious, passionate Eve to whom Keats' unconscious being turns—pure woman without the arts and artifices of the petty man-entangler, a woman who is what she is and with whom a man can be what he is. Man's natural enemy, it may be, but an open and above-board enemy, and also his natural mate.

But Keats stifled in himself the thought of her as 'a much greater crime than the feverous relief of poetry.' This refuge was not for him. Nevertheless the letter in which he wrote of Charmian to his brother is filled, as is no other of his letters, with his devouring desire for a woman's love. It begins with an uprush of tenderness at the thought of Georgiana; it passes on to Charmian; then to a meeting with the lady he had met at Hastings sometime in 1817. He went home with her.

> As I had warmed with her before and kissed her, I thought it would be living backwards not to do so again—she had a better taste: she perceived how much a thing of course it was and shrunk from it—not in a prudish way but in as I say a good taste. She continued to disappoint me in a way which made me feel more pleasure than a simple kiss could do. She said I should please her much more if I would only press her hand and go away. Whether she was in a different disposition when I saw her before—or whether I have in fancy wrong'd her I cannot tell. I expect to pass some pleasant hours with her now and then: in which I feel I shall be of some service to her in matters of knowledge and taste: if I can I will. I have no libidinous thought about her—she and your George are the only women à peu près de mon age whom I would be content to know for their mind and friendship alone.

Then the depth of his preoccupation and the manner in which he is stifling it are unmistakably revealed.

> I shall in a short time write you in as far as I know how I intend to pass my Life—I cannot think of these things now Tom is so unwell and weak. Notwithstanding your Happiness and your recommendation I hope I shall never marry. Though the most beautiful Creature were waiting for me at the end of a Journey or a Walk; though the Carpet were of Silk, the Curtains of the morning Clouds; the chairs and Sofa stuffed with Cygnet's down; the food Manna, the Wine beyond Claret, the Window opening on Winander mere, I should not feel—or rather my happiness would not be so fine, as my Solitude is sublime.

Nothing in Keats strikes the careful reader with deeper admiration than his absolute integrity. In this letter it is palpable. He was going to say: 'I should not feel so happy as I do in my solitude'—but in the very act of saying it he feels it is not true, and he breaks off. He knows he would be happier with the woman of his dreams; but he consoles himself with the thought that his happiness, though greater, would not be so fine as the happiness of his solitude.

> Then instead of what I have described there is a sublimity to welcome me home. The roaring of the wind is my wife and the Stars through the window pane are my Children. The mighty abstract idea I have of beauty in all things stifles the more divided and minute domestic happiness—an amiable wife and sweet Children I contemplate as part of that Beauty, but I must have a thousand of those beautiful particles to fill up my heart. I feel more and more every day, as my imagination strengthens, that I do not live in this world alone but in a thousand worlds. No sooner am I alone than shapes of epic greatness are stationed around me, and serve my Spirit the office which is equivalent to a King's bodyguard—then 'Tragedy with scepter'd pall comes sweeping by'. . . . These things, combined with the opinion I have of the generality of women—who appear to me as children to whom I would rather give a sugar Plum than my time, form a barrier against Matrimony which I rejoice in.

He rejoiced in the barrier, no doubt: without it he would have suffered more deeply still: but he did not rejoice in the fact that the barrier was necessary. He could take refuge amid his bodyguard of epic shapes and hide himself in *Hyperion:* but the importunate longing for a woman's love remained. And if he could stay the pangs of his hunger with the thought that the generality of women were children to whom a man should give a sugar plum rather than his time, he also knew that there were women of another kind, not so easily dismissed, whom he did not desire to dismiss, whom on the contrary he longed to take into his heart. There were real women, and he had known two of them: Georgiana was one, Charmian was another.

The letter to his brother and sister was ended on 31st October. A month later, on 1st December, Tom was dead. The ordeal was over, and the need of refuge from it in the abstraction of Miltonic poetry was past, for now Keats no longer thought it a crime to suffer a woman to enter his heart. On the contrary, the gates were flung wide: the first woman who was beautiful and who did show signs of caring whether Mister John Keats five feet high liked her, could enter in triumph. She entered in at once; she was Fanny Brawne.

After Tom's death Keats could not bear to remain in his lonely lodgings with Bentley the postman in Well Walk any more; his friend Charles Brown invited him to share his little house at Wentworth Place, and Keats eagerly accepted. Brown was in the habit of letting his house during the summer and going away; this year, while he was away with Keats in Scotland, he had let it to a Mrs. Brawne, who had liked Hampstead so well that when her term was up she had taken another house hard by. While living in Brown's house, she had naturally made friends with the Dilkes next door, and was now with her daughter a fairly constant visitor to Wentworth Place. In his next letter to George, begun about the middle of December, Keats tells his brother of his change of quarters, and soon afterwards for the first time mentions Fanny Brawne:

> Mrs. Brawne, who took Brown's house for the Summer, still resides in Hampstead—she is a very nice woman—and her daughter senior is I think beautiful and elegant, graceful, silly, fashionable and strange—we have a little tiff now and then—and she behaves a little better, or I must have sheered off.

Probably George had not read Keats' October letter with the same care as we read it now, or the fact that Keats had not sheered off instantly would have told him all. For the moment Keats was reentering life gaily: he is to be invited to a dance, and he is going.

> I find by a sidelong report that I am to be invited to Miss Millar's birthday dance. Shall I dance with Miss Waldegrave? Eh! I shall be obliged to shirk a good many there. I shall be the only Dandy there—and indeed I merely comply with the invitation that the party may not be entirely destitute of a specimen of that race. I shall appear in a complete dress of purple, Hat and all—with a list of the beauties I have conquered embroidered round my Calves.

On the next day he tells George that Bentley the postman has just brought his books round from Well Walk in a clothes-basket.

> I am passing a Quiet day—which I have not done for a long while—and if I do continue so, I feel I must again begin with my poetry—for if I am not in action mind or Body I am in pain—and from that I suffer greatly by going into parties where from the rules of society and a natural pride I am obliged to smother my Spirit and look like an Idiot—because I feel my impulses given way to would too much amaze them—I live under an everlasting restraint—never relieved except when I am composing—so I will write away.

At that point he broke off his letter and tried to take up *Hyperion*. But in vain. On the next day, 18th December, he continues his letter:

I think you knew before you left England, that my next subject would be 'the fall of Hyperion.' I went on a little with it last night, but it will take some time to get into the vein again.

He never was to get into the vein again. The vein belonged to a period of his life that was past and done with. A new period had begun. He had been out in the world again, smothering up his spirit at parties so often that the day before was the first quiet day he had passed. He had plunged into life and straightway met his destiny. 'Shall I give you Miss Brawne ?' he asks Georgiana abruptly, and proceeds to give her. The all-important fact comes first:

She is about my height—with a fine style of countenance of the lengthened sort—she wants sentiment in every feature—she manages to make her hair look well—her nostrils are fine—though a little painful—her mouth is bad and good—her Profile is better than her full face which indeed is not full but pale and thin without showing any bone. Her shape is very graceful and so are her movements—her arms are good, her hands bad-ish—her feet tolerable—she is not seventeen*—but she is ignorant—monstrous in her behaviour, flying out in all directions, calling people such names—that I was forced lately to make use of the term *Minx*—this is I think not from any innate vice but from a penchant she has for acting stylishly. I am however tired of such style, and shall decline any more of it. She had a friend to visit her lately—you have known plenty such—her face is raw as if she was standing out in a frost—her lips raw and seem always ready for a Pullet—she plays the Music without one sensation but the feel of the ivory at her fingers. She is a downright Miss without one set-off. We hated her and smoked her and baited her and I think drove her away. Miss B. thinks her a Paragon of fashion, and says she is the only woman she would change persons with. What a stupe—She is as superior as a Rose to a Dandelion.

Georgiana would have understood the meaning of that letter, and she might also have understood how inevitable it was that the letter should break off almost immediately and continue thus:

It is some days since I wrote the last page—and what I have been about I have no Idea. . . . Just now I took out my poem to go on with it—but the thought of my writing so little to you came upon me and I could not get on—so I have begun at random and I have not a word to say—and yet my thoughts are so full of you that I can do nothing else.

Here for once, and on this subject forever, Keats was disingenuous. His mind was filled with Fanny Brawne. He cannot go on with *Hyperion*, not merely because Fanny Brawne fills his mind, but because he is plunged into a new and crucial experience that will change all that he is. He is in the fever of love, and *Hyperion* belongs to the past. If his mind had really been filled with his brother and sister he would have found plenty to say to them; he always did. He is writing to them simply because he must do something, and he does not keep at that long. Nearly a fortnight later, on 31st December, he has added but a couple of printed pages. 'I received a note from Haslam yesterday—asking if my letter was ready—now this is only the second sheet—notwithstanding all my promises. But you must reflect what hindrances I have had.' They would have needed to reflect a good deal, for no hindrances had been mentioned. But Georgiana may have guessed at them. However, Keats promises better for next month: he will begin a journal for them immediately. (Nearly two months passed before he wrote the first word of it.) He will not copy any extracts from his large poem because it is 'scarce begun.' 'Scarce begun,' indeed, for Apollo had not yet entered it, yet almost at an end. The truth was that *Hyperion* and letter-writing, even to his beloved brother and sister, had both gone to the dogs. But Haslam's demand for the letter is imperative: so Keats, with a sense of shame, makes the effort on 2nd January 1819, to get on with it:

> I am afraid a great part of my Letters are filled up with promises and what I will do rather than a great deal written—but here I say once for all—that circumstances prevented me from keeping my promise in my last, but now I affirm that as there will be nothing to hinder me I will keep a journal for you. That I have not yet done so you would forgive if you knew how many hours I have been repenting of my neglect. For I have no thought pervading me so constantly and frequently as that of you—my Poem cannot frequently drive it away—you will retard it much more than you could by taking up my time if you were in England. I never forget you except after seeing now and then some beautiful woman—but that is a fever—the thought of you is a passion with me but for the most part a calm one.

Keats thus lets fall a hint of the real truth and no more. Not until his brother George came to England a year later did Keats mention to him his love for Fanny Brawne; and then he seems to have confined himself to the bare fact. His love was already what it was always to be, a subject on which he could speak to no one, save only to herself. As he was silent afterwards when his love had become an anguish, so now when it was an ecstasy he was silent. This utter silence on the subject of his love is an essential part of Keats' nature; his love was too tremendous, too devouring and too sacred a thing ever to be spoken of save to the woman for whom he felt it.

Instead of extracts from *Hyperion* he sends them two poems he has just written: *Ever let the Fancy roam* and *Bards of Passion and of Mirth*. They are poems of delighted happiness—' a sort of rondeaus ' he calls them, and he thinks he will become partial to them. They permit one idea to be 'amplified with greater ease and more delight and freedom than in the sonnet.' One has only to read these poems after the first two books of the first *Hyperion* to feel how completely Keats' mood has changed. These two poems spring from the same emotion as the lines of the third book of *Hyperion* which begin: ' Flush everything which hath a vermeil hue.'

Ever let the fancy roam,
Pleasure never is at home:
At a touch sweet Pleasure melteth,
Like to bubbles when rain pelteth . . .

may possibly seem to those who read poetry as they would read a blue-book a poem tinged with melancholy. If so, they must compare it with *The Ode to Melancholy*. *Ever let the Fancy roam* is pure allegro; so is *Bards of Passion and of Mirth*. Keats was not to know the mood for long; even in *The Eve of St. Agnes* there is a tinge of sadness and mistrust. For all its opulent sensuous confidence, it is a dream-fulfilment of his love. The two ' rondeaus ' more exactly mark the pinnacle of his happiness. Even in them it is by a hair's-breadth overpast.

Oh, sweet Fancy, let her loose!
Every joy is spoilt by use,
Every pleasure, every joy—
Not a Mistress but doth cloy.
Where's the cheek that doth not fade
Too much gaz'd at? Where's the Maid
Whose lip mature is ever new?
Where's the eye however blue
Doth not weary? Where's the face
One would meet in every place?
Where's the voice, however soft,
One would hear too oft and oft?
At a touch sweet pleasure melteth
Like to bubbles when rain pelteth.
Let then winged fancy find
Thee a Mistress to thy mind:
Dulcet-eyed as Ceres' daughter
Ere the God of torment taught her
How to frown and how to chide;
With a waist and with a side

White as Hebe's, when her Zone
Slipp'd its golden clasp and down
Fell her Kirtle to her feet
While she held the goblet sweet,
And Jove grew languid.

Mistress fair!
Thou shalt have that tressed hair
Adonis tangled all for spite,
And the mouth he would not kiss,
And the treasure he would miss;
And the hand he would not press
And the warmth he would distress.
O the Ravishment—the Bliss!
Fancy has her—there she is—
Never fulsome, ever new,
There she steps! And tell me who
Has a Mistress so divine?
Be the palate ne'er so fine
She cannot sicken.

Break the Mesh
Of the Fancy's silken leash
Where she's tether'd to the heart.
Quickly break her prison string
And such joys as these she'll bring.
Let the winged fancy roam,
Pleasure never is at home.

Those are the concluding lines of *Ever Let the Fancy Roam* as Keats copied it into his letter, except that italics are used for the lines which he afterwards omitted when he published the poem. In those suppressed lines the intimate connection of Keats' poem as he originally wrote it with his love is manifest. It also is a dream-consummation of his passion. Perhaps the most revealing of all the lines suppressed is:

Break the mesh
Of the Fancy's silken leash
Where she's tethered to the heart.

Poor Keats! So quickly to feel that his love would not be consummated in living reality; so quickly to feel that he must let his imagination fly free of the real woman he coveted and take its delight of love in the castle of fancy.

Aye, in the very temple of delight
Veil'd Melancholy hath her sovran shrine.

So he was to write more sadly a little later. But even now, when the ecstasy of love had almost swallowed up foreboding, the poison sting was there. There was that ominous and incessant ' sore throat.' All he can say of it, just as he begins to copy the poem, is not that it has gone, but only that ' it is much better.'

So far, from his own reticent letters of the time, we have followed the birth of his love for Fanny Brawne. That the story is true and unexaggerated we may learn from his letters to her. To no other living soul, save to Brown in the moment of his death agony, did Keats speak anything of the truth of his love. His friends, of course, saw what they could see afterwards with their own eyes; but probably it was long before any one of them guessed a fraction of the true condition of things. Even if he had told them, they would not have understood. Some six months later, looking back upon the beginnings he wrote to her (8th July 1819):

> I never knew before, what a love as you have made me feel, was; I did not believe in it; my Fancy was afraid of it, lest it should burn me up. . . . Why may I not speak of your Beauty, since without that I never could have lov'd you?—I cannot conceive any beginning of such love as I have for you but Beauty. There may be a sort of love for which, without the least sneer at it, I have the highest respect and can admire it in others: but it has not the richness, the bloom, the full form, the enchantment of love after my own heart.

And, a little later (25th July 1818), he said:

> The very first week I knew you I wrote myself your vassal; but burnt the Letter as the very next time I saw you I thought you manifested some dislike to me. If you should ever feel for Man at the first sight what I did for you, I am lost.

Keats was not romanticizing: he never did romanticize. He was speaking the absolute truth. Moreover, the letter to Reynolds (22nd September 1818) shows how real had been his fear that love should burn him up. ' I feel escaped from a new and threatening sorrow. There is an awful warmth about my heart like a load of Immortality.' Keats was describing to Fanny Brawne exactly what had happened to him, and he had been in the condition when exactly this thing does happen. He had fallen a prey to devouring, passionate, physical love of a woman. Fanny Brawne was beautiful, Fanny Brawne was about his height, Fanny Brawne had cared whether Mister John Keats liked her; and she took possession of his heart for ever.

Keats was ill; Keats had little money, and on the little money that he had Haydon was making demands. Although his sore throat recurs continually in his letters of January, and he was obviously in no condition to be abroad, yet in order to get money for Haydon he made exhausting visits to the City and vexed his spirit with interviews with his intractable guardian, Abbey.

> I shall have a little trouble in procuring the Money (he wrote to Haydon) and a great ordeal to go through—no trouble indeed to anyone else—or ordeal either. I mean I shall have to go to town some thrice and stand in the Bank an hour or two—to me worse than anything in Dante. . . .
>
> I have been writing a little now and then lately: but nothing to speak of—being discontented and as it were moulting. Yet I do not think I shall ever come to the rope or the Pistol, for after a day or two's melancholy, although I smoke more and more my own insufficiency—I see by little and little more of what is to be done and how it is to be done, should I ever be able to do it. On my soul, there should be some reward for that continual 'agonie ennuyeuse.' I was thinking of going into Hampshire for a few days. I have been delaying it longer than I intended.

He went into Hampshire; and he was kept indoors by his sore throat all the while he was there. He took down with him some sheets of thin paper that his friend Haslam had given him for writing to America. Probably he took them in order to write to America. Instead he wrote on them *The Eve of St. Agnes*.

To describe *The Eve of St. Agnes*, we shall find no apter words than those used by Keats himself to Fanny Brawne of his love for her. It has 'the richness, the bloom, the full form, the enchantment of love after his own heart.' It is the poem of awakened sensuous love, not quite confident—was not Keats at the very moment he wrote it kept indoors by his sore throat?—for it is a dream that vanishes. Yet we may fairly call it a poem of opulent and triumphant love. It has the rapture and enchantment, the rich and deep and right sensuousness, of complete surrender to the god; it is the brief dayspring of Keats' passion translated into terms of the poetic imagination. If the crude equation be taken with enough imaginative margin, we may say that Madeline is Fanny and Keats Porphyro.

> A casement high and triple-arch'd there was
> All garlanded with carven imag'ries
> Of fruits, and flowers, and bunches of knot-grass,
> And diamonded with panes of quaint device,
> Innumerable of stains and splendid dyes,
> As are the tiger-moth's deep-damask'd wings;
> And in the midst, 'mong thousand heraldries,
> And twilight saints, and dim emblazonings,
> A shielded scutcheon blush'd with blood of queens and kings.

Full on this casement shone the wintry moon,
And threw warm gules on Madeline's fair breast,
As down she knelt for heaven's grace and boon;
Rose-bloom fell on her hands, together prest,
And on her silver cross soft amethyst,
And on her hair a glory, like a saint:
She seem'd a splendid angel, newly drest,
Save wings, for heaven:—Porphyro grew faint:
She knelt, so pure a thing, so free from mortal taint.

Anon his heart revives: her vespers done,
Of all its wreathed pearls her hair she frees;
Unclasps her warmed jewels one by one;
Loosens her fragrant boddice; by degrees
Her rich attire creeps rustling to her knees;
Half-hidden, like a mermaid in sea-weed,
Pensive awhile she dreams awake, and sees,
In fancy, fair Saint Agnes in her bed,
But dares not look behind, or all the charm is fled.

Soon, trembling in her soft and chilly nest,
In sort of wakeful swoon, perplex'd she lay,
Until the poppied warmth of sleep oppress'd
Her soothed limbs, and soul fatigued away;
Flown, like a thought, until the morrow-day;
Blissfully-haven'd both from joy and pain;
Clasp'd like a missal where swart Paynims pray;
Blinded alike from sunshine and from rain,
As though a rose should shut, and be a bud again. . . .

Beyond a mortal man impassion'd far
At these voluptuous accents, he arose,
Ethereal, flush'd, and like a throbbing star
Seen mid the sapphire heaven's deep repose;
Into her dream he melted, as the rose
Blendeth its odour with the violet,—
Solution sweet. . . .

That is essentially Keats' dream-consummation of his love for Fanny Brawne; and it is worth remarking that in the following September he shocked the generous and discriminating but slightly prudish Woodhouse by his insistence that the 'solution sweet' meant that Porphyro and Madeline enjoyed the supreme felicity of physical love.

We may thank heaven that this condition of comparative confidence lasted long enough for Keats to immortalize it in *The Eve of*

St. Agnes; for it did not last long. The pain of doubt soon entered in, and the pain quickly passed into an agony of despair. Of this pain and despair there were two practical and palpable causes. The ' sore throat ' was obstinate, and Keats, who was himself a doctor and had watched his brother die, knew too much about ' sore throats.' The thought of death soon resumed its permanent abode in his mind. Then there was the thought of money. His efforts to raise the wind for Haydon were finally to reveal that a lawsuit in Chancery would be begun against his small patrimony, and that the supplies which he had counted on to keep him going economically for two or three years would be altogether stopped. In fact, he had no money at all. Without money how was he to marry Fanny? And how was he to get money? By another book of poems, when his last had been fly-blown into rottenness on the review-shambles?

Death and poverty—either of these might deprive him of the possession of his love. And long before the time it would take to earn the smallest competence, he might be dead. So in a single month Keats passed through the ecstasy of love to the ecstasy of despair, a despair deeper than any he had felt before, a despair as deep as any that man can feel. Therefore he told Haydon that he felt he was ' as it were moulting ' as a poet. He was on the brink of that ' dying into life ' which was to be endured by Apollo as the condition of his full divinity, and by the poet of the second *Hyperion* as the price of his vision of the face of Mnemosyne.

CHAPTER IX

'DYING INTO LIFE'

FANNY BRAWNE was beautiful and young and small. She liked Keats; perhaps she liked him chiefly for liking her. She liked to be liked, and to be liked by someone whom their mutual friends were inclined to think a poet of genius was very pleasant to her. She wanted to be admired by everybody. Perhaps she had a vague feeling that to be loved by Keats was more worth than to be admired by military men with shiny boots and fine moustaches. She may even have felt that she was positively fond of him. At all events she was willing to be half-engaged to him. But she was young, she wanted to be stylish, and she wanted to enjoy life. And the life to be enjoyed consisted for her chiefly—she was only eighteen—in routs, and flirtations, and parties, and dances. Keats did not shine in such assemblies. He was miserable at parties, and he did not even know how to dance. He wrote to his sister Fanny in February regretting that their guardian Abbey did not look on him with a kindlier eye, so that he might come to the lawn at Walthamstow. 'I should like to take possession of those Grassplots for a Month or so and send Mrs. Abbey to town to count coffee berries instead of currant Bunches, for I want you to teach me a few common dancing steps.' A fortnight later he wrote to her: 'I went lately to the only dance I have been to these twelve months or shall go for twelve months again.'

No, Keats did not shine in society; the life which Fanny Brawne most enjoyed was not a life that he could share. And there could be no thought of her giving up her delights for his sake. He would have given up everything for hers, it is true. But unfortunately one thing was obvious, and Keats knew it well: Fanny Brawne did not love him as he loved her. That he accepted as a fact from the beginning. 'If you should ever feel for Man at first sight what I did for you,' he wrote to her in July, 'I am lost,' and again and again he insists in his letters to her on that which he knows, that she does not love him as he loves her. She liked him well enough to be engaged to him if the engagement was not too serious, and perhaps to marry him if he for his part had success and position enough to support her. If he would become a figure in the world like Mr. Thomas Moore or Lord Byron, that would be very nice indeed. But of the passionate and self-destroying love which will take risks there is not a trace in what we know of Fanny Brawne.

Why should there be? There are thousands of Fanny Brawnes in the world to-day: in one class of society they talk of their various 'boys,' and they say, and feel, that one is 'a nicer boy' than the others; but in all classes the thought, though not the speech, is the same. Keats was 'a nice boy' to Fanny Brawne; she really liked him. She may sometimes have thought that it was rather a pity he could not afford to marry her; and then again she thought it was just as well, on the whole rather better, for if she were to be married to him then she supposed she would have to give up flirtations and parties too if he wanted it, as he probably would. But until she was married to him, and that would take a conveniently long while, she could not be expected to give up these things, could she? And the thousands of Fanny Brawnes that are in the world to-day, and a good many thousands of others, will agree with her in replying: No, she could not be expected to. They are substantially right, but for the wrong reason. If she had felt for Keats what he felt for her, then her gaieties and her stylishness and her flirtations would have fallen from her naturally; they would have become intolerable to her. Since she did not feel for Keats what he felt for her, it was better that she should not have pretended.

To tell the truth, she seems to have made no effort to pretend so much; nor even to have pretended that she regarded their engagement as very binding upon her. Keats' first letter to her after he had left Hampstead for the country at the end of June tells us a great deal:

> I almost wish we were butterflies and liv'd but three summer days—three such days with you I could fill with more delight than fifty common years could ever contain. But however selfish I feel, I am sure I could never act selfishly: as I told you a day or two before I left Hampstead, I will never return to London if my Fate does not turn up Pam or at least a Court-card. Though I could centre my happiness in you, I cannot expect to engross your heart so entirely—indeed if I thought you felt as much for me as I do for you at this moment I do not think I could restrain myself from seeing you again to-morrow for the delight of one embrace. But no—I must live upon hope and Chance. In case of the worst that can happen, I shall still love you—but what hatred shall I have for another!

That is a singular letter from a lover to his mistress: in it he comes very near to telling her outright that if a more eligible suitor than the penniless Keats were to present himself, she would choose the man with the money. I doubt whether Fanny Brawne, with all her faults, deserved so bitter an imputation. She did not love Keats enough to take a risk—and it was no small risk. Keats knew it and it was torture to him.

He felt that his love was utterly precarious, not only from his poverty and the chance of death, but because of Fanny Brawne herself; and from what we can glean from Keats' letters he had good reason to be afraid. What man would not be afraid of the faithfulness of a betrothed who said that she looked forward complacently to a long engagement? And the scraps of her letters which Keats quotes in his during the summer of this year are not reassuring. She was very young; she had her 'penchant for acting stylishly,' and perhaps the real Fanny Brawne could not express herself in letters. But her phrases have a touch of coquettish affectation that is very unpleasant. She speaks of 'horrid people' and wonders whether it depends on them whether she shall see Keats again. 'Horrid people'—one can almost see the *moue* of acquired petulance. She meets Severn and writes: 'But you must be satisfied in knowing that I admired you much more than your friend'—it is the arch voice of the suburban belle. On this occasion Keats confessed that her words hurt him. They must have made him wince. To be coquetted with when he was wholly hers; to have it proved again and again that she felt for him nothing of what he felt for her. It was no wonder that Keats felt that his love was precarious indeed.

Death that might snatch him away, poverty that might delay his love for years, a love that might itself fail him—such was the knowledge that changed Keats' ecstasy of happiness to an ecstasy of despair. It is this despair and his victory over it which changed the rapture of *Ever let the Fancy roam* and *The Eve of St. Agnes* into the rich and strange temper which underlies the *Odes*. Their most familiar phrases:

> Joy whose hand is ever at his lips
> Bidding adieu. . . .
>
> She cannot fade, though thou hast not thy bliss;
> Forever wilt thou love and she be fair . . .
>
> Where Beauty cannot keep her lustrous eyes
> Or new Love pine at them beyond to-morrow . . .

are thrilled with the aching hopelessness of Keats' love for Fanny Brawne. There is more, far more in the *Odes* than that; but that is there, and in a sense it is dominant in them. That is the immediate life-experience which inspires and colours them; as the dying of his brother Tom is the life-experience which inspires and colours the first *Hyperion;* as the sudden flowering of his impassioned and sensuous love for Fanny Brawne is the life-experience which inspires and colours *The Eve of St. Agnes*. Or to speak still more exactly, by anticipating a division of man's knowledge which Keats discovered at this time—heart-knowledge, mind-knowledge, soul-knowledge—the hopelessness of his love for Fanny Brawne is the heart-knowledge that inspires and colours his *Odes*.

But much was to happen to Keats before that heart-knowledge could be so richly sublimated; many operations were to be worked upon it in the crucible of his being before it could become the substance of poems which are incommensurable with any in the English language save those of Shakespeare's maturity. It was at this time, mid-February, that Keats wrote at the beginning of the letter to George (which he had but just commenced) the profound words:

> They are very shallow people who take everything literally. A Man's life of any worth is a continual allegory, and very few eyes can see the Mystery of his life—a life like the scriptures figurative—which such people can no more make out than they can the Hebrew Bible. Lord Byron cuts a figure but he is not figurative, Shakespeare led a life of Allegory; his works are the comments on it.

Fortunately for the eyes that care to see the mystery of Keats' life, his letters remain; and by a double fortune they are fullest at this critical moment of 'dying into life.' We can, with a little patience and a little 'learning in spiritual hieroglyphics,' follow the secret movement of his mind.

While he was at Bedhampton in Hampshire, Keats had been unwell. He had not gone beyond the garden gate more than two or three times; but he had written *The Eve of St. Agnes* and *The Eve of St. Mark*. When he returned to London at the end of January his sore throat had remained persistent, and he was confined to the house again. He told George that on 23rd February he had been to town for the first time for three weeks. So that for nearly six weeks he had been more or less an invalid. The three weeks' confinement at Hampstead were the beginning of a period of creative quiescence. 'I have not gone on with *Hyperion*,' he told George on 24th February, 'for to tell the truth, I have not been in great cue for writing lately.' This disinclination or inability to write was not directly caused by his ill-health, because during the same ill-health he had composed *The Eve of St. Agnes*. Keats was quiescent because he was brooding over his experience: of that experience, which has been described, ill-health was but one of the elements. On 8th March he wrote to Haydon, 'I have experienced the satisfaction of having great conceptions without the trouble of sonnetteering. I will not spoil my love of gloom by writing an Ode to Darkness.' On 13th March he writes to George: 'I know not why poetry and I have been so distant lately,' and says that he is considering whether to go to Edinburgh to qualify as a physician, but he is afraid he would not take kindly to it; and yet he would like to do it: making his living as a doctor is 'not worse than writing poems and hanging them up to be fly-blown on the review-shambles.' Then, for about a month, there is silence in his journal-letter to George. The silence ends in mid-April. We learn of what it had chiefly consisted from a letter to Haydon, who has been worrying him for money, on 13th April: 'I dread as much as plague the idle fever of two months more without any fruit.' And two days later (15th April) he tells George that 'he is still at a standstill in versifying—I cannot do it yet with any pleasure—I mean however to look round on my resources and means—and see what I can do without poetry. To that end I shall live in Westminster.' Living in Westminster meant trying to make a living by journalism, or as we say now, 'working in Fleet Street.' A fortnight later, the time of silence and brooding and idle fever is at an end. He copies the *Ode to Psyche* into his letter to George. 'The following poem,' he says, 'is the first and the only one with which I have taken even moderate pains. I have for the most part dash'd off my lines in a hurry. This I have done leisurely—I think it reads the more richly for it, and will I hope encourage me to write other things in even a more peaceable and healthy spirit.' The creative period of the great *Odes* had begun.

Those are the outward and tangible facts of the crucial period during which Keats became a great and completely original poet. Nearly three months of 'idle fever,' in which he tastes the satisfaction of having great conceptions without the trouble of expressing them in poetry. Slowly the tension of this feverous brooding relaxes, and he finds serene and sovereign expression for a temper which for strangeness and richness and profundity cannot be paralleled outside the work of Shakespeare. The essential history of this mysterious change is given, as I have said, in the third book of *Hyperion*, which was written at intervals during this period of fever. The pangs with which the god of poetry on looking into the eyes of Mnemosyne dies into life and puts on full divinity are the pangs of the earthly poet. Apollo's first exercise of his new divinity is the writing of Keats' Odes.

By some divine fortune Keats' letter to his brother George during this period is such that we can trace the details of the process in the poet's soul. As a preliminary to examining them, we may note that on the very first day of this year 1819, Keats had enounced to George once more and more clearly his own peculiar criterion of truth. 'I can never feel certain of any truth but from a clear perception of its beauty.' It may be well to insist once more that Keats means precisely what he says: that he is unable to recognize truth except by the sign of beauty. His faculty of truth-perception, as the logician might say, is of a different kind from the ordinary. And on 8th March, when the brooding fever is full upon him, in a letter to Haydon, he confesses that he finds none among his acquaintance who are bent upon this search for truth:

> Men and tin-kettles are much the same in these days. They do not study like children at five-and-thirty—but they talk like men

> of twenty. Conversation is not a search after knowledge, but an endeavour at effect. . . . I am convinced of this, and from this I have come to this resolution—never to write for the sake of writing or making a poem, but from running over with any little knowledge or experience which many years of reflection may perhaps give me; otherwise I will be dumb.
>
> With respect to my livelihood I will not write for it—for I will not run with that most vulgar of all crowds, the literary. Such things I ratify by looking upon myself and trying myself at lifting mental weights, as it were. I am three-and-twenty, with little knowledge and middling intellect. It is true that in the height of enthusiasm I have been cheated into some fine passages: but that is not the thing.

What then was 'the thing'? More knowledge of that truth which could be recognized only by the sign of beauty; a more secure possession of that knowledge which would not leave him dependent on the glimpses of enthusiasm for the apprehension of the beauty of all things wherein their truth consists; a changing of that 'mighty abstract idea of the Beauty of all things' into a concrete perception. Out of this knowledge when it came, he would write; but 'not for the sake of writing' and it would take him 'many years of reflection.'

Many indeed, had Keats been one of the ruck; but it is in this very letter to Haydon that he speaks of his having had 'the satisfaction of having great conceptions without the trouble of sonnetteering.' Keats was speaking of a knowledge that he had at last begun to touch. Ten days later in his letter to George (19th March) he expresses one of these conceptions: he reveals his mind in the very act of this discovery of truth by the sign of beauty, which is knowledge. The whole passage is of consuming interest:

> This morning I am in a sort of temper, indolent and supremely careless—I long after a stanza or two of Thomson's *Castle of Indolence*—my passions are all asleep, from my having slumbered till nearly eleven, and weakened the animal fibre all over me, to a delightful sensation, about three degrees on this side of faintness. If I had teeth of pearl and the breath of lilies I should call it languor, but as I am (especially as I have a black eye) I must call it laziness. In this state of effeminacy the fibres of the brain are relaxed in common with the rest of the body, and to such a happy degree that pleasure has no show of enticement nor pain no unbearable power. Neither Poetry, nor Ambition, nor Love have any alertness of countenance as they pass by me; they seem rather like figures on a Greek vase—a Man and two women whom no one but myself could distinguish in their disguisement. This is the only happiness, and is a rare instance of the advantage of the body overpowering the Mind.

Miss Amy Lowell has discovered a lost fragment of this letter, which shows that Keats had got his black eye not, as had been previously supposed, in a ding-dong fight with a Hampstead butcher-boy who had been tormenting a kitten, but in playing very early cricket. However, we have already learned to be on our guard, or at least to be particularly alert when Keats chronicles a mood of indolence. His indolence was indeed 'diligent indolence,' a kind of creative brooding, a going-in of the soul to be renewed in its own darkness, a rest and recuperation from intellectual fever.

> I have this moment received a note from Haslam, in which he expects the death of his Father. . . . This is the world—thus we cannot expect to give away many hours to pleasure. Circumstances are like Clouds continually gathering and bursting. While we are laughing, the seed of some trouble is put into the wide arable land of events—while we are laughing it sprouts, it grows, and suddenly bears a poison-flower which we must pluck. Even so we have leisure to reason on the misfortunes of our friends; our own touch us too nearly for words.
>
> Very few men have ever arrived at a complete disinterestedness of Mind: very few have been influenced by a pure desire of the benefit of others—in the greater part of the Benefactors of Humanity some meretricious motive has sullied their greatness—some melodramatic scenery has fascinated them. From the manner in which I feel Haslam's misfortune I perceived how far I am from any humble standard of disinterestedness. Yet this feeling ought to be carried to its highest pitch, as there is no fear of its ever injuring society—which it would do, I fear, pushed to an extremity.

By 'disinterestedness,' it is worth pointing out, Keats means a completely unselfish love of one's fellow creatures: it is a positive and not a negative quality.

There follows immediately another glimpse of that 'eternal core of fierce destruction' of which he had written in his *Epistle to Reynolds* a year before. To perceive the profound and subtle change which has come over Keats' vision of the same reality we need to have his former words fresh in our minds. Then he had cried in despair:

> O never will the prize,
> High reason, and the love of good and ill,
> Be my award!

and he had gone on to tell of the vision which had brought him to that despair:

> Dear Reynolds! I have a mysterious tale,
> And cannot speak it: the first page I read

> Upon a Lampit rock of green sea-weed
> Among the breakers: 'twas a quiet eve,
> The rocks were silent, the wide sea did weave
> An untumultuous fringe of silver foam
> Along the flat brown sand; I was at home
> And should have been most happy,—but I saw
> Too far into the sea, where every maw
> The greater on the less, feeds evermore—
> But I saw too distinct into the core
> Of an eternal fierce destruction,
> And so from happiness I far was gone.
> Still am I sick of it, and tho', to-day,
> I've gathered young spring-leaves, and flowers gay
> Of periwinkle and wild strawberry,
> Still do I that most fierce destruction see,—
> The Shark at savage prey,—the Hawk at pounce,—
> The gentle Robin, like a Pard or Ounce,
> Ravening a worm. . . .

But now the light in which that same reality is seen is utterly changed. Keats has touched that 'love of good and ill' of which he despaired. He has been saying that if disinterestedness were to prevail throughout life, life would be injured.

> For in wild nature (he goes on) the Hawk would lose his Breakfast of Robins, and the Robin his of Worms—the Lion must starve as well as the Swallow. The greater part of Men make their way with the same instinctiveness, the same unwandering eye from their purposes, the same animal eagerness as the Hawk. The Hawk wants a Mate, so does the Man—look at them both, they set about it and procure one in the same manner. They both want a nest and they both set about one in the same manner—they get their food in the same manner. The noble animal Man for his amusement smokes his pipe—the Hawk balances about the clouds—that is the only difference of their leisures. This it is that makes the Amusement of Life—to a speculative Mind—I go among the Fields and catch a glimpse of a Stoat or a field-mouse peeping out of the withered grass—the creature hath a purpose, and its eyes are bright with it. I go among the buildings of a city and I see a man hurrying along—to what? the creature hath a purpose, and his eyes are bright with it. . . .

One is loth to interpose a comment; but the occasions are rare when we can watch a pure poet in the act of creative perception. And surely we cannot fail to see what is happening, what has happened. The truth which Keats is discovering is a terrible truth, but it is being made beautiful. Or more exactly, this beauty which Keats is discovering and revealing in life is the truth. He is discovering the harmony which unites man to the animal universe; he is revealing to himself and to us that things must be as they are. Our good and our evil are but partial; were our good—'disinterestedness'—to prevail, the strange beauty of life would be gone. In this vision is that 'love of good and ill,' which he had despaired to attain; for now good and evil are seen as a harmony and loved as a harmony. This is no conjuring trick by which beautiful words are made to throw a gleam over an ordinary thought; this beauty emanates from the instantaneous recognition by the poetic mind of a truth which it alone can perceive. At this moment we are perhaps as near to the actual miracle of great poetry as we may ever approach it; for this is poetic comprehension in act.

There follows a further and a still higher effort of poetic comprehension, by which Keats stands as it were outside himself and brings himself and his thinking within the scope of his vision: he sees himself as an element of the beauty and a constituent atom of the truth:

> Even here (he goes on), though I myself am pursuing the same instinctive course as the veriest human animal you can think of—[though] I am, however young, writing at random, straining at particles of light in the midst of a great darkness, without knowing the bearing of any one assertion, or any one opinion, yet may I not in this be free from sin? May there not be superior beings, amused with any graceful, though instinctive, attitude my mind may fall into as I am entertained with the alertness of the Stoat or the anxiety of a Deer? Though a quarrel in the Streets is a thing to be hated, the energies displayed in it are fine: the commonest Man shows a grace in his quarrel. [Seen] by a Superior Being our reasonings may take the same tone—though erroneous, they may be fine. This is the very thing in which consists Poetry. . . .

This statement is one of the profoundest ever made concerning the nature of poetry; it is 'a verisimilitude caught from the Penetralium of mystery.' Keats is saying that the attitude of the poet is instinctive, the thought of the poet's mind is spontaneous; but he is saying this not in the abstract and lifeless language of rational thought, but in the concrete and living speech of poetry. It may have been noticed how little abstraction there is in this swift and subtle argument; and for that reason it may have escaped notice that it *is* an argument. The failure to perceive this may well be excused, because it is at once an argument and not an argument at all. It is the poetic equivalent for argument, but it is an independent and far rarer process of mind. The thought moves organically from concrete perception to concrete perception, from image to image, from similitude to similitude. In this passage we have a thing which, so far as

I know, is unique in our literature, poetic thought of the highest making a sustained movement in its own medium towards an apprehension of its own nature. As the Stoat is to him, so is Keats to the Superior Being, in whose eyes the poet has the spontaneous grace and beauty of a creature who ' hath a purpose and its eyes are bright with it.' By that act of self-detachment Keats is himself become the Superior Being, and from that pinnacle of authority he declares that ' this is the very thing in which consists Poetry.'

It is not an easy thought, but it is a simple one; though I should perhaps hesitate to say so when even Professor Bradley confesses that he has never been able to understand it. And I confess that I had read that passage many times before it suddenly became transparently clear to me; and even now I recognize that its simplicity is the simplicity of a pure act of poetic thought, and therefore impossible to translate. One can give only a meagre paraphrase: ' Poetry consists in an instinctive attitude taken by the complete being.' It may be that Professor Bradley was troubled by the next words:

> If so [that is, if this is the very thing in which consists Poetry] then it is not so fine a thing as philosophy, for the same reason that an eagle is not so fine a thing as a truth.

But in order to understand this we must read on:

> Give me this credit—Do you not think I strive—to know myself? Give me this credit, and you will not think that on my account I repeat Milton's lines—
>
> How charming is divine Philosophy,
> Not harsh and crabbed, as dull fools suppose
> But musical as is Apollo's lute—
>
> No, no[t] for myself—[but] feeling grateful as I do to have got into a state to relish them properly. Nothing ever becomes real till it is experienced—even a Proverb is no proverb to you till your Life has illustrated it.

Do not misunderstand him; Keats is not saying that *The Critique of Pure Reason* is finer than poetry, or musical as is Apollo's lute. In Keats' mind ' philosophy ' never meant abstract metaphysical speculation; it meant for him one thing and one thing alone—a comprehension of the mystery of life. That is to say, it meant precisely the kind of speculations of which his letter is composed; and the conclusions he reached through them are what he meant by Truth. So that when he said that Poetry was not so fine a thing as Philosophy, he was saying simply that one kind of poetry is not so fine as another kind of poetry: and that one kind of poet is not so fine as another kind of poet. Or, if my meagre paraphrase be accepted, whereas all true poetry is the utterance of an instinctive attitude of the complete being, one complete being may be more comprehensive than another, and the poetry of that more comprehensive being will be finer. An eagle is indeed not so fine a thing as a man perceiving the beauty which is truth with an eagle's swiftness: that is what Keats is saying. Or, to put it more nakedly still, he is saying that the Keats of 1818 was not so fine a thing as the Keats of 1819: which was true, and Keats knew it.

The contrast is between Keats the spontaneous and unconscious poet; and Keats the conscious, yet still spontaneous poet. And this is the great poet: the poet who remains loyal to his own spontaneous poetic nature when he confronts the burden of the mystery, who knows by a secret sign that beauty is in all things and that in that beauty is their truth, who cannot rest until he has discovered it. Such a great poet Keats had now become.

Then comes an apparent change in the movement of the letter:

> I am ever afraid (he goes on) that your anxiety for me will lead you to fear for the violence of my temper continually smothered down: for that reason I did not intend to have sent you the following sonnet—but look over the last two pages and ask yourselves whether I have not that in me which will bear the buffets of the world. It will be the best comment on my sonnet: it will show you that it was written with no Agony but that of ignorance; with no thirst of anything but Knowledge, when pushed to the point though the first steps to it were through my human passions—they went away and I wrote with my Mind—and perhaps I must confess a little bit of my heart:
>
> Why did I laugh to-night? No voice will tell:
> No God, no Demon of severe response
> Deigns to reply from heaven or from Hell—
> Then to my human heart I turn at once—
> Heart! thou and I are here sad and alone;
> Say, wherefore did I laugh? O mortal pain!
> O Darkness! Darkness! ever must I moan
> To question Heaven and Hell and Heart in vain.
> Why did I laugh? I know this being's lease,
> My fancy to its utmost blisses spreads:
> Yet could I on this very midnight cease
> And the world's gaudy ensigns see in shreds.
> Verse, fame, and Beauty are intense indeed,
> But Death intenser—Death is Life's high meed.
>
> I went to bed and enjoyed uninterrupted sleep. Sane I went to bed, and sane I arose.

That is not an easy sonnet; but is a strangely powerful one. The reference is too intimate to be superficially understood. In order that the connection of thought should be plain, we need to know what manner of laugh it was that occasioned it. At this, we have to guess; and for our conjecture to begin, we need to have made up our minds as to what is the inward movement of feeling which shapes the poem.

I have no doubt that the sestet is antiphonal to the octet: it is not a reply to his own question: 'Why did I laugh ?', but it is a renunciation of the feeling expressed in the laugh. A deeper Keats is disowning and putting away the Keats who laughed. It is the conquering of a despair by a deeper faith. And the faith itself is not an easy one. 'I know all the joys of life,' he declares, 'not one is hidden from my mind. Yet would I gladly die to-night. Poetry, Fame, and Beauty are glorious: they fire the soul. But none is so glorious, none lights so great a flame in the soul as Death. Death is the crown of life.'

Thus it is clear that the laugh had been one of cynical despair. It was a laugh of bitterness, of the sudden sense: 'Vanity of vanities: all is vanity.' The fearful imminence of death, with its looming menace to the love he desired, the poetry he dreamed, the fame he coveted, the beauty he adored, jarred him to the depths, and he laughed. But the laughter was not he. For him, the true Keats, Death is not a mockery, but a triumph; not a darkness that blots out the soul's ecstasies, but the greatest ecstasy of all. 'Eloquent, just and mighty Death !'*

The relation of this sonnet to the beginning of the passage of his letter written on 19th March with which we have been concerned is plain. At the beginning he had said that in his present mood of 'indolence,' 'Neither Poetry, nor Ambition, nor Love have any alertness of countenance as they pass by me.' Poetry—Ambition—Love; Verse—Fame—Beauty: it is the same trinity in the same order. The thought of these three of life's desirables had been vexing his spirit; now on this morning they have become faint and shadowy. It may well have been that the sonnet was written on the night before: when he wrote it he had conquered the agony of the thought that these three would be denied him, by an ecstatic acceptance of death; in the morning he had passed onward to a vision of the beauty of life as it is.

Then comes a month's silence. What passed in this month of silence we might guess from what we already know. During this period of silence, I believe, the final passage of the third book of *Hyperion* was written. The letter, broken off on 19th March, is resumed on 15th April. There is a touch of gaiety in what he now writes, and soon after resuming he copies two poems which also belong to the month of silence. The first is a sonnet which he introduces with these words:

The fifth canto of Dante pleases me more and more—it is that one in which he meets with Paulo and Francesca. I had passed many days in rather a low state of mind, and in the midst of them I dreamt of being in that region of Hell. The dream was one of the most delightful enjoyments I ever had in my life. I floated about the whirling atmosphere as it is described with a beautiful figure, to whose lips mine were joined, as it seemed for an age—and in the midst of all this cold and darkness I was warm. . . . I tried a sonnet upon it—there are fourteen lines but nothing of what I felt in it—O that I could dream it every night:

> As Hermes once took to his feathers light
> When lulled Argus, baffled, swoon'd and slept
> So on a delphic reed my idle spright
> So play'd, so charm'd, so conquer'd, so bereft
> The dragon world of all its hundred eyes
> And seeing it asleep, so fled away:—
> Not to pure Ida with its snow-cold skies,
> Nor unto Tempe where Jove grieved that day;
> But to that second circle of sad hell,
> Where in the gust, the whirlwind and the flaw
> Of Rain and hailstones lovers need not tell
> Their sorrows. Pale were the sweet lips I saw,
> Pale were the lips I kiss'd, and fair the form
> I floated with about that melancholy storm.

And a few days later he copies abruptly into his letter the famous and lovely *La Belle Dame sans Merci*. The connection between it and the sonnet on Paolo and Francesca is manifest, and it may well be that the actual dream which directly inspired the sonnet, was the inspiration at a second remove of the dream of the palely loitering knight at arms.

However that may be, behind both poems is the anguish of an impossible love. La Belle Dame is Fanny Brawne; she is also the beauty of life itself which is claiming, through Fanny, Keats for its sacrifice and victim. Life, with its beauty and its pain, has taken hold of him; Love and Death have twined their arms about him. These two poems have their origin in the struggle to conquer his agonized longing for that one of the three desirables which he calls in one place Love and in another Beauty. And now when he has finished copying *La Belle Dame sans Merci* he adds this:

> Why four kisses—you will say—why four because I wish to restrain the headlong impetuosity of my Muse—she would fain have said 'score' without hurting the rhyme—but we must temper the imagination as the Critics say with Judgment: I was obliged

to choose an even number that both eyes might have fair play, and to speak truly I think two apiece quite sufficient. Suppose I had said seven there would have been three and a half apiece—a very awkward affair and well got out of on my side.

That is not the bitter detachment of the laugh of *Why did I laugh to-night?* It is the detachment of a man who has uttered his heart and must turn away from what he has said. It is the irony of the pain of self-revelation; it is the irony of Hamlet, the unembittered irony of the soul which begins to see beyond its pain, and to comprehend that the pain must be.

The second desirable with the thought of which he struggled in this month of silence was Fame. A little later, on 30th April, in the same long letter to his brother George, he tells him that he will copy out two or three sonnets which he has lately written: one of them is a sonnet on Fame. But he cannot copy that because Brown is transcribing it at the very moment he writes. 'I must employ myself perhaps,' says Keats, 'in a sonnet on the same subject.' And he straightway does. He composes directly into his letter a sonnet *On Fame*. The corrections prove beyond all doubt that it was a first draft. He writes at the top: 'You cannot eat your cake and have it too—*Proverb*,' and then composes:

> How fever'd is that man who cannot look
> Upon his mortal days with temperate blood,
> Who vexes all the leaves of his Life's book
> And robs his fair name of its maidenhood
> It is as if the rose should pluck herself
> Or the ripe plum finger its misty bloom
> As if a clear Lake meddling with itself,
> Should cloud its pureness with a muddy gloom.
> But the rose leaves herself upon the Briar
> For winds to kiss and grateful Bees to feed
> And the ripe plumb still wears its dim attire,*
> The undisturbed Lake has crystal space—
> Why then should man teasing the world for grace
> Spoil his salvation by a fierce miscreed?

Had that sonnet been without a title, it would have occurred to no one to call it a sonnet *On Fame*, and even when we know it was written *On Fame* the reference may be still obscure. But what has happened we can discover from the sonnet *Why did I laugh to-night?* Fame has her two sisters still in her company—Poetry and Love. She is but one aspect of a single thought, the thought of all that Keats desires in life, and that may be denied him. It is the fevered desire to hold in his grasp all that life might give that 'vexes all the leaves of his life's book': and against this fever he calmly enjoins upon himself serenity. He must 'look upon his mortal days with temperate blood'; he must grow towards his appointed end, untroubled by the menace of death and of the desirables from which it will for ever shut him out. If he fails in this, he will 'spoil his salvation by a fierce miscreed.' The fever must be no more; and the sonnet shows that the fever is no more; for its slow, quiet movement and its rich natural imagery* are but the translation into words of a condition of being which is the same, profoundly the same, as that expressed so magically by Edgar in *King Lear:*

> We must endure
> Our going hence even as our coming hither:
> Ripeness is all.

At this point Keats began to compose the *Odes*. The sonnet *On Fame* was written into his letter on 30th April: either the next day or the day after he copied the *Ode to Psyche*. The 'idle fever' had been past days before 30th April. Probably its passing was the cause of his resuming the letter to George on 15th April. But nothing depends upon the exact dating of so profound an evolution in Keats' being. The main facts are clear. Somewhere in the six weeks which followed 19th March, Keats had passed from despair to acceptance. On 19th March we can mark the beginning of the change. In the sonnet *Why did I laugh to-night?* he conquers, and we can watch him conquering, despair by an ecstatic acceptance of death; in the 'indolent' letter, he conquers, and we can watch him conquering, despair by an acceptance of life and a knowledge of the true nature of that Poetry which was the third of life's desirables; but the struggle is not at end. There follows a month of silence; at the end of it he emerges into that condition of calm and serene acceptance which is uttered in the sonnet *On Fame:* and he is a great poet.

If we could know the process by which that inward victory was accomplished, a great secret would be ours. I may be under an illusion; but I believe that the process and the secret can in some measure at least be known. But in order to know them we must first be clear as to the change itself. It is, as I have said, essentially a movement from ecstatic to serene acceptance. Acceptance of what? First, acceptance of death—that is primary. And the beginning and end of the movement from an ecstatic to a serene acceptance of death are marked in the sonnet '*Why did I laugh to-night?* and the sonnet *On Fame*. But true acceptance of death, as Keats' was, is acceptance of life, for death is the greatest fact of life. To accept death is to accept life; it is to accept the whole of one's mortal destiny, to see it as necessary and inevitable and beautiful. This vision may be momentary, or it may be a secure possession. The distance between those two things—the flash of intuition and the security of knowledge—is vast. Keats traversed it in that month of silence. Yet though the distance between these two conditions is vast, it evades expression in ordinary speech. If one has no experience of these doubts and despairs and agonies, it is perhaps impossible to understand them, or the visions or the knowledge by which they are conquered. These things cannot be imagined, they must be experienced, not contemplated in the mind, but ' proved on the pulses.' This is what Keats meant when he said: ' We never really understand fine things until we have gone the same steps as the author.' And the momentous and supremely important changes in the condition of soul which depend upon such experiences are impossible to express save by means of poetry, which is the natural and only speech of the complete being. Take, for instance, those words of Edgar in *King Lear* which have been used to describe Keats' condition of serene acceptance in the sonnet *On Fame*.

> We must endure
> Our going hence even as our coming hither;
> Ripeness is all.

Try to separate that thought, or that knowledge, from the words which are its necessary garment, and the quality and tone of it is gone; and quality and tone in such a thought as this is of its very essence. Expressed in the language of discourse, the thought must dwindle and be changed into a mere Stoic indifferentism. In the living reality it is nothing of the kind. Those few magical words are an act of the soul, and not a thought at all; they are a warm, rich, loving act of acceptance of human destiny—a yea-saying to the sum of things, an act not of the mind but of the complete being, which is ' the very thing wherein consists Poetry.'

The sonnet *On Fame* is such an act of the soul; the sonnet *Why did I laugh to-night?* is not. The earlier sonnet is an assertion, a vision of a truth; but it has not the calm serenity which is the visible proof that the truth is known and possessed. Such a distinction may appear subtle and intangible; but it is vital; it is the distinction between the utterance of the divided and the utterance of the harmonious being, it is the distinction between pure poetry and poetry that is still struggling towards purity. In the earlier sonnet the deeper and truer Keats is renouncing the Keats who laughed so bitterly. It marks the very moment of the pangs of that death in life and rebirth which Apollo endured. In the ' indolent ' letter the deeper Keats is, as it were, consolidating his desperate victory. He is passing into that new condition of acceptance; he is on the verge of ' becoming a god.' Such victories are not won in a day even by a poet like Keats; by the rest of mankind they are not won in their mortal lives at all.

We need not wonder at the month of silence, or at 'his low state of mind,' or at his wandering in 'that region of Hell' in which Paolo and Francesca wandered, or at the agony of *La Belle Dame sans Merci*.

It is possible to know how that act of acceptance was made by Keats; but whether it is possible to explain how it was made, I cannot tell. Keats did his utmost to explain it in his letters to his brother; but I have never seen any evidence that those letters have been understood. And where so eminent and masterly a critic as Professor Bradley has confessed that he had never been able to understand the crucial sentence: 'This is the very thing wherein consists Poetry,' where he has proposed to change the crucial sentence of the *Epistle to Reynolds:*

'Never will the prize,
High reason, and the *love* of good and ill,
Be my award!

into 'high reason and the *lore* of good and ill'—how can I hope to succeed? These two confessions of the greatest living English critic fill me with despair. I admire them as acts of great critical integrity. These two phrases which Professor Bradley does not understand are crucial. If they cannot be understood, Keats cannot be understood. For the 'love of good and ill' is precisely that which Keats dreamed of attaining, set himself to attain, and did attain; and this spontaneous attitude of the complete being 'which is the very thing wherein consists Poetry' is the means by which he attained it. When a mind such as Professor Bradley's loyally acknowledges that it is precisely these two things, the living core of all that Keats was and did, that he has never been able to understand, a sense of sheer impossibility takes hold of me.

For the moment one may speak briefly of the *Odes* which Keats wrote when the inward victory was accomplished. The relation between the sonnet *Why did I laugh to-night?* and the *Ode to a Nightingale* is manifest; the sonnet is doubtless one of those 'musèd rhymes' in which Death had been called soft names. But although the *Ode to a Nightingale* is a poem which everybody knows by heart, something of its movement may be recalled.

The poet is drowsy with happiness at the nightingale's song, and he dreams that he might follow the voice of the bird into a realm of utter forgetfulness of the pain of the world,

Where but to think is to be full of sorrow
And leaden-eyed despairs,
Where Beauty cannot keep her lustrous eyes
Or new Love pine at them beyond to-morrow.

Suddenly the dream is real. 'On the viewless wings of Poesy' he is fled after the voice to a place of 'embalmed darkness,' where he is conscious only of the bird's song.

> Darkling I listen; and for many a time
>   I have been half in love with easeful Death,
> Called him soft names in many a musèd rhyme,
>   To take into the air my quiet breath;
> Now more than ever seems it rich to die,
> To cease upon the midnight with no pain,
>   While thou art pouring forth thy soul abroad
>   In such an ecstasy!
> Still wouldst thou sing, and I have ears in vain—
>   To thy high requiem become a sod.

In part the *Ode to a Nightingale* is a very triumph-song to Death; in part it is a song of despair; as the song of the bird is in part an invitation to the supreme ecstasy of Death, in part the voice of immortality sounding clear amid the agony of mortality. Those two movements of the divided soul which were antiphonal in *Why did I laugh to-night?* are now blent into one strange and unearthly harmony; it is as though that deep division of the soul had been reconciled, with no joy diminished and no pain denied. All that Keats had felt and thought is there, with all its contradictions; but now the contradictions are made one.

It is no part of the purpose of this book to appreciate Keats' poems objectively as poetry; its concern is solely to elucidate the deep and natural movement of the poet's soul which underlies them. This movement is towards a complete acceptance of a peculiar kind, most peculiar in this that it is really complete. This acceptance—this 'love of good and ill'—is manifest in all Keats' poetry in this period of sudden opulence. As it is in the *Ode to a Nightingale*, so it is in the *Ode to Melancholy*.

> She dwells with Beauty—Beauty that must die
>   And Joy whose hand is ever at his lips
> Bidding adieu; and aching Pleasure nigh,
>   Turning to poison while the bee-mouth sips:
> Ay, in the very temple of Delight
>   Veil'd Melancholy has her sovran shrine,
>   Though seen of none save him whose strenuous tongue
>   Can burst Joy's grape against his palate fine;
> His soul shall taste the sadness of her might
>   And be among her cloudy trophies hung.

Only those who have no sense for the true speech of Poetry will call that a poem of despair; it is a poem of triumph through despair.

And the same acceptance, the same triumph through despair, is in the *Ode on a Grecian Urn*, of which the final words are so often and so pitifully misunderstood as the utterance of a sort of æstheticism.*

> Thou shalt remain, in midst of other woe
> Than ours, a friend to man, to whom thou say'st,
> 'Beauty is truth, truth beauty,'—that is all
> Ye know on earth, and all ye need to know.

Those who have read the 'indolent' letter as it should be read will be in a position to understand something of the full significance of these lines, and to feel what they contain of deep wisdom purchased at the full price of deep suffering. The *Ode on a Grecian Urn* is not a dream of unattainable beauty, nor is the urn itself the sign of an impossible bliss beyond mortality. It has a precious message to mankind, not as a thing of beauty which gives an exquisite delight to the sense, but as a symbol and prophecy of a comprehension of human life to which mankind can attain.

Though the delight of pointing to the sheer loveliness of the *Odes* as poetry must be forgone, it is impossible to refrain from insisting on the consummate mastery with which Keats' poetic thought is uttered; for this sustained and miraculous felicity and daring of the concrete imagination is new in Keats' poetry. At this point he is become a master with none beside him save Shakespeare. That this should have been so is necessary to the truth of our argument. He has become a pure poet; he utters himself in pure poetry:

> What little town, by river or sea shore,
> Or mountain-built with peaceful citadel,
> Is emptied of its folk, this pious morn?
> And, little town, thy streets for evermore
> Will silent be; and not a soul to tell
> Why thou art desolate, can e'er return.

Shakespeare himself never made a more perfect or more dazzling flight of the imagination. We can no more analyze it, though it moves lucid and serene before the inward eye, than we can analyze the similar sweep of the imagination by which the nightingale is suddenly endowed with immortality:

> Thou wast not born for death, immortal bird;
> No hungry generations tread thee down. . . .

The nightingale is mortal as any son of man; if indeed those townsfolk left their little town, they could return to it. So speaks the rational mind; but the poetic mind is of another order: it can move sovereign through the dimensions, it can impose eternity on the temporal, it reveals miracles by performing them.

Keats' poetic mastery at this moment can be compared with nothing in English literature save Shakespeare's in his maturity. Keats was twenty-three. How was this miracle—for indeed it is nothing less—accomplished? That question can never be wholly answered; but it can be answered in part, and the partial answer is an answer to the more important part of the question. We can know what Keats meant, and how he achieved his knowledge, when he said:

> 'Beauty is truth, truth beauty,'—that is all
> Ye know on earth, *and all ye need to know.*

CHAPTER X

SOUL-MAKING

AT the beginning of the month of silence, out of which he emerged with mastery of his art and in possession of the knowledge which he expressed by its means, Keats had made in his ' indolent ' letter two discoveries at the same moment. He had discovered that the truth of human life was beautiful, and that its truth was its beauty; and he had discovered that poetry consisted in that instinctive and spontaneous attitude taken by his mind in making that discovery. These discoveries were made by flashes of sudden vision. The tormenting question which confronted him was how to make his knowledge of the truth he had glimpsed secure. He had for a moment become a 'Superior Being' and seen himself and his searchings as a part of the organic beauty of life. How was he, who had seen so much, who had by the very fact of his seeing been lifted out of that pattern of life of which he saw the beauty and the truth, to remain within it? Were not those gnawing thoughts of his own ineffectuality, his own unsatisfied hunger for the happiness of Love, of Fame and of Poetry, part of himself? How could he submit them to the vision? He had seen the beauty and the truth of life; but how could he declare it, when his soul was divided within him? Unless he could accept it in his own soul, for himself, and could believe that his own menacing destiny was beautiful and true, what he had seen was a lie, and he could not declare it.

There was the beauty, there was the truth: but something in him rebelled against it, and so long as he rebelled he betrayed the vision. He was a poet, and he had seen that poetry essentially consisted in a spontaneous attitude of his being. How, with all his knowledge, was he to remain spontaneous? Spontaneous, faced by a vision that all his most agonizing pains were endorsed by the universe? Spontaneous, when life was robbing him of all he held most dear? No, it was too much. Too much was asked of him; he could not pay that price for remaining a poet. And surely there is no man in the world who has the imagination to realize what Keats suffered but would say: The price *is* too great. He cannot be asked to accept *his* destiny. If the cup will not pass from him, then he must rebel; he must arraign for ever, in words that shall be immortal, the injustice and cruelty of whatever gods there be.

And what every man in the world must feel, if he has the power to feel anything at all, Keats must have felt a thousand times more deeply in that month of silence and fever. Yet he emerged from it with these words:

> How fever'd is that man who cannot look
> Upon his mortal days with temperate blood!

and with these words spoken by 'the friend to man':

> 'Beauty is truth, truth beauty,'—that is all
> Ye know on earth, and all ye need to know.

Somehow the victory was accomplished; he had accepted his destiny, he had put away the fever, he had not 'spoiled his salvation by a fierce miscreed.'

The sonnet *On Fame* which marks the victory, not by asserting it but by being it, was written in the long journal-letter to his brother on 30th April. It follows immediately after the most astonishing portion of this, the greatest of all Keats' letters. Probably the sonnet was composed in the morning following the night on which the letter was written; it came into his head as the truer, because purely poetic, utterance of a thought which he had been struggling to convey in other terms to his brother.

This portion of the letter has become famous; it has been quoted many times, but I have never seen any attempt to grapple with the thought which it contains. It is famous and quoted and remembered, I suppose, for the same reason that many of the greatest things in poetry are famous and quoted and remembered. They contain some haunting beauty that is mysteriously knit up with some vaguely apprehended truth. It is not so much that we remember them, as that they cling to our minds in our own despite. They are not merely beautiful, or they could be admired and let us go; they are not merely true, or they could be understood and put away. But with such things as these we cannot have done, nor they have done with us.

Let us try to follow this one, if only because it comes at the crucial moment of Keats' inward growth, to the last verge of implication, no matter where it leads. The letter opens quite gently and simply. Keats has been reading two books of history.

> I have been reading lately two very different books, Robertson's America and Voltaire's 'Siècle de Louis XIV.' It is like walking arm in arm between Pizarro and the great-little Monarch. In how lamentable a case do we see the great body of men in both instances; in the first when Men might seem to inherit quiet of Mind from unsophisticated senses; from uncontamination of civilization and especially from their being as it were estranged from the mutual helps of Society and its mutual injuries—and

thereby more immediately under the Protection of Providence—even there they had pains to bear as bad, or even worse than Bailiffs, Debts and Poverties of civilized life.

The whole appears to resolve itself into this: that Man is originally a poor forked creature subject to the same mischances as the beasts of the forest, destined to hardships and disquietude of some kind or another. If he improves by degrees his bodily accommodations and comforts—at each stage, at each ascent there are waiting for him a fresh set of annoyances—he is mortal and there is still a heaven with its Stars above his head.

The thought is clear: the pains of humanity keep pace with its progress in the mechanics of civilization. To each advance in outward civilization a new pain corresponds:

The most interesting question (Keats continues) that can come before us is, How far by the persevering efforts of a seldom-appearing Socrates Mankind may be made happy—I can imagine such happiness carried to an extreme—but what must it end in? Death—and who could in such a case bear with death? The whole troubles of life which are now frittered away in a series of years, would then be accumulated for the last days of a being who instead of hailing its approach would leave this world as Eve left Paradise.

Again the thought is clear. Human happiness to be perfect must include the abolition of death. If pain were to be blotted out of the world, the result would merely be that death would be a thousand times greater agony than it is. For now the pains of life are such that we are prepared for death and accustomed to the thought of death. But it is surely of himself alone that Keats is thinking when he speaks of 'hailing its approach.'

But in truth (he goes on) I do not at all believe in this sort of perfectibility—the nature of the world will not admit of it—the inhabitants of the world will correspond with itself. Let the fish Philosophise the ice away from the Rivers in winter time and they shall be at continual play in the tepid delight of summer. Look at the Poles and the Sands of Africa, whirlpools and volcanoes. Let men exterminate them and I will say that they may arrive at earthly Happiness. The point at which Man may arrive is the parallel state in inanimate nature and no further. For instance suppose a rose to have sensation, it blooms on a beautiful morning, it enjoys itself, but then comes a cold wind, a hot sun—it cannot escape it, it cannot destroy its annoyances—they are as native to the world as itself—no more can man be happy in spite, the worldly elements will prey upon his nature.

This is yet another example of the pure poetic thought of Keats, of his attainment of truth through the recognition of beauty. Keats' mind is once more elucidating a harmony in the world; he is discerning a pattern and divining that man also must obey the pattern and be of one nature with the world which he inhabits. If the condition of man were perfectible, he would become a discordant element in the harmony.

If we were to analyse thought of this peculiar kind from the point of view of the logician, we should have to say that it was based upon an assumption; and that the assumption was that reality is harmonious. It is true: this is the fundamental assumption that the pure poetic mind does make; this is the central axiom of all poetic thought. It is made for the most part unconsciously, and can be discovered only by analysis of such primary acts of poetic thought as the seizing of images and making of metaphors; in other and higher forms of poetic thought it is made with knowledge. This is what Keats meant when he said to Bailey in November 1817: 'I have never yet been able to perceive how anything can be known for truth by consecutive reasoning,' and when he reaffirmed this perception of the nature of his own mind at the beginning of 1819 by saying to George: 'I can never feel certain of any truth but from a clear perception of its beauty.' This is what one who is among the greatest of all French poets, Charles Baudelaire, meant when he said: 'La première condition nécessaire pour faire un art sain est la croyance à l'unité intégrale.' The process of poetic comprehension moves from the perception of harmony to the perception of harmony, and these successive harmonies are its truths.

That may sound singularly irrational, and indeed it is completely irrational. But we have to make the simple, though difficult, sideway leap with our minds, and see that rational thought is based, not one whit less than poetic thought, upon an assumption which is also for the most part unconscious. Rational thought *assumes* that reality is rational. Once we have seen that this is an assumption, we shall also see the futility of criticizing poetic thought because it is irrational. One might as well criticize rational thought for being unpoetic. What we have to understand and to accept is the fact that there are two orders or kinds of thinking, and that the only means of deciding which of them brings us nearer to reality is by the completeness of the ultimate satisfaction which they bring. There is absolutely no objective criterion by which one can be preferred to the other. They exist, each in its own right. It is for us to choose between them; and probably our choice will not be deliberate, but will be determined by some instinctive and unconscious inclination towards one or the other.*

Keats offers an almost pure case of poetic thought. Apprehension of truth was for him always apprehension of harmony. We have been watching his faculty at work in the contemplation of the human universe: he now advances further to the discovery of a more comprehensive harmony still.

> The common cognomen of this world among the misguided and superstitious is 'a vale of tears,' from which we are to be redeemed by a certain arbitrary interposition of God and taken to Heaven. What a little circumscribed straightened notion! Call the world if you please 'The vale of Soul-making'. Then you will find out the use of the world (I am speaking now in the highest terms for human nature admitting it to be immortal which I will here take for granted for the purpose of showing a thought which has struck me concerning it) I say '*Soul-making*'—Soul as distinguished from an Intelligence. There may be intelligences or sparks of the Divinity in millions—but they are not Souls until they acquire identities, till each one is personally iteslf. Intelligences are atoms of perception—they know and they see and they are pure, in short they are God.
>
> How then are Souls to be made? How then are these sparks which are God to have identity given them—so as ever to possess a bliss peculiar to each one's individual existence? How but by the medium of a world like this? This point I sincerely wish to consider because I think it a grander system of salvation than the christian religion—or rather it is a system of Spirit creation. This is effected by three grand materials acting the one upon the other for a series of years. These three materials are the *Intelligence*—the *human heart* (as distinguished from intelligence or Mind) and the *World*, or *Elemental space* suited for the proper action of *Mind and Heart* upon each other for the purpose of forming the *Soul* or *Intelligence destined to possess the sense of Identity*. I can scarcely express what I but dimly perceive—and yet I think I perceive it—that you may judge the more clearly I will put it in the most homely form possible.
>
> I will call the *world* a School instituted for the purpose of teaching little children to read. I will call the *human heart* the *horn Book* read in that School. And I will call the *Child able to read, the Soul* made from that *School* and its *horn book*. Do you not see how necessary a World of Pains and troubles is to school an Intelligence and make it a Soul? A Place where the heart must feel and suffer in a thousand diverse ways. Not merely is the Heart a Hornbook. It is the Mind's Bible, it is the Mind's experience, it is the test from which the Mind or Intelligence sucks its identity. As various as the Lives of Men are, so various become their Souls, and thus does God make individual beings, Souls, Identical Souls of the sparks of his own essence. . . .

In this remarkable passage Keats is discovering a harmony in the world within man which completes the harmony he had previously discovered in the world without him. There is, as ever, a deceptive simplicity about his statement. That it is not really simple, or rather that its simplicity is the simplicity of a directly apprehended mystery, will quickly be apparent to anyone who sincerely tries to grasp his thought. And that this is so is proven by his own words: 'I can scarcely express what I dimly perceive, and yet I think I perceive it.' Keats was making a supreme effort at comprehension; it stands to reason that what cost Keats so great an effort to comprehend and express will cost us no small one.

Let us return for a moment to Keats' 'indolent' letter. In it he had seen the world of men and women as forming a harmony with the animal world. Essentially all human beings are instinctive as animals, and if they are so seen, they have the grace and beauty of animals. When a man's mind works with the same instinctiveness, when instead of working in a vacuum of abstract thought it retains this spontaneity, when, in short, man's mind is in harmony with his instinctive being, then you have the essential condition of poetry.

But there remained an urgent problem, which Keats had left unsolved save by implication. How was this harmony of the mind with the instinctive being to be achieved? Keats was indeed achieving it as he wrote his 'indolent' letter, and he was aware of it. But how was he achieving it? Was it merely an accident? How was this spontaneity of the mind to be made a permanent possession, when his mind seemed for the most part to have an existence of its own which it spent in vexing his spirit and gnawing at his life with tormenting and impossible questions? For we must remember that the day on which he wrote his letter was a day of respite and peace. His words are perfectly clear. 'In this state of effeminacy the fibres of the brain are relaxed in common with the rest of the body, and to such a happy degree that pleasure has no show of enticement and pain no unbearable power. Neither Poetry, nor Ambition, nor Love have any alertness of countenance as they pass by me. . . .' That is to say, the mind had sunk back into harmony with the instinctive being, and the three most agonizing thoughts with which Keats' mind was torturing him had lost their power to pain. But such felicity was rare, and accidental. Keats says so. 'This is the only happiness, and is a rare instance of the advantage of the body overpowering the mind.'

It is clear that this condition was very far indeed from being a condition of laziness or effeminacy. Out of it directly sprang one of the two profoundest of all Keats' letters; and Keats himself was aware that the condition was truly creative. It is precisely this condition of subordination of the mind to the instinctive being, which, at the climax of his letter, he declares to be 'the very thing in which consists Poetry.' This is the condition in which the faculty of pure poetic perception can work, and it works in that letter with a sovereign power.*

But the condition was accidental and rare; it was an oasis in the desert of agonizing thought. How could it be made his own for ever? That and no other is the question Keats is answering in his letter on 'Soul-making.' It was the most urgent and vital question of all. Everything depended upon it, and above all else the question whether Keats could remain a poet. Poetry, for him, must come naturally as the leaves to a tree, or it had better not come at all; it was the natural product of a spontaneous attitude of the complete being. If he was to depend upon accident for the submission of rebellious mind to instinctive being, then it was better not to be a poet at all. Keats was above all things else, a man; and a man does not trust to accident to possess his own being.

One need not enlarge upon the implications of this problem, over which Keats was brooding during his month of silence. It is the deepest of all problems, and everything depends upon it, not only for Keats, but for mankind at large. The burden of consciousness, the burden of the mystery, is upon us all: Keats shows us the way to face it and conquer.

He has brushed aside, with sovereign ease, all shallow notions of the perfectibility of the conditions of human life. Were there to be realized conditions in which the human universe were freed from pain, death would become intolerable and, more than this, man would become a discordant element in the great harmony of which he is a part. No, Keats says, not the conditions of human life but the individual man is perfectible. Man has it in him to become a complete man, by possessing his own soul. This, and this alone, is the purpose of human life, and he tries to declare the way by which the purpose can be achieved.

He makes a threefold division of man's being: into Heart and Mind and Soul. The Soul exists only as a potentiality; it has to be created in the process of man's life. The original elements are only two: Mind and Heart. Mind is both 'an atom of intelligence' and, more strangely, 'a spark of the Divinity'; these atoms of intelligence —to use Keats' own simple and mysterious words—'know and see and are pure, in short they are God.'* Let us not pause over the stranger part of this definition for the moment, but remember only that it has been stated so. Mind shall be simply 'an atom of intelligence.' Heart is defined by Keats further on in this letter as 'the seat of the Human Passions.' We might call it Body; it is, in the widest sense, man's instinctive being. It is the instrument of all immediate knowledge, whether through sensation or intuition. In the language of modern psychology, Mind is 'consciousness' and Heart is 'unconsciousness.'

It is important to realize that both Mind and Heart 'know,' but with different kinds of knowledge, for which there is unfortunately no corresponding distinction in modern language.* Adapting the terms of modern psychology, let us call the knowledge of the Mind 'conscious knowledge,' and the knowledge of the Heart 'unconscious knowledge.' Then, according to Keats, the 'conscious knowledge' of the Mind works upon the 'unconscious knowledge' of the Heart. But in a peculiar and unexpected way. Not by judging and rejecting, but rather by assimilating. Above all, 'conscious knowledge' does not assume any attitude of superiority towards 'unconscious knowledge.' 'The Heart', Keats says emphatically, 'is the Mind's Bible'—the phrase is important, for Keats' mind thinks not with the logic of discourse, but with the finer instruments of analogy and metaphor, and such a phrase as this, which may easily be passed over as a mere phrase by those unfamiliar with the process of Keats' thinking, contains the equivalent of a vital definition. It means that the attitude of 'conscious knowledge' towards 'unconscious knowledge' must be one not of superiority, but of deference; not of judgement, but of reverence; not of condescension, but of loyalty. At the extreme its function is but one of interpretation, and it must be one of faithful interpretation.

It will be a temptation for those who are not prepared to struggle to grasp Keats' thought, which cost him a struggle to grasp, to diminish and degrade it into a commonplace. 'Mind works upon experience,' they will say. 'Of course: it has nothing else to work on.' But Keats is saying far more than this; he is saying Mind must be utterly loyal to immediate and unintellectual experience—to the passions, to the affections, to the intuitions. These are the Bible of the Mind, not its own constructions and vaticinations.

By this loyalty, by this submission of consciousness to unconsciousness is slowly created—the Soul. Keats describes this achievement of Soul as 'the possession of a sense of identity' by the Mind or consciousness. The Mind comes to be 'personally itself,' and to possess 'a bliss peculiar to its individual existence.' This condition, in which the Soul, or true Self, has now come into existence, is quite different from 'conscious knowledge'; it involves a change in the very nature of 'conscious knowledge.' 'Conscious knowledge' is somehow merged together with 'unconscious knowledge,' to form this deeper knowledge of an indefeasible self-existence. This self-existence is the soul, and that which knows it is the soul. The soul knows itself, and a true and inviolable personality is achieved. And now we have reached yet a third kind of knowledge, born of the union of the two previous kinds of knowledge. This knowledge may be called 'soul-knowledge.'

This condition of 'soul-knowledge,' which appears, when approached in this way, to be primarily a knowledge that the soul *is*, a knowledge of the individual's true self-existence, has strange consequences; for it results immediately in a knowledge of the harmony and necessity of that universe, whose workings upon the Heart are the primary source of 'soul-knowledge.' 'Do you not see,' cries Keats, 'how necessary a world of Pains and Troubles is to school an Intelligence and make it a Soul?' The answer to that from anyone who trusts his intellect alone, and for whom his Heart is not the Bible of his Mind, will assuredly be: 'No, I do *not* see.' And there is an end. No argument is possible. But Keats did see.

In saying that the achievement of this condition of soul-knowledge results immediately in a knowledge of the harmony and necessity of the universe, I have assumed that Keats himself had at that moment himself reached the condition of 'soul-knowledge.' That may appear an unwarrantable assumption. But it is not so; it is, and it evidently must be, inherent in the nature of such knowledge as Keats here is trying to describe, that it should be a record of personal experience. Leaving aside what we have come to know of Keats' character—his own complete loyalty to experience, his instinctive refusal of all abstract speculation, his refusal to speak save from the complete being—it is obvious that knowledge of this kind *cannot* be merely speculative. Keats is trying to put into words, and thereby to make wholly conscious to himself, a process which he has actually lived through. We are reading his own account of the manner in which he achieved his soul; and more than that, we are reading an account of it written at the very moment when the process was being finally completed. For this consciousness of its own nature after which Keats is now struggling is the perfection of soul-knowledge itself. At the moment when Keats finally achieves his soul he sees immediately the necessity and harmony of the universe of which he is a part, and which, acting first upon his heart and through his heart upon his mind, has finally created the soul which knows the universe as necessary and harmonious.

Probably there are two orders of minds: one for whom such things as these are mysterious and unintelligible, and another for whom they are mysterious and simple. And it may be that a gulf is for ever fixed between them. This is the re-living in the nature of a pure poet of that strange happening which is known to mystical experience as the simultaneous knowledge of the soul and the knowledge of God. Soul-knowledge is God-knowledge, for the reality in the phrase 'to know God' is nothing other than the knowledge of the necessity and harmony of the universe which Keats declared when he cried: 'Do you not see how necessary a world of Pains and Troubles is to school an Intelligence and make it a Soul?' No man can *explain* that mystery. It came to pass in Keats, and Keats tried to communicate to his brother the process by which it came to pass.

'Soul-knowledge is God-knowledge.' I have not dragged in the word or the thought; I know only too well that it is an offence against decorum in modern criticism, and I would never have ventured it upon my own authority. I am not expounding my own beliefs, but Keats'; and if I deviate by a hair's breadth from his own meaning, then so far as my purpose is concerned, I have failed. But Keats himself uses the word 'God' with no uncertain voice in this letter. Not only does he say that 'the atoms of intelligence,' the germs of consciousness, 'know and see and are pure, in short they are God,' but he concludes his account of the system of soul-creation with the emphatic words: 'Thus does God make individual beings, Souls, Identical Souls, of the sparks of His own essence.' And I should not be adding a fraction of a thought of my own to Keats' thought if I were to describe the process of soul-creation which he has apprehended, as a knowledge of life as a necessary means by which the atom of God comes to self-consciousness of its own divine nature. But, indeed, Keats may speak for himself:

> I am convinced (he goes on) that many difficulties under which Christians labour would vanish before this system—there is one which even now strikes me—the salvation of Children. In them the spark or intelligence returns to God without any identity—it having no time to learn of and be altered by the heart—or seat of the human Passions. It is pretty generally suspected that the Christian scheme [he means, of theology] has been copied from the ancient Persian and Greek philosophers. Why may they not have made this simple thing [it will be noticed that though 'he could scarcely express what he dimly perceived,' the thing is, nevertheless, 'simple'] even more simple for common apprehension by introducing Mediators and Personages in the same manner as in the heathen mythology abstractions are personified? Seriously I think it probable that this system of Soul-making may have been the parent of all the more palpable and personal schemes of Redemption among the Zoroastrians, the Christians and the Hindoos. For as one part of the human species must have their carved Jupiter; so another part must have the palpable and named Mediator and Saviour, their Christ, their Oromanes and their Vishnu.

Once more, Keats means what he says: that he seriously thinks that the system of soul-making he has apprehended is the fundamental and essential religious truth, of which all religions are partial and simplified statements. That I also believe this to be true is of no account save in so far that it may have made me more than others liable to the conviction that Keats means what he says, and that what he is saying is something of importance to all men. And it will be clear from what Keats now says that those would do violence to his thought who should endeavour to identify the God of whom he speaks with the God of a particular sect. Keats' God is not the God of the Christian, if that God is different from the God of the Hindoo, or the Persian, or the Greek. His God is the God whom exclusive religions can, by reason of their partiality, apprehend only in part. He is, indeed, God.

And, for that very reason, it is only here in his letters that Keats makes deliberate and considered use of the name, for the purpose of revealing the nature of his thought, or his knowledge, to his brother. What his God really is cannot be expressed directly in speech; but it can be quite simply apprehended from the terms of this letter and the 'indolent' letter of 19th March. God is that with which the human soul comes into contact and communion at the moment it knows itself for a soul; God *is* that harmony of the universe which flowers into a consciousness of its own nature through the human being who can make his Heart his Mind's Bible, and thereby achieve his soul. And because God was this for Keats at the moment that he knew Him through the knowledge of his own soul, when he came in his *Odes* to declare Him, he did not make use of the dangerous word; he declared what he knew as he knew it, he proclaimed the truth as he apprehended it and not otherwise:

> 'Beauty is truth, truth beauty,'—that is all
> Ye know on earth, and all ye need to know.

In a sense the truth which Keats expressed in those words, and in the letter in which he tried to show the means by which man could attain to the knowledge of the truth, is indeed simple, as Keats implied in his poem and asserted in his letter, because true mysteries are simple, just as true simplicities are mysterious; but they are mysteries. What is a simple act of apprehension for soul-knowledge is a complicated and impossible one for mind-knowledge. Theology can only be truly interpreted by those who have no need of it; and so with all attempts, inevitable though they are, to translate soul-knowledge into terms of mind-knowledge. In this realm of soul-knowledge, those more mysterious and terrible words do literally apply: 'To him that hath shall be given, and from him that hath not it shall be taken away, even that which he hath.' In the realm of soul-knowledge the tiniest gleam, loyally followed, flames slowly into full comprehension; but the most arduous and subtle efforts of mind-knowledge to enter that realm end only in confusion and bitterness. This tiny gleam is given to everyone who is thrilled and haunted by some strange validity in a line of pure poetry, of which he can render to himself no rational account: if he will stick faithfully to what he has felt, take it for a proven and incontrovertible fact, no matter what his mind may tell him, then by slow degrees fact will join itself to fact until there is formed within him a body of certitude concerning the nature of poetry and the nature of the reality to which it alone can give complete and palpable expression. This process is, in miniature at least, what Keats meant when he said that the Heart must be the Mind's Bible.

In this matter, we have to make a choice: on the one side, the rationalists, on the other Keats and Shakespeare, and the whole fact of religion and great art. For it is not really possible to compromise, as many would like to do, by regarding this, the strangest and most astonishing of all Keats' letters—as a mere speculation, or as the groping of 'an untrained mind' into the mysteries of metaphysics. That attitude is taken by those critics who deign to pay any real attention to the letter at all. But the Keats who wrote that letter was not an apprentice to knowledge; he was one of the most marvellous human beings of whom the world holds record. He was twenty-three; and at the moment he wrote this letter he was writing day after day the *Odes*, to Psyche, to the Nightingale, on a Grecian Urn, on Melancholy—poems comparable to nothing in English literature save the work of Shakespeare's maturity. We cannot have it both ways: we must choose. Either we choose a Keats who is homogeneous, whose poetry and thought and knowledge are one and homogeneous; or we choose a Keats who thought childish thoughts with 'an untrained mind' and by some miracle wrote poems which surpass for profundity of experience and splendour of statement anything that 'a trained mind' has ever conceived. If we can believe in this monster we may; but it is worth while to pause a moment to consider whether we are not, for the sake of allegiance to a rigidly rational prejudice concerning reality, being forced to accept a naked impossibility.

What I am now contending for is not to prove that what Keats thought is true—that cannot be *proved*, and what Keats thought or wrote must be left to make its own impression on men's minds—but that Keats was indeed homogeneous and at one within himself, that he conquered this oneness, that in his letter on 'Soul-making' he gave the most faithful account he could of the process by which he conquered it. This was the process by which Keats himself believed he attained the condition of soul in which he wrote the first poetry which was undubitably and unmistakably Keats' and Keats' alone; by which he became, in fact, a great English poet, second only to Shakespeare. It may be said that Keats was mistaken about himself. If Keats was mistaken in this, he was mistaken in everything. This letter is but the inevitable and harmonious outcome of all his thinking: it is utterly consistent with all that he thought and was. If we choose to believe that Keats was mistaken in everything, and that out of this abysm of error he sent forth the great *Odes*,—then we will believe anything.

But, indeed, this letter, and all Keats' letters in their profoundest parts, are of such a kind that if we understand them at all, we know that they are true, just as we know that his highest poetry is true. In a sense the letter is difficult to understand, and it may be that in order to understand it fully we have to bring to it some fragment of a like experience. But what has impressed me is the evident reluctance of the many critics and biographers of Keats to take the hint given by his confession ' I can scarcely express what I dimly perceive ' and to make a serious effort to grasp the thought. The reason of this reluctance, I have concluded, is that it is difficult for us really to admit that a pure poet knows the truth differently and knows more of it than ourselves. Unconsciously we accept the conception of the poet as a monster with unrelated faculties—a child in thought, a magician in words. We do not take poetry or the poet seriously. I believe this is one form of a terrible mistake, for which our so-called civilization has paid heavily and will, if this temper is not changed, pay more heavily still. For poetry in its highest and purest forms is one of the few roads that remain open to the eternal reality that is less directly and less fully expressed in religion. We have lost contact with that reality; and we have to regain it. We have to learn to think on matters which do most vitally concern us in other and truer and older ways; we have to put out of our temple those gods by which we have all unconsciously replaced the older and truer gods. Very likely we cannot return to those truer and older gods; we have grown out of them, we have forgotten what they meant, and there is no taking up the thread of history once it has been broken. But we must dethrone the false gods we worship; we must put out of our hearts that blind faith—a blinder faith than any of those at which our wisdoms sneer—in the ideas of Civilization and Progress as powers which work for good apart from ourselves. We have to remember the war, which wrote across the face of the heavens in letters of flame, that there is no progress save of the individual soul.

One way, and perhaps the best and surest way towards the supersession of these sham truths by a real one, is to take great poetry seriously. It is not an easy way; by no means as easy as it sounds. In order to advance along it we have sooner or later to take the *salto mortale*, the perilous leap. We have to take seriously knowledge that is not, and by its own nature cannot be, expressed in propositions; we have to believe that such knowledge exists and that men have possessed it in the past, and that they can possess it to-day. If we can make the leap, all will in the last resort be well; if we cannot, then the greatest poet on earth will remain for us ' the idle singer of an empty day.'

At this point in Keats' history, if not long before, the perilous leap must be made. For henceforward, if not long before, Keats must be regarded as a man made of a mind and a body, and a soul which included them both; he must be regarded as thus made, because he knew himself as thus made. His soul was the truest and most real of these three, because he knew it was the truest and most real: only those have a soul who know they have a soul. The soul of Keats had passed beyond agony and despair into the knowledge of itself as part of the Beauty and the Truth which is the Divine. In his letter on 'The Vale of Soul-making,' he tells of the process of this passing; by this process he had reached his knowledge that 'Ripeness is all.'

And there, it might be thought, the story ends. But it is not so. This achievement of his soul, and its necessary outcome in a serene acceptance is the inward and spiritual grace of which Keats' magnificent poetical achievement at this moment is the outward and visible sign. Keats had become a pure poet, because he had achieved his soul completely; he was now second only to Shakespeare, and far in advance of the Shakespeare of twenty-three. But mind and body still existed; they were real: Keats had not passed beyond them, for no complete man ever can. But Keats had touched a final knowledge: whether he could maintain it, how he could maintain it, was the question. It was the same question with Shakespeare.

Therefore in order to understand Keats henceforward, we must be able to contemplate him under the three aspects of mind and body and soul: to make a true contact with what he was, we have permanently to enlarge our conception of man's nature. To me, I confess, this strange proposition appears the veriest common sense. A pure poet is not an ordinary man; nor can he be, as criticism too often assumes, an ordinary man with an extraordinary faculty tacked on to him. Such portentous births, though they are apparently accepted by minds which would not accept similar phenomena in other realms, are really more incredible than the Anthropophagi. An unrelated faculty is inconceivable. That we are unable to perceive the relation should be a reason not for tacitly denying that the relation exists, but for mistrusting our own knowledge. We are reluctant to do that. For some reason, the Western mind has become very complacent in its knowledge. Possibly we have good right to be complacent in the knowledge of the external world. But there is not the faintest reason to suppose that we know more about the internal world of the human soul than did our misty forefathers thousands of years ago. I believe that we do not know so much; that we know in truth far less; that in this realm at least—and it is an important one—our ignorance is abysmal and our pretensions childish. By our presumption we shut ourselves off from knowledge. We do not believe, we cannot believe, that poetry has really something to tell us of importance to our lives. We laugh at the old theory of direct inspiration without pausing to think whether it meant anything, and whether the belief that the poet (the *vates sacer*) brought men a message from God has not a profound symbolic significance which is not adequately replaced by the conception of him as 'abnormal,' or at best as the incalculable provider of some exotic thrill called an 'æsthetic emotion.' Our modern rationalism, which is so deep in our bones that we are scarcely conscious of it, will reduce everything to its own terms. There is no God, it says, therefore the poet cannot be inspired by him; there is no supra-rational truth, therefore the poet cannot declare it.

I hold, and hold fast, to a different philosophy. I have been gradually forced into it, not least through an instinctive and ineradicable conviction that pure poetry is not irrelevant to life, but on the contrary more exactly relevant to it than any other creation of the human spirit. I believe, for I have found it so by experience, that pure poetry contains a revelation, and I would far rather stand with the ancients in their belief that the poet is directly inspired by God than with the moderns in theirs that the poet is a *lusus naturae* and poetry an amusing accident. What the ancients said—though I might not care, or dare, to use their language—corresponds with my experience; their explanation is at least adequate to the revelation which pure poetry brings: what the moderns say is almost an insult to my knowledge. And the fundamental cause of this inadequacy of the modern theory to the actual reality of experience lies in our ignorance of the nature of the human soul. This is the price we have paid for the 'enlightenment' of the Renaissance. For it is all very well to turn God out of the universe rather than to suffer a parody of the divine reality to remain: but if you turn out God, without taking upon yourself the full responsibility for what you have done, you run the risk of turning out also that secular human faculty which finds its exercise and purpose in the apprehension of the divine reality. Remove God from the universe, and you may very well remove a faculty from the human soul.

Such surgery is impossible, you say? I am afraid it is not. Faculties of the human soul can be atrophied as surely as limbs of the human body, when they have no opportunity of exercise. And the worship of God, the true reverential and mystical worship of God, was the most universal exercise ever established for a great faculty of the human soul. Not only was participation in a mystery as a contact with the divine reality one of the highest human approximations to an ultimate truth; it was also an enduring witness, an incessant declaration of the nature of the human soul itself. For that act of worship was not performed by the mind, neither was it performed by the body, yet it was performed by both of these in their most real function as co-existent parts of a third being, which was the human soul in its individual completeness. The symbolic act of all true religious worship includes at the same moment an act of the mind and an act of the body; the mind apprehends, the body partakes of, the real existence of God. But these are only the outward moments of the act of real communion. The inward act is a knowledge of God by the soul: a knowledge that is independent both of the knowledge of the mind and the knowledge of the body,—a direct and ineffable contact of soul with Soul, which can be outwardly *expressed* only by these two acts of the soul's two members.

This act of worship is not an easy act; it calls for a real achievement in the life of the individual who makes it. And the tendency is for it to become abstract, or perfunctory, or emotional. For this knowledge of God by the soul is essentially a concrete knowledge, of the necessity and harmony of all that is. Knowledge of God is acceptance of life. But this meaning becomes overlaid and hidden, in the pullulation of theology and the multiplication of ceremonies. The accidental and outward parts of religion suffocate its inward life. The fundamental truth that the knowledge of God is a consummation of the progress of the individual soul, that 'the kingdom of Heaven is within us,' is always forgotten, and the Church becomes a temporality. Therefore true men rebel against it. Sometimes they can rebel, like Francis of Assisi, and remain within the Church and revolutionize it for a moment into reality; or like Christ himself they can rebel and found a new Church; and sometimes, as at the Renaissance, they rebel against the whole conception of a Church, as something which must inevitably deny the freedom of the individual to fulfil his own destiny. For we must remember that in the long history of human civilization which we know, a Church, in our sense of the word, is a comparatively modern invention; it is a temporary expedient, which may well become permanently inexpedient. But the truth which is expressed in religion remains. The rebels rediscover it, if they are true men; and they rediscover it by a path which the Church against which they rebel has long since left, the path of loyalty to their complete humanity; and they rediscover the reality which the Church has lost.

That reality is twofold: it is a knowledge of the unity and harmony of the universe which can be reached only through the individual's knowledge of unity and harmony in himself. This twofold knowledge is achieved by the pure poet, and in him it never becomes abstract and schematic: he does not assert a harmony, he reveals it, and he gains the power to reveal this through the completeness of his achieved humanity. In the pure poet, who makes his mind the faithful instrument of his heart, who neither allows mind to tyrannize over heart, or heart to tyrannize over mind, completeness of humanity and true personality are achieved. We have an instinctive sense that this is so; quite instinctively we feel that there was in both Shakespeare and Keats a greater richness of the poetic gift, and a greater completeness of common manhood, than in any other of our English poets save Chaucer. And this appears a strange paradox to our intellectual minds, which have been nurtured on the false assumption that pure poetry is a thing abnormal and inhuman. But the sense of paradox is due to the fact that we have forgotten the nature of the human soul, and we have forgotten that chiefly because religion ceased to be a reality after the Rennaissance. There would have been no harm done, but on the contrary a great good, if men had lived up to the responsibility of their freedom, and had not run away from it by enthroning deities more trivial by far than those they had overthrown. If men had fought out the battle for themselves, they would have understood the poet, who fought out the battle on their behalf; they would have understood that the poetic gift in a Shakespeare or a Keats is more complete because they are completer men; because they did, in a very precise sense, possess their souls; because they more completely achieved this fusion of mind and body into the immanent reality of the soul, having a life and knowledge of its own.

Argument of this kind, because it is unfamiliar, will be said to be obscure and transcendental. It will be objected that this is a mystical theory. It may be so; but the names we give to such things are not very important. It is the realities that matter. This obscure or transcendental or mystical theory is what Keats believed, and he did not reach it by any obscure or transcendental or mystical road. He followed his destiny as a man and a poet; he knew that poetry must be the spontaneous utterance of the complete self, and he strove against incredible suffering to achieve that necessary wholeness in himself. He won the victory and he tried to tell his brother how he did it. If that account is obscure or transcendental or mystical, it is because the greatest victories won in human life are themselves obscure or transcendental or mystical. I do not believe they are; they are at once simple and mysterious—simple to know, mysterious to understand. And Keats' letter on 'Soul-making' is, in this, like the process it records.

Keats, by this process which I have tried to expound, achieved in April 1819 his own complete individuality, and the knowledge which inevitably accompanies that achievement. 'The mighty abstract idea of Beauty in all things' had become concrete and his own. Could he maintain his victory?

CHAPTER XI

THE FINAL STRUGGLE

BETWEEN mid-March and mid-April Keats had won a great victory; between mid-April and the end of May he wrote the *Odes*. But life took no account of that. He was in love, he was ill, he was all but penniless; by the middle of June, he heard that a suit in Chancery had been begun against his small estate and for the time being (which might in those days of Jarndyce *v.* Jarndyce be twenty years) his money was non-existent. But before that news reached him, he must have learned, in his efforts to raise the wind for Haydon, that it was likely. Long before the end of May he knew that he had to make his living, and to begin to make it without delay.

There is no knowing what were the relations between Keats and Fanny Brawne during the late spring months of this year 1819. At some time in 'the month of silence,' the Brawnes had moved into Dilke's house next door; Keats and his beloved were under the same roof. Whether Fanny was kind to him, no one can say: certainly she was not kind enough to make Keats believe even for a moment that his chance of an earthly fruition of his love was anything but hazardous. Nor is it pertinent to ask whether he was happy in her neighbourhood during that month of May: for the *Odes* alone reveal him as beyond happiness. He was pressing out a quintessence of beauty from the contemplation of his thwarted destiny.

The great creative moment over, he turned to face the urgencies of life. He must put money in his purse without delay. His former plan of qualifying for a physician at Edinburgh, which would cost money instead of making it, inevitably went by the board. The next thing that occurred to him was to ship as surgeon on an East Indiaman. He had almost decided upon this on 26th May. Five days later he is undecided again. He thinks of trying to live cheaply in the English country and writing more poetry. So he sends a letter to a Teignmouth friend, Miss Jeffrey, to ask her if she knows of a cheap lodging in the neighbourhood:

> I have the choice as it were of two Poisons (yet I ought not to call this a Poison) the one is voyaging to and from India for a few years; the other is leading a fevrous life alone with Poetry—This latter will suit me best; for I cannot resolve to give up my studies.

What had made the second poison possible was the offer of his friend, Charles Brown, to lend Keats the modest sum he needed to live on while he wrote another book of poetry and collaborated with

Brown in writing a play for Kean, of which Brown would provide the scenario.

Charles Brown was a figure scarcely less important than Fanny Brawne herself during these months of Keats' life. He has been obscured in clouds of glory by benevolent biographers. The real Charles Brown was different from this legendary figure, and it was the real Charles Brown who had a crucial influence upon Keats.

Charles Brown was a shrewd and canny Scot, an honest man and a good fellow. He was about ten years older than Keats, and lived rather modestly, after a failure in commerce, on a small income left him by a brother. He liked Keats and Keats liked him; and on Tom's death he had invited Keats to share his little house. He genuinely admired Keats' talent, and wished somehow to be identified with him. He was something of an amateur man of letters, and had done what was easier for the amateur to do in those days than these, namely, written a serio-comic opera which was actually produced at Drury Lane. Out of this he made some £300. Now his acquaintance with a real poet had fired him with the idea of collaborating with Keats in a successful play. He would lend Keats the money to live while it was written; and Keats would repay him out of his half-share of the profits.

It was a straightforward business arrangement; generous it would appear only to those who disregard the fact that Brown was a man of literary ambitions. Brown was a scrupulously honest man, but no more. When Keats died he presented George with a bill for all he had lent Keats, which would have been reasonable enough had he not kept the play for himself. Moreover, he charged George with interest in addition. The total amount was a little over £70. That is not the action of a generous man, and Brown was not a generous man: much less was he, as he has been represented, a sort of Maecenas to Keats.

As in money-affairs, so in affairs more subtle, Brown was a realist. There was ' no humbug about him,' as the phrase goes; and Keats, who was a realist of another kind, liked him for it. But the fundamental contrast between the two men emerges plainly in the contrast between Keats' action in moving heaven and earth, when he was ill, to raise money for Haydon, and Brown's in presenting George with a bill for all he had lent Keats, plus interest, and keeping the play for himself. Keats was generous, too generous; Brown was not.

But in no point were the characters of the two men more utterly opposed than in their attitude to women. In this matter Brown's realism was carried to an extreme. Keats wrote some humorous verses upon him in April 1819 in which his knowledge of this side of Brown's character is expressed with an amused and amusing tolerance. The description goes, of course, by contraries:

Ne cared he for wine, or half and half;
Ne cared he for fish or flesh or fowl,
And sauces held he worthless as the chaff;
He 'sdeign'd the swine head at the wassail bowl,
Ne with lewd ribbalds sat he cheek by jowl,
Ne with sly Lemans in the scorner's chair;
But after water brooks this pilgrim's soul
Panted, and all his food was woodland air,
Though he would ofttimes feast on gilliflowers rare—

The slang of cities in no wise he knew;
Tipping the wink to him was heathen greek;
He sipp'd no olden Tom or ruin blue,
Or nantz or cherry brandy drank full meek
By many a damsel hoarse and rouge of cheek;
Nor did he know each aged watchman's beat;
Nor in obscured purlieus would he seek
For curled Jewesses with ankles neat
Who, as they walk abroad, make tinkling with their feet.

That admirable piece of humorous poetry (for poetry it is rather than verse) was written, it is worth noting, as a riposte to some stanzas Brown was writing against Fanny Brawne and Keats.

Keats knew the name of one at least of the 'curled Jewesses'—she was called Jenny Jacobs. But what Keats apparently did not know was an interesting and characteristic episode in Brown's life in this very year 1819, which has since been revealed in a memoir of Brown by his son. In this year Brown made a journey to Ireland in order to marry a peasant girl called Abigail Donohue, who seems to have been at one time a servant in Brown's house. The marriage, being performed by a Catholic priest, was illegal; it was also kept secret by Brown. In fact, Brown seems to have gone through the ceremony simply for the sake of getting a son, who was duly born in 1820. So soon as the child was old enough to be taken from his mother, in 1822, Brown took him, and went off to Italy, to avoid the danger of a suit claiming custody of the child. The whole affair was a perfectly cold-blooded exercise in eugenics; and as such was, no doubt, concealed from Keats.

Brown's attitude to Keats' passion for Fanny Brawne is obvious: he could not understand its nature at all, and what little he did understand of it seemed to him thoroughly deplorable. The mere idea that a man should suffer from love of a woman seemed to him fantastic. 'Put the woman out of your head, my dear Keats,' would have been about the kindest consolation of which Brown was capable. Inevitably, Keats kept his devouring love to himself.

Brown was utterly opposed to what he knew of Keats' love, on principle: and he can have known very little about it, beyond the obvious and tangible facts. Of its whole nature he was ignorant. Were it not for this ignorance it would be impossible to forgive him for the torture he inflicted upon Keats in the following winter, by flirting with Fanny Brawne in Keats' presence when Keats was ill. Keats confessed his suffering in an agonized letter to Fanny Brawne (5th July 1820):

> I cannot forget what has pass'd. What? nothing with a man of the world, but to me dreadful. I will get rid of this as much as possible. When you were in the habit of flirting with Brown you would have left off, could your own heart have felt one half of one pang mine did. Brown is a good sort of Man—he did not know he was doing me to death by inches. I feel the effect of every one of those hours in my side now; and for that cause, though he has done me many services, though I know his love and friendship for me, though at this moment I should be without pence were it not for his assistance, I will never see or speak to him until we are both old men, if we are to be. I *will* resent my heart having been made a football.

That is generally dismissed as one of the outpourings of 'sick passion.' Sick passion! One can only say to the comfortable persons who use the phrase concerning Keats what Keats himself said to Fanny: 'You do not feel as I do—you do not know what it is to love.' But there, in that heart-rending letter, is the difference between Brown and Keats: 'Nothing with a man of the world, but dreadful to me.'

Brown was undoubtedly 'a good sort of person,' but he was crudity and coarseness itself compared with Keats. That Keats forgave him was due not to Brown's merit, but to Keats' magnanimity. After all, Brown did not know what he was doing. But it is no wonder that Keats should have kept his love to himself, and come to make Brown's absence a condition of his visits to Fanny or hers to him.

With this Brown Keats had agreed to retire in the country to collaborate in a play for Kean, on a business arrangement. During their time together Brown tried his utmost (for he was certainly not as reticent in the matter as Keats was) to influence his friend against Fanny Brawne. Keats was to put her out of his mind: she was not worth a thought. And Keats, from very different motives, longed to be able to put her out of his mind. If only he could forget her all might yet be well. If only he could forget her for the time he might be able to write poems that the world would not willingly let die. Yet where, in this, was the acceptance he had learned? His heart told him that he longed for her. Could he uproot that knowledge from his heart? And if he could, was *that* the victory he had won?

It is impossible to analyse fully the mood in which Keats left London 'to lead a fevrous life alone with poetry,' for he was involved in an impossibility. He was going to try his fortune in poetry once more, chiefly for the sake of making some money; and he wanted money chiefly for the chance it would give of making him able to marry Fanny. Yet in order to write the poetry he would have to keep the thought of Fanny out of his mind. He who believed that poetry must come as naturally as the leaves to a tree, had to force himself into an utterly unnatural posture to write it. He who knew that his heart must be the Bible of his Mind, had to face a situation in which his heart could not be the Bible of his Mind.

It was primarily for money that Keats left Hampstead for the country in mid-June and agreed to clothe with rhetoric the preposterous skeleton of Brown's *Otho the Great*. In his first letter to Fanny Brawne from the Isle of Wight, he said: 'As I told you a day or two before I left Hampstead, I will never return to London if my Fate does not turn up Pam or at least a Court-card.' At that moment it was in his mind to retire permanently into the country, if his new effort failed and all thought of marrying Fanny had consequently to be abandoned. He wrote to his sister (9th June) that his Teignmouth friend, Miss Jeffrey, had told him of a pleasant place in Devonshire 'which I think I shall eventually retire to', and a week later (16th June) he wrote to her:

> I am going to try the Press once more, and to that end shall retire to live cheaply in the country and compose myself and verses as well as I can. . . . I was preparing to enquire for a situation with an apothecary, but Mr. Brown persuades me to try the press once more; so I will with all my industry and ability.'

On the next day he wrote to Haydon, explaining that he was penniless. 'My purpose is now to make one more attempt in the Press—if that fail, "ye hear no more of me" as Chaucer says. Brown has lent me some money for the present. Do borrow or beg somehow what you can for me.'

Nothing could be more eloquent of Keats' condition than his having written that letter to Haydon, which must have cost an effort to his pride. Keats was penniless, he was also ill. Twice in mid-June he wrote to his sister that he could not come to see her at Walthamstow because he was not well enough to walk nor rich enough to pay the coach-fare, which can only have been a matter of a shilling or two.

Money at this moment meant everything to Keats. The possibility of his love depended on it. The practical causes for despair were in this month of June greater than ever. But it was scarcely despair which he uttered (9th June) to Miss Jeffrey, who had advised him against the Indiaman:

Your advice about the Indiaman is a very wise advice, because it just suits me, though you are a little in the wrong concerning its destroying the energies of Mind: on the contrary, it would be the finest thing in the world to strengthen them—To be thrown among people who care not for you, with whom you have no sympathies, forces the Mind upon its own resources and leaves it free to make its speculations of the differences of human character and to class them with the calmness of a Botanist. An Indiaman is a little world. One of the great reasons that the English have produced the finest writers in the world is, that the English world has ill-treated them during their lives and foster'd them after their deaths. They have in general been trampled aside into the bye-paths of life and seen the festerings of Society. They have not been treated like the Raphaels of Italy. And where is the Englishman and Poet who has given a magnificent Entertainment at the christening of one of his Hero's Horses as Boyardo did? He had a Castle in the Appenine. He was a noble Poet of Romance; not a miserable and mighty Poet of the human Heart. The middle age of Shakspeare was all clouded over; his days were not more happy than Hamlet's who is perhaps more like Shakespeare himself in his common everyday Life than any other of his Characters. . . .

For all this I will not go on board an Indiaman, nor for example's sake run my head into dark alleys: I dare say my discipline is to come, and plenty of it too. I have been very idle lately, very averse to writing; both from the overpowering idea of our dead poets and from abatement of my love of Fame. I hope I am a little more of a Philosopher than I was, consequently a little less of a versifying Pet-lamb.

We have come to know what Keats meant by his being a little more of a philosopher, and a little less of a versifying pet-lamb; and how his love of fame had abated. For his overpowering idea of our dead poets the letter itself is witness, in which he coins for Shakespeare the magnificent title: 'A miserable and mighty Poet of the human Heart.' From his previous letter to Miss Jeffrey (31st May) we may glean a little more knowledge of his inward mood:

Yes, I would rather conquer my indolence and strain my nerves at some grand Poem—than be in a dunderheaded Indiaman. . . . I have been always till now almost as careless of the world as a fly—my troubles were all of the Imagination—My Brother George always stood between me and my dealings with the world. Now I find I must buffet it—I must take my stand on some vantage ground and begin to fight—I must choose between despair and Energy—I choose the latter—though the world has taken on a quakerish look with me, which I once thought was impossible—

'Nothing can bring back the hour
Of splendour in the grass and glory in the flower.'

I once thought this a Melancholist's dream.

It is plain that Keats does not really want to write. His deepest inclination is that which he expressed to Haydon in his letter of 8th March—'never to write for the sake of writing or making a poem, but from running over with any little knowledge or experience which many years of reflection may perhaps give me: otherwise I will be dumb. . . . With respect to my livelihood, I will not write for it.' Such writing, unforced and overflowing, had been the writing of the *Odes*. But Keats could not keep his resolution. Fate had decided against it. He must strain his nerves and write poetry for a living. And the posture was forced and unnatural to him: how unnatural appears from a sentence in a letter he wrote a month later from the country to his friend Reynolds (12th July). 'The first time I sat down to write I could scarcely believe in the necessity for so doing. It struck me as a great oddity.'

This working against the grain, this necessary but conscious betrayal of his own deepest knowledge concerning his own genius, underlies the whole of the creative period which began early in July, when Keats retired to the Isle of Wight. The next two months were amazingly productive: in them Keats wrote the whole of *Otho the Great*, the whole of *Lamia*, and the second *Hyperion*. The mere amount of poetic writing was prodigious. But this immense productivity was all to some degree unnatural. It had not, and Keats knew from the beginning it had not, that essential spontaneity which was the true perfection of poetry for him. *Otho the Great* was, of course, mere hack-work: Keats wrote act after act from Brown's scenario without knowing what was to come. Against this wholly unnatural method of 'making a livelihood' Keats naturally reacted. He had, as it were for his own salvation's sake, to plunge into original work as a relief. Inevitably the relief itself was feverous.

During these two months we can watch Keats becoming more and more fevered in the act of writing. He had been forced at the beginning into an unnatural attitude, and all his attempts to free himself ended only by exacerbating his position. Beneath his agonized contortions—for they reach an extremity which can be only thus described—the reality was that Fanny Brawne was denied him. It was to achieve her that he had put the dunderheaded Indiaman out of his mind and determined to try the press once more; it was for her that he had forced himself into the unnatural posture, and his longing for her and his mistrust of her racked him with agony:

Though I could centre my Happiness in you (he wrote to her on 1st July, on reaching the Isle of Wight) I cannot expect to engross your heart so entirely—indeed if I thought you felt as much for me as I do for you at this moment I do not think I could restrain myself from seeing you again to-morrow for the delight of one embrace. But no—I must live upon hope and Chance. In case of the worst that can happen, I shall still love you—but what hatred I shall feel for an other!

On 12th July he wrote to Reynolds that he had finished the first act of *Otho* and before beginning the second act he had finished the first part of *Lamia*. *Lamia*, to which Keats had to turn for relief from the artificialities of *Otho*, was based on a passage of Burton's *Anatomy*. The reading of that disappointed and embittered old idealist was one of the drugs to which Keats now had recourse, and his marginal notes which have been preserved probably belong to these days. One or two of these notes will throw more illumination on Keats' temper at this moment than many pages of description. For instance, on Burton's curious encomium of the virtues of precious stones 'to pacify the affections of the mind,' Keats comments: 'Precious stones are certainly a remedy against Melancholy: a valuable diamond would effectually cure mine.' Again, Burton gives from Jacopus de Voragine a list of nine arguments 'to persuade to, or commend marriage,' and immediately after, as his method was, gives nine counter-arguments of his own. 'Hast thou meanes?' says Jacopus. 'Thou hast one to keep and increase it.' 'Hast thou meanes?' retorts Burton. 'Thou hast one to spend it.' Against which Keats simply writes 'Aye, aye.' Finally, as a note on the whole subsection, 'Love's Beginning, Object, Definition, Division,' Keats wrote this:

Here is the old plague-spot: the pestilence, the raw scrofula. I mean there is nothing disgraces me in my own eyes so much as being one of a race of eyes, nose and mouth beings in a planet called the earth who all from Plato to Wesley have always mingled goatish, winnyish, lustful love with the abstract adoration of the deity. I don't understand Greek—is the Love of God and the Love of women expressed by the same word in Greek? I hope my little mind is wrong—if not I could—Has Plato separated these loves? Ha! I see how they endeavour to divide—but there appears to be a horrid relationship.

Keats is bitter, with the bitterness of a man who loves passionately and sees no term to his desire; the 'horrid relationship' exists indeed, as Keats knew better than most men. It had been the theme of *Endymion*.

From his reading of Burton at this time Keats took the story of *Lamia*:

Philostratus, in his fourth book *de Vita Apollonii*, hath a memorable instance in this kind, which I may not omit, of one Menippus Lycius, a young man twenty-five years of age, that going betwixt Cenchreas and Corinth, met such a phantasm in the habit of a fair gentlewoman, which taking him by the hand, carried him home to her house, in the suburbs of Corinth, and told him she was a Phœnician by birth, and if he would tarry with her, he should hear her sing and play, and drink such wine as never any drank, and no man should molest him; but she, being fair and lovely, would live and die with him, that was fair and lovely to behold. The young man, a philosopher, otherwise staid and discreet, able to moderate his passions, though not this of love, tarried with her awhile to his great content, and at last married her, to whose wedding, amongst other guests came Apollonius; who, by some probable conjectures, found her out to be a serpent, a lamia; and that all her furniture was, like Tantalus' gold, described by Homer, no substance but mere illusions. When she saw herself descried, she wept, and desired Apollonius to be silent, but he would not be moved, and thereupon she, plate, house, and all that was in it, vanished in an instant: many thousands took notice of this fact, for it was done in the midst of Greece.

That is the story as old Burton gave it. It was singularly appropriate to Keats' situation—a young man of twenty-three, a philosopher, able to moderate his passions, though not this of love, who must have wondered many times whether Fanny Brawne had not entangled him to his own perdition. 'I have never known any unalloy'd Happiness,' he was writing to her at the very moment of beginning *Lamia* (1st July) 'for many days together: the death or sickness of some one has always spoilt my hours—and now when none such troubles oppress me, it is you must confess very hard that another sort of pain should haunt me. Ask yourself, my love, whether you are not very cruel to have so entrammelled me, so destroyed my freedom.' Already the story fitted well. Keats made it fit better still. In Burton there is no hint of a relation between Lycius and Apollonius. Apollonius is but a wedding-guest. In the poem *Lamia*, Apollonius is Lycius' friend and master. In Burton there is no hint of anything untoward happening to Lycius as the result of the exposure of the Lamia. She dissolves into thin air, and that is all. In Keats' poem, Lycius struggles to prevent the exposure, and when it is made, he dies.

Lamia, as Keats wrote it, is imaginative autobiography, and of the most exact and faithful kind. Keats is Lycius, Fanny Brawne is the Lamia, and Apollonius is Charles Brown the realist, trying to break Fanny's spell over Keats by insisting upon her as the female animal. The identification seems transparent. *Lamia* is a poem of real and living experience; Keats wrote it from his heart. And that explains two things: it explains why Keats definitely and deliberately preferred it to *The Eve of St. Agnes*, because it showed more ' experience of life ': it explains the bewilderment which some critics have felt concerning the poem as a whole.

> But to me (says Sir Sidney Colvin in his *Life of Keats*) the fundamental flaw in *Lamia* concerns the moral. The word is crude: what I mean is the bewilderment in which it leaves us as to the effect intended to be made on our imaginative sympathies. Lamia is a serpent-woman, baleful and a witch, whose love for Lycius fills him with momentary happiness but must, we are made aware, be fatal to him. Apollonius is a philosopher who sees through her and by one steadfast look withers up her magic semblance and destroys her, but in doing so fails to save his pupil, who dies the moment his illusion vanishes. Are these things a bitter parable of universal application, meaning that all love-joys are but deception, and at the touch of wisdom and experience they melt away? If so, the tale might have been told either tragically or satirically, in either case leaving the reader impartial as between the sage and his victim. But Keats in this apostrophe, which I wish he had left out, deliberately points a moral and expressly invites us to take sides:
>
> What wreath for Lamia? What for Lycius?
> What for the sage, old Apollonius?
> Upon her aching forehead be there hung
> The leaves of willow and of adder's tongue;
> And for the youth, quick, let us strip for him
> The thyrsus, that his watching eyes may swim
> Into forgetfulness; and, for the sage,
> Let spear-grass and the spiteful thistle wage
> War on his temples. Do not all charms fly
> At the mere touch of cold philosophy?
> There was an awful rainbow once in heaven:
> We knew her woof, her texture; she is given
> In the dull catalogue of common things.
> Philosophy will clip an Angel's wings,
> Conquer all mysteries by rule and line,
> Empty the haunted air and gnomed mine—
> Unweave a rainbow, as it erewhile made
> The tender-person'd Lamia melt into a shade.
>
> These lines (Sir Sidney continues) have not only the fault of breaking the story at a critical point and anticipating its issue, but challenge the mind to untimely questionings and reflections. The wreaths of ominous growth distributed to each of the three

personages may symbolize the general tragedy: but why are we asked to take sides with the enchantress, ignoring everything about her except her charm, and against the sage? If she were indeed a thing of bale under a mask of beauty, was not the friend and tutor bound to unmask her, even though the pupil lacked strength of soul to survive the loss of his illusion? Is there not in all this a slackening of the intellectual and imaginative grasp?

The answer to the last question may wait for a moment. The reason why we are asked to take sides with the enchantress in *Lamia* is that Keats was in love with her. The truth about the Lamia is that Keats himself did not know whether she was a thing of beauty or a thing of bale. He only knew that if he were to be deprived of her, he would die, which he did, in the poem and in fact. He believed her a thing of beauty; Brown believed her, and for that matter any woman, a thing of bale. Keats knew it was not so simple: she was a thing of beauty who might by that very fact become a thing of bale to him. What Sir Sidney Colvin calls 'the bewilderment in which *Lamia* leaves us as to the effect intended to be produced on our imaginative sympathies' is the projection into the objective world of poetry of Keats' real anguish of soul. There are plenty of examples of a like bewilderment in Shakespeare—*Measure for Measure* is one; *Troilus and Cressida* another—but no more than *Lamia* do they show a weakening of the imaginative and intellectual grasp; they show, like *Lamia*, the struggle of the true poet to be faithful to the reality of his experience.

But why, it may yet be asked, should we assume that during the summer weeks when he and Keats were together at Shanklin and at Winchester, Brown's influence on Keats was such as it has been described? Whether what seems an inevitable deduction from what we know of Brown's character and actions can fairly be called an assumption is open to doubt; happily, however, there is proof. In a letter to Brown which Keats wrote on 22nd September, telling him of his determination to live apart from and independently of Brown—a determination with which in all its bearings we shall be closely concerned—he says, quite abruptly: 'If you live at Hampstead next winter— I like Fanny Brawne and I cannot help it. On that account I had better not live there.' That is all: and in that one abrupt sentence the whole nature of Keats' and Brown's relations in respect of Fanny during these summer months of 1819 is made plain. The subject is one on which Keats will not talk any more to Brown. 'I like Fanny Brawne and cannot help it,' addressed to Charles Brown, is the key to *Lamia*.

The first part of *Lamia* was finished by 12th July; then it was put aside. It was too real; it was a refuge from his love that Keats wanted, not a contemplation of it.

On 25th July he wrote to Fanny Brawne: 'You must forgive me if I wander a little this evening, for I have been all day employ'd in a very abstract poem and I am deep in love with you—two things which must excuse me.' *Lamia* is not an abstract poem at all. The phrase means precisely what it had meant in the previous winter—*Hyperion.* Keats was once more taking refuge in 'abstract images,' and he had begun to rewrite *Hyperion.* That this was so is proved by his telling Bailey on 15th August: 'I have been writing parts of my *Hyperion,*' and by his letter to Woodhouse on 22nd September which includes passages from the beginning, the middle, and the end of the revised induction to *Hyperion,* and thus establishes that it was the second *Hyperion* on which Keats had been engaged. During the two months following 12th July, Keats was feverishly occupied during the time when he was not engaged in the hack-work of *Otho the Great,* with the second part of *Lamia* and the rewriting of *Hyperion.* What *Lamia* meant we have seen, what the rewriting of *Hyperion* meant we shall see hereafter. For the moment it must suffice that on these two poems Keats was feverishly intent.

We can watch the fever growing. On 12th July, when he told Reynolds that he had finished the first half of *Lamia*—the half of the poem, that is to say, in which the enchantment and not the pain of his love is expressed—he is calm and determined.

> I have great hopes of success (he says), because I make use of my judgment more deliberately than I have yet done; but in case of failure with the world, I shall find my content. And here (as I know you have my good at heart as much as a Brother), I can only repeat to you what I have said to George—that however I should like to enjoy what the competencies of life procure, I am in no wise dashed at a different prospect. I have spent too many thoughtful days and moralized through too many nights for that, and fruitless would they be indeed, if they did not by degrees make me look upon the affairs of the world with a healthy deliberation. I have of late been moulting: not for fresh feathers and wings: they are gone, and in their stead I hope to have a pair of patient sublunary legs. I have altered, not from a Chrysalis into a butterfly, but the contrary; having two little loopholes, whence I may look out into the stage of the world: and that world on our coming here I almost forgot. The first time I sat down to write, I could scarcely believe in the necessity for so doing. It struck me as a great oddity. Yet the very corn which is now so beautiful, as if it had only took to ripening yesterday, is for the market; so, why should I be delicate?

There speaks calm determination. What the competencies of life would have procured for him was Fanny; what his failure with the world would deprive him of was Fanny. Yet, in case of failure, he is certain that he will find his content.

Was it so certain? A few days later he wrote to Fanny wondering why he was in such good spirits.

> What reason? When I have to take my candle and retire to a lonely room, without the thought as I fall asleep, of seeing you to-morrow morning? or the next day, or the next—it takes on the appearance of impossibility and eternity—I will say a month—I will say I will see you in a month at most, though no one but yourself should see me; if it be but for an hour. I should not like to be so near you as London without being continually with you: after having once more kissed you Sweet I would rather be here alone at my task than in the bustle and hateful literary chit-chat.

In a few days more (25th July) the yearning to be with her again had become an anguish.

> You cannot conceive how I ache to be with you: how I would die for one hour—for what is in the world? I say you cannot conceive; it is impossible you should look with such eyes on me as I have upon you: it cannot be. . . . You absorb me in spite of myself. . . . I have two luxuries to brood over in my walks, your Loveliness and the hour of my death. O that I could have possession of them both in the same minute. I hate the world, it batters too much the wings of my self-will, and would I could take a sweet poison from your lips to send me out of it.

A week later (5th August) he confesses that he is using work as a drug to dull the importunacy of his love.

> Thank God for my diligence! (he writes). Were it not for that I should be miserable. I encourage it, and strive not to think of you—but when I have succeeded in doing so all day and as far as midnight, you return, as soon as this artificial excitement goes off, more severely for the fever I am left in. . . . So you intend to hold me to my promise of seeing you in a short time. I shall keep it with as much sorrow as gladness: for I am not one of the Paladins of old who liv'd on water grass and smiles for years together. What though would I not give to-night for the gratification of my eyes alone? This week we shall move to Winchester. Brown will leave me there to pay a visit to Mr. Snook at Bedhampton: in his absence I will flit to you and back. I will stay very little while, for as I am in a train of writing now I fear to disturb it—let it have its course bad or good—in it I shall try my own strength and the public pulse. . . .

The next week—they had arranged to write to each other weekly—Keats did not write. He had moved from the Isle of Wight to Winchester, and he had been in Winchester for days without sending her word. The next letter (16th August) explains itself, and expresses far more vividly than any description would do the strange fever into which Keats had worked himself.

What shall I say for myself? I have been here four days and not yet written you—'tis true I have had many teasing letters of business to dismiss—and I have been in the Claws, like a serpent in an Eagle's, of the last act of our Tragedy. This is no excuse; I know it; I do not presume to offer it. I have no right either to ask a speedy answer to let me know how lenient you are—I must remain some days in a Mist—I see you through a Mist: as I daresay you do me by this time. Believe in the first Letters I wrote you: I assure you I felt as I wrote—I could not write so now. The thousand images I have had pass through my brain—my uneasy spirits—my unguess'd fate—all spread as a veil between me and you. Remember I have had no idle leisure to brood over you—'tis well perhaps I have not. I could not have endured the throng of jealousies that used to haunt me before I plunged so deep into imaginary interests. I would fain, as my sails are set, sail on without interruption for a Brace of Months longer—I am in complete cue—in the fever; and shall in these four Months do an immense deal. This Page as my eye skims over it I see is excessively unloverlike and ungallant—I cannot help it—I am no officer in yawning quarters; no Parson-romeo. My Mind is heap'd to the full; stuff'd like a cricket-ball—if I strive to fill it more it would burst. I know the generality of women would hate me for this; that I should have so unsoftened, so hard a Mind as to forget them; forget the brightest realities for the dull imaginations of my own Brain. But I conjure you to give it a fair thinking; and ask yourself whether 'tis not better to explain my feelings to you, than write artificial Passion—Besides you would see through it. It would be vain to strive to deceive you. 'Tis harsh, harsh, I know it. My heart seems now made of iron—I could not write a proper answer to an invitation to Idalia . . . You see how I go on—like so many strokes of a hammer. I cannot help it—I am impell'd, driven to it. I am not happy enough for silken Phrases, and silver sentences. . . .

Then with an obvious effort he tries to give a little picture of his journey from the Isle of Wight to the mainland, and breaks off.

Forgive me this flint-worded letter, and believe and see that I cannot think of you without some sort of energy—though mal à propos. Even as I leave off it seems to me that a few more moments' thought of you would uncrystallize and dissolve me. I must not give way to it—but turn to my writing again—if I fail I shall die hard. O my love, your lips are growing sweet again to my fancy—I must forget them.

It is impossible to mistake the meaning of that extraordinary letter. Keats is making and has been making a frenzied effort to shut his love out of his mind and heart. With an extreme tension of the intellectual will, he is striving to hide himself from the thought of his mistress in feverish work; and the tension is so great that it shapes every phrase of the letter itself. It is, in very truth, 'like so many strokes of hammer'; but those hammer-strokes are falling on Keats' heart, not on hers. He does not keep his promise of seeing her; he obviously dare not; when the thought of her will 'uncrystallize' him, what would her warm kiss have done?

There are no more letters to Fanny Brawne for a month. I believe that he did not write to her for a month. When he did write to her again, on 13th September, he was in London, but he did not go to see her. He was in London because yet another disaster had befallen him. He had received a letter from his brother George in America to say that he too was ruined, and begging Keats to see their guardian Abbey and endeavour to get some money from him. This is Keats' letter to Fanny Brawne:

I have been hurried to town by a Letter from my brother George; it is not of the brightest intelligence. Am I mad or not? I came by the Friday night coach and have not yet been to Hampstead. Upon my soul it is not my fault. I cannot resolve to mix any pleasure with my days: they go one like another, indistinguishable. If I were to see you to-day it would destroy the half-comfortable sullenness I enjoy at present into downright perplexities. I love you too much to venture to Hampstead, I feel it is not paying a visit, but venturing into a fire. *Que feraije?* as the French novel-writers say in fun, and I in earnest: really what can I do? Knowing well that my life must be passed in fatigue and trouble, I have been endeavouring to wean myself from you: for to myself alone what can be much of misery? As far as they regard myself I can despise all events: but I cannot cease to love you. This morning I scarcely know what I am doing. I am going to Walthamstow. I shall return to Winchester to-morrow; whence you shall hear from me in a few days. I am a Coward, I cannot bear the pain of being happy: 'tis out of the question: I must admit no thought of it.

'I have been endeavouring to wean myself from you.' That is the explanation of the month of silence towards Fanny that followed 'the flint-worded letter'.

During this month Keats was working, in what frame of mind we now partly know, on the second part of *Lamia* and the rewriting of *Hyperion*. With a fierce effort of the intellectual will he was flinging himself into the world of imagination to escape the anguish of his heart. It was an effort of precisely the same kind as that which had inspired the first two books of the first *Hyperion*, but now it was by far more cruel.

Keats does not speak to Fanny Brawne of his actual writing. But he, if ever man was, was homogeneous. How indelibly the pain of his heart was printed on the thought of his brain appears from the four letters to his men-friends during the month between mid-August and mid-September, in which he was making this agonized attempt to shut his love out of his heart.

The first of these letters is the one to Bailey of 15th August, in which he tells him that he has been writing parts of *Hyperion*:

> One of my Ambitions is to make as great a revolution in modern dramatic writing as Kean has done in acting. Another, to upset the drawling of the blue-stocking literary world—if in the Course of a few years I do these two things, I ought to die content, and my friends should drink a dozen of claret on my tomb. I am convinced more and more every day that (excepting the human friend philosopher), a fine writer is the most genuine being in the world. Shakespeare and the Paradise lost every day become greater wonders to me. I look upon fine phrases like a lover.

The implications of that passage, so far as they concern Kean and Keats' conviction that a fine writer was 'the most genuine being in the world' have already been considered. Now, the sentence to be remarked and remembered is the simple one: 'Shakespeare and the Paradise lost every day become greater wonders to me.'

On the following day (16th August) Keats wrote his final 'flint-worded letter' to Fanny—the letter like 'so many strokes of a hammer.' The next letter of his we have is one written to Taylor, his publisher, just a week later, on 23rd August.

> I feel every confidence that, if I choose, I may be a popular writer. That I will never be; but for all that I will get a livelihood. I equally dislike the favour of the public with the love of a woman. They are both a cloying treacle to the wings of independence. I shall ever consider them (People) as debtors to me for verses, not myself to them for admiration—which I can do without. I have of late been indulging my spleen by composing a preface AT them; after all resolving never to write a preface at all. 'There are so many verses,' would I have said to them, 'give so much means

for me to buy pleasure with, as a relief to my hours of labour.'—
You will observe at the end of this, if you put down the letter,
'How a solitary life engenders pride and egotism!' True—I know
it does: but this pride and egotism will enable me to write finer
things than anything else could—so I will indulge it. Just so much
as I am humbled by the genius above my grasp am I exalted and
look with hate and contempt upon the literary world.—A drummer-
boy who holds out his hand familiarly to a field Marshal,—that
drummer-boy with me is the good word and favour of the public.
Who would wish to be among the common-place crowd of the
little famous—who are each individually lost in a throng made up
of themselves? Is this worth louting or playing the hypocrite for?
To beg suffrages for a seat on the benches of a myriad-aris-
tocracy in letters? This is not wise—I am not a wise man. 'Tis
pride—I will give you a definition of a proud man. He is a man
who has neither Vanity or Wisdom—one filled with hatreds cannot be vain, neither can he be wise. Pardon me for hammering
instead of writing.

Is it not clear that this letter is the exact counterpart, in another
realm, of the flint-worded letter to Fanny? Both are, confessedly,
'hammering instead of writing,' and the relation between them is
avowed by Keats' own words: 'I equally dislike the favour of the
public with the love of a woman. They are both a cloying treacle to
the wings of Independence.' Just as Keats the man is trying to shut
out the thought of Fanny from his heart, so Keats the poet is trying
to shut out the thought of the public from his mind. In the modern
phrase, he is hiding himself within 'the ivory tower.' Now, he con-
vinces himself that 'pride and egotism' will enable him to write
finer things than anything else could. To live remote from human
concerns, to turn his face away from the fever and the fret, to look
with contempt and hatred on the literary world,—this is what he
desires to do.

Two days later (25th August) he writes in the same strain to
Reynolds.

I have indeed scarcely anything to say, leading so monotonous
a life, except I was to give you a history of sensations, and day-
nightmares. You would not find me at all unhappy in it, as all my
thoughts and feelings which are of the selfish nature, every day
continue to make me more iron—I am convinced more and more,
every day, that fine writing is, next to fine doing, the top thing in
the world: the Paradise Lost becomes a greater wonder. The more
I know what my diligence may in time probably effect, the more
does my heart distend with Pride and Obstinacy—I feel it in my
power to become a popular writer—I feel it in my power to refuse

> the poisonous suffrage of a public. My own being which I know to be becomes of more consequence to me than the crowds of Shadows in the shape of men and women that inhabit a kingdom. The soul is a world of itself, and has enough to do in its own home. Those whom I know already, and who have grown as it were part of myself, I could not do without: but for the rest of mankind, they are as much a dream to me as Milton's Hierarchies. I think if I had a free and healthy and lasting organization of heart, and lungs strong as an ox's, so as to be able to bear unhurt the shock of extreme thought and sensation without weariness, I could pass my life very nearly alone though it should last eighty years. But I feel my body too weak to support me to the height, I am obliged continually to check myself, and be nothing. It would be vain for me to endeavour after a more reasonable manner of writing to you. I have nothing to speak of but myself, and what can I say but what I feel? If you should have any reason to regret this state of excitement in me, I will turn the tide of your feelings in the right Channel, by mentioning that it is the only state for the best sort of Poetry—that is all I care for, all I live for.

In that letter the fever has reached an extreme: his heart is distended with Pride and Obstinacy: the suffrage of the public is now become 'poisonous': every day he becomes more and more iron: if he were only physically stronger he could banish the world for ever: but he can scarcely stand the strain of extreme thought and sensation: still, this condition of fierce excitement is, he asserts, the only state for 'the best sort of poetry.' But the crucial words of the letter are these:

> I am convinced more and more, every day, that fine writing is, next to fine doing, the top thing in the world; the Paradise Lost becomes a greater wonder.

It is almost the same thought, in almost the same words, that he had written to Bailey ten days before:

> I am convinced more and more every day that (excepting the human friend philosopher), a fine writer is the most genuine being in the world. Shakespeare and the Paradise lost every day become greater wonders to me.

The thought is almost the same: yet how profoundly different. Shakespeare has disappeared: Milton alone remains. A casual and unimportant discrepancy, it may be said. Were the writer another than Keats, and the subject another than Shakespeare, it might be so: but it is Keats and it is Shakespeare. Something of vital importance has happened, is happening.

And what is happening is clear. Keats knows he cannot invoke Shakespeare any more, being what he is become. He has shut Fanny Brawne, he has shut the world of men and women out of his heart; and with them he has shut Shakespeare. Keats was too honest not to know that he had not the right to claim Shakespeare any more as his forerunner. Shakespeare had endured a bitter love; Shakespeare had accepted the world of men and women; Shakespeare had made his terms with the public; and in these things Shakespeare had shown his greatness. Keats could not follow him.

And Keats knew what he was doing. When he came to write the phrase again, his hand surely paused before he wrote simply: 'The Paradise Lost becomes a greater wonder.' He was making *il gran rifiuto,* and he knew it: and in his superb integrity, he could not praise Shakespeare with his lips when his heart was far from him. Consider, too, the subtle yet profound difference between 'a fine writer is the most genuine being in the world'—a deep and mysterious truth which Keats had learned in following Shakespeare and his own complete self—and 'fine writing is, next to fine doing, the top thing in the world.' The fatal severance has been made: whereas before 'fine writing' was itself 'fine doing' because it was a function of 'fine being,' now they are separated and distinct.

Keats, in the agony of his fever, was trying to do once more what he tried to do in the winter at Tom's bedside. He was trying desperately to make the remoteness and abstraction of Milton his ideal; to find in the deliberate art of Milton and his proud neglect of human destinies for his majestic but inhuman theological drama a refuge from the torment of life. But now, as his suffering was more bitter, so his passion for the abstract art of Milton had reached a pitch of frenzy. In this frenzy he was rewriting *Hyperion.*

Then came a fresh blow. Keats heard that Kean, for whom *Otho the Great* had been written, without whom there was no chance of its being accepted, had suddenly left England for America. The chief labour of the summer had been wasted; the one serious chance of his fortune turning up Pam or at least a court card, was lost. And upon that came yet another: George had suffered catastrophe in America, and Keats must send him all the money he could lay hold on. When this news reached him on 10th September, he was alone in Winchester. Brown had gone off on a mysterious three weeks' visit. The same night Keats took the coach to London to see Abbey, his guardian. In London he did not see Fanny Brawne. 'Am I mad or not?' he wrote to her. He well might ask, when disaster after disaster was being thus heaped upon him. 'I am a Coward, I cannot bear the pain of being happy: 'tis out of the question: I must admit no thought of it.'

On Tuesday 15th September Keats returned to Winchester, alone with his thoughts. On the following Sunday he wrote the most beautiful, the most calm, the most perfectly serene of all his poems. Two days later, on 22nd September, he wrote to Reynolds, telling him that he had written it. 'I am surprised myself', he says, 'at the pleasure I live alone in.'

> How beautiful the season is now—How fine the air—a temperate sharpness about it. Really, without joking, chaste weather—Dian skies—I never liked stubble-field so much as now—Aye better than the chilly green of the Spring. Somehow, a stubble-field looks warm—in the same way that some pictures look warm. This struck me so much in my Sunday's walk that I composed upon it.

What he composed was the *Ode to Autumn*. The miracle had happened.

> When in midway the sickening east wind
> Shifts sudden to the south, the small warm rain
> Melts out the frozen incense from the flowers. . . .

Not otherwise, nor less sudden was the miracle with Keats. And in the next lines of his letter to Reynolds he says:

> I have given up *Hyperion*—there were too many Miltonic inversions in it—Miltonic verse cannot be written, but in an artful, or rather, artist's humour. I wish to give myself up to other sensations.

Shakespeare had triumphed in Keats' soul.

CHAPTER XII

THE SECOND *HYPERION*

IN those crucial four days which Keats spent alone in Winchester between 15th September and 20th September, Shakespeare had triumphed over Milton. But a victory for Shakespeare in Keats' soul was a victory for himself; it was the triumph of his own complete, spontaneous, and natural being over its own internecine division. In that momentous decision, many decisions were involved, for it meant simply that Keats was to be Keats. The attempt will be made hereafter to show in what ways he was to be Keats, and to follow out in every province of his being the consequences of that triumph of his own spontaneity.

Though Keats abandoned the revised *Hyperion*, it remains the profoundest and most sublime of his poems. He did not abandon it because he had abandoned the thought it contains, but because he knew that the thought could not be uttered ' in an artful or rather artist's humour '; the knowledge he was trying to reveal, he knew he must reveal in another way and in another mood. The acceptance that is in the revised *Hyperion* could not be truly spoken save from the complete being; and then its utterance would be concrete and spontaneous and 'come as naturally as the leaves to a tree.' One cannot compare a poem of three stanzas with one of as many hundred lines; nevertheless it is exact to say that the highest poetic truth of the revised *Hyperion* is in the *Ode to Autumn.*

To use the terms which have been adopted from Keats himself, Keats abandoned the revised *Hyperion* because he was committing the sin of uttering soul-knowledge through an effort of mind-knowledge. That is a sin absent from the Decalogue, and unknown to ordinary experience; it is known only to poetic genius: it consists in the effort to utter what can only be revealed. It is in some sort a betrayal of the soul's knowledge, it is also a betrayal of the soul itself. This statement neither contains nor implies a criticism of Keats: the man has not yet lived who has the right to criticize Keats in such a matter; it is simply an attempt to explain Keats' own criticism of himself. He had involved himself in an impossible situation in his revision of *Hyperion*; out of a mood in which he did not accept he was writing a poem in which the mystery of acceptance was to be revealed. At the moment that he was trying to shut out of his heart and mind Fanny and the world of men and women he was trying also to utter his knowledge that all things must be accepted. He was trying to deny and accept at once.

In other words, though the revised *Hyperion* is the profoundest of Keats' poems, it is not the most perfect, for it is but a partial and in a sense a forced expression of himself. We can learn from it his deepest and truest thoughts, but we shall not learn them as he would have had us learn them. His was a still deeper knowledge than that which he expressed in his abandoned poem: his knowledge was so deep and true that it did not need to be torn out of himself as this was. But to express his own knowledge completely in his own way was forbidden him by destiny: let us be thankful that the revised *Hyperion* remains. It was written in a fever. 'I want to compose without this fever,' he said to his brother after abandoning it, 'I hope one day I shall.' Nothing is more certain than that he would have done. The *Ode to Autumn* proves it. But the revised *Hyperion* written without the fever would have been one of the greatest poems in the world.*

In the revision *Hyperion: a Fragment* becomes *The Fall of Hyperion: a Dream.* We need not stress the variation of title. *Hyperion* was always in Keats' mind *The Fall of Hyperion.* Hyperion was to be dethroned by Apollo, who had come at the abrupt end of the first version of the poem, through the pain of a death into life, to a full consciousness of his own godhead. 'Knowledge enormous makes a god of me.' That was the projection, into an imagined world of immortals, of the knowledge which the mortal poet Keats had achieved through the death into life which has been described. It happened, and the third book of the first *Hyperion* was written, in March and April of this year 1819. Then Keats himself read what Apollo read in the eyes of silent Mnemosyne:

> Names, deeds, gray legends, dire events, rebellions,
> Majesties, sovran voices, agonies,
> Creations and destroyings——

This knowledge of the beauty and necessity of human destinies, Keats personified in Mnemosyne. In the new *Hyperion* the liquid and lovely name is changed to a sterner one: the Greek Mnemosyne becomes the Latin Moneta. It may have been simply that Keats felt the Greek name discordant among the Latin names; but it is more probable that when he began to rewrite *Hyperion* at the end of July 1819 he desired a sterner name for a sterner knowledge. However, that may be, Moneta is the new name for Mnemosyne: and if further proof is needed of the identification of Apollo with Keats himself, it is to be found in the simple fact that the whole of the new *Hyperion* is concerned with the poet's own encounter with Moneta. The second *Hyperion* is a rewriting, compelled by a yet fuller experience, of the third book of the first *Hyperion*.

With so much by way of preamble we may embark upon the poem itself: *The Fall of Hyperion: A Dream.* The brief induction of eighteen lines is greatly relevant:

> Fanatics have their dreams, wherewith they weave
> A paradise for a sect; the savage, too,
> From forth the loftiest fashion of his sleep
> Guesses at heaven; pity these have not
> Traced upon vellum or wild Indian leaf
> The shadows of melodious utterance.
> But bare of laurel they live, dream, and die;
> For Poesy alone can tell her dreams,—
> With the fine spell of words alone can save
> Imagination from the sable chain
> And dumb enchantment. Who alive can say,
> 'Thou art no Poet—may'st not tell thy dreams'?
> Since every man whose soul is not a clod
> Hath visions and would speak, if he had lov'd,
> And been well nurtured in his mother tongue.
> Whether the dream now purposed to rehearse
> Be poet's or fanatic's will be known
> When this warm scribe my hand is in the grave.

Such is the brief, staccato prelude to the poems, in timbre it precisely recalls 'the hammer-strokes' of his August letters. It is worth a careful reading, and it needs one. With the sombre last line ringing in one's ears, one would be tempted to call it the gasping speech of a dying man. But we know something of the mood in which it was written. However—all men have their dreams, says Keats, but the poet alone may utter them. Then he thinks: But many men are poets, who have not the gift of poetic speech: many men, that is to say, have the soul and vision of the poet, which they would utter if—the first qualification is in the context quite unexpected but not strange to our knowledge—'*if they had loved* . . . and been well-nurtured in their mother-tongue.' Then he concludes: 'When I am dead it will be known whether my dream was a poet's or a fanatic's.'

The thought is not easy: it is terribly compressed. He has used the words poetry and poet in two senses. Poetry is that which makes men's dreams immortal whether they be fanatics or savages; the poet is also the man who 'hath visions and hath loved.' These two ideas of poetry—as utterance making dreams immortal, and as a condition of soul—are different. Suddenly, in the last lines they are blent into one. It will be known when he is dead whether his dream is a fanatic's, that is 'a paradise for a sect,' or a poet's, that is—what that is Keats was going to try to say. To declare this is the essential purpose of the new *Hyperion*. For the moment we must be satisfied with the obvious opposite to a paradise for a *sect*—a paradise for all humanity. Whether Keats' dream offered this will be known

> When this warm scribe my hand is in the grave.

The thought is threefold—the thought of approaching death, the thought that only after death will it be known whether his dream is a balm to all humanity, and that it will only then be known whether he has given his dream immortality.

That is a very long commentary on a very few verses. But the verses are tense with meaning, and they have haunted my mind for days together. There is a quality in that last line: 'When this warm scribe my hand is in the grave,' which takes hold of me and will not let me go. In that line I feel the actual presence of Keats with a vividness that is almost pain. These are my last words, it says, this is my hand writing them: watch. And I watch; I have watched those lines being written many times, till it seemed they were written on my brain. Finally, when at last I understood them, there came flooding into my mind other lines written by Keats, concerning that same warm hand of his. They were discovered written on the margin of *Cap and Bells*.

> This living hand, now warm and capable
> Of earnest grasping, would, if it were cold
> And in the icy silence of the tomb,
> So haunt thy days and chill thy dreaming nights
> That thou would'st wish thine own heart dry of blood
> So in my veins old life might stream again
> And thou be conscience-calm'd—see here it is—
> I hold it towards you.

Those terrible lines are supposed to have been addressed to Fanny Brawne. No doubt they were; but in the deathly stillness in which they were written no mortal speaks to a mortal. Keats was at that moment on the thither side of death, watching his hand. So now, at the moment of beginning the new *Hyperion*, Keats is watching his hand. It calls up in him more thoughts than he utters,—one thought above all others that he shuts back into his heart with the words ' if he had lov'd.' The effort is in the opening lines of the poem: what was suppressed by the effort is in those other lines to Fanny Brawne. After such an effort the dream begins.*

The poet dreams that he is standing in an earthly Eden; spread on a mossy mound are the remnants of an ethereal banquet. With a yearning appetite he eats, and, ' after not long ', thirsts. A vessel of nectar stands near by—

> the which I took
> And, pledging all the mortals of the world,
> And all the dead whose names are on our lips,
> Drank. That full draught is parent of my theme.

It has been generally agreed that in this vision of an earthly Eden Keats is symbolically expressing that phase of his development which in his letter to Reynolds (3rd May 1818) he described as *The Chamber of Maiden Thought*—the phase in which he passes from the Infant Chamber of instinctive and thoughtless enjoyment of the beauty of the world to the intoxication of the atmosphere of thought. It is pertinent to recall his description of the effect of that intoxicating air.

> However, among the effects this breathing is father of is that tremendous one of sharpening one's vision into the heart and nature of Man—of convincing one's nerves that the world is full of misery and heartbreak, Pain, Sickness and oppression—whereby this Chamber of Maiden Thought becomes gradually darkened. . . .

Here, in the poem, the darkening is not gradual but sudden, and it comes in consequence of the draught of delicious liquor. He struggles hard against the ' domineering potion,' but he is conquered, and sinks down in a swoon.

> When sense of life return'd, I started up
> As if with wings, but the fair trees were gone,
> The mossy mound and arbour were no more.

To this the exact parallel is the line from Wordsworth quoted by Keats in his letter to Miss Jeffrey (31st May 1819): ' The world has taken on a quakerish look with me which I once thought was impossible:

> Nothing can bring back the hour
> Of splendour in the grass and glory in the flower.

I once thought this a Melancholist's dream.' So, in the poet's vision, ' the fair trees were gone.' In their stead, he looks around upon

> the carved sides
> Of an old sanctuary with roof august,
> Builded so high, it seem'd that filmed clouds
> Might spread beneath, as o'er the stars of heaven.
> So old the place was, I remember'd none
> The like upon the earth: what I had seen
> Of grey cathedrals, buttress'd walls, rent towers,
> The superannuations of sunk realms,
> Or Nature's rocks toil'd hard in waves and winds,
> Seem'd but the faulture of decrepit things
> To that eternal domed monument.

It is the sublime and awful temple of an unknown religion. North and south an illimitable range of columns ' ending in mist of nothing '; to the east ' black gates '

> Were shut against the sunrise evermore.
> Then to the west I look'd, and saw far off
> An image, huge of feature as a cloud,
> At level of whose feet an altar slept
> To be approached on either side by steps
> And marble balustrade, and patient travail
> To count with toil the innumerable degrees.
> Towards the altar sober-pac'd I went,
> Repressing haste, as too unholy there;
> And coming nearer saw beside the shrine
> One minist'ring; and there arose a flame.

It is rash to press meanings from the details of a symbolic imagination, but the shutting out of the sunrise to the east and the placing of the image and the altar and the ministrant to the west, certainly have their significance. There are to be no more dawns; the poet is born to his destiny, and truth lies toward the sunset, of death and accomplished life. The temple is the temple of life become conscious of itself in man, and now in one man more than all others, the poet. Ignorance has been; he must accept his destiny of knowledge and make the fearful effort towards mastery and comprehension, travelling along the road from birth to death. North and south, to his right hand and his left, the vista is illimitable; profitless, therefore, to turn aside.

From the altar arises a sweet savour, once more intoxicating the sense to forgetfulness of everything but bliss. But immediately a voice is heard, of awful summons

> If thou canst not ascend
> These steps, die on that marble where thou art . . .
> The sands of thy short life are spent this hour
> And no hand in the universe can turn
> Thy hour-glass, if these gummed leaves be burnt
> Ere thou canst mount up these immortal steps. . . .

He struggles to obey the summons; and the struggle is terrible. A palsied chill strikes upward from the paved floor. He is on the very brink of death.

> One minute before death, my iced foot touch'd
> The lowest stair; and, as it touch'd, life seem'd
> To pour in at the toes; I mounted up
> As once fair angels on a ladder flew
> From the green turf to heaven.

In the first *Hyperion* Apollo also had ' died into life.' Now the mortal poet turns to the veiled ministrant, and cries: ' What am I that should be so saved from death '? And the answer comes:

> Thou hast felt
> What 'tis to die and live again before
> Thy fated hour; that thou hadst power to do so
> Is thine own safety: thou hast dated on
> Thy doom.

This death in life, which is also a death into life, is necessary to the progress of the poet, as Keats conceives it. It is hard to explain to those who do not intuitively comprehend it, or have not some correspondent experience of their own. It is a profound acceptance of death, which is a death; it is a deliberate submission of the conscious self which rebels against death. Keats is speaking of that which he knows and has passed through. To his further question:

> ' None can usurp this height,' returned that shade,
> ' But those to whom the miseries of the world
> Are misery, and will not let them rest.'

For this acceptance of death, which is a death, is the bowing down of the soul before the supreme misery of the world. It is, as it were, the pressing to one's heart of the pang that includes all pangs. Not a mere intellectual realization of the miseries of the world can save the poet. Having that alone in the temple of consciousness he would die, beyond reprieve; he is saved only by his power to feel in the depths of his being 'what it is to die and live again before his fated hour.'

This mysterious conception, which is indeed the conception of a mystery, passes beyond the conception of the death into life which is undergone by Apollo in the final book of the first *Hyperion*. That death and deification comes through the 'knowledge enormous' seen in the eyes of Mnemosyne: something of the same kind was, as we shall see, to befall the poet. But the later Keats has entered into a fuller possession of his own intuition; now he declares that the power to feel what it is to die and live again before his fated hour is the very condition of achieving his ' knowledge enormous'. It is only after he has passed through this death that he is told the secret, namely, that he has been suffered to reach the altar steps and to live again because he is one of those ' to whom the miseries of the world are misery and will not let them rest.' That is, in truth, the meaning of his death; by it he has proved—once more ' on his pulses '—his right to usurp the height.

This mysterious thought of Keats' contains a profound and ultimate human wisdom; Keats has passed now clean out of Wordsworth's range. In Shakespeare, and in Shakespeare alone, can be found the full equivalent of this deep knowledge. Keats has left far behind that younger Keats who had reached the point that Wordsworth reached in *Tintern Abbey*, and which Wordsworth himself was never to pass beyond. No momentary gleam of vision ' into the heart of things ' could satisfy this poet upon whom life lavished all her pains. He had struggled for an abiding knowledge, and in the new *Hyperion* he recounts the steps of his strange progress. They are not easy to follow; it is impossible that they should be easy to follow: and, above all, no purely intellectual understanding of them is possible. By the fragments of kindred experience we may have, by a complete submission of ourselves to the inward and vital movement of the poet's soul, we may come if not to a full, at least to a partial comprehension of his meaning. It is mysterious, but not more mysterious than the meaning of certain strange words that we learn from our childhood, whose beauty sinks into our hearts, but whose meaning comes to us only after many years. ' He who loseth his life shall save it.' And if any should feel impatient of mystery, or puzzled why the study of a pure poet should lead to those seemingly ambiguous issues, they can only be reminded of the old saying: *Omnia abeunt in mysterium.* The study of all things end in a mystery, and the knowledge that does not end in a mystery is not a true knowledge at all.

We have followed the poet through his living death to the altar-steps, to the moment at which the voice of Moneta has told him that only those to whom the miseries of the world are misery can reach where he has come. The voice goes on:

> All else who find a haven in the world,
> Where they may thoughtless sleep away their days,
> If by a chance into this fane they come,
> Rot on the pavement where thou rotted'st half.

To enter into the temple of consciousness and not to bear the burden of the pain of the world to the last extreme is death. Then the poet asks:

> ' Are there not thousands in the world,' said I,
> ' Who love their fellows even to the death,
> Who feel the giant agony of the world,
> And more, like slaves to poor humanity,
> Labour for mortal good? I sure should see
> Other men here, but I am here alone.'
> ' Those whom thou spak'st of are no visionaries,'
> Rejoin'd that voice,—' they are no dreamers weak;
> They seek no wonder but the human face,
> No music but a happy-noted voice—
> They come not here, they have no thought to come—
> And thou art here, for thou art less than they.

What benefit canst thou or all thy tribe
Do the great world? Thou art a dreaming thing,
A fever of thyself; think of the earth;
What bliss, even in hope, is there for thee?
What haven? Every creature hath its home,
Every sole man hath days of joy and pain—
The pain alone, the joy alone, distinct;
Only the dreamer venoms all his days
Bearing more woe than all his sins deserve.
Therefore, that happiness be somewhat shar'd,
Such things as thou art are admitted oft
Into like gardens thou didst pass erewhile,
And suffer'd in these Temples: for that cause
Thou standest safe beneath this statue's knees.'

Not to enter the temple of the consciousness of life but to live in the simple doing of good, in the simple enjoyment of joy, in the simple suffering of pain, is best. Keats seems here to strip himself even of the final consolation of the *Ode on Melancholy*.

Aye, in the very temple of Delight
Veil'd Melancholy has her sovran shrine,
Though seen of none save him whose strenuous tongue
Can burst Joy's grape against his palate fine;
His soul shall taste the sadness of her might
And be among her cloudy trophies hung.

But in truth a finer consolation remains. It were better indeed, Keats is saying, not to have entered the temple of consciousness, not to suffer unending pain. But for that pain there is a reward: at last he stands safe on the altar steps.

But the most searching question has been asked: 'What benefit canst thou or all thy tribe do the great world?' In the first draft of the poem Keats answered the question directly, through the lips of Moneta. First he asks:

Majestic shadow, tell me, sure not all
Those melodies sung into the world's ear
Are useless: sure a poet is a sage:
A humanist, physician to all men.
That I am none, I feel, as vultures feel
They are no birds when eagles are abroad:
What am I then: thou spakest of my tribe:
What tribe?

The reply comes:

> Art thou not of the dreamer tribe?
> The poet and the dreamer are distinct,
> Diverse, sheer opposite, antipodes.
> The one pours out a balm upon the world,
> The other vexes it.

These lines are taken from a MS. that belonged to Woodhouse; in which he had deleted them in pencil with the remark that Keats seems to have intended to erase them. That he did erase them in his own copy is fairly certain from the fact that they do not appear in the printed version of *The Fall of Hyperion*, published by Lord Houghton. It seems unwarrantable to include them in the text of the poem as one modern editor has done.

The argument by which their inclusion in the text is justified is that the thought is necessary. Without these lines, it is said, there is no answer to the great question: 'What benefit canst thou or all thy tribe do the great world?' The question will go by default, and poetry be rejected as useless. The situation is supposed to be saved by those lines wherein Keats admits that he is a dreamer, and of the tribe of dreamers—whereas the true poet is in this sense no dreamer at all. Keats deleted the lines. The reason of his doing so is quite clear.

He did not admit that he was a mere dreamer: he knew—had he not spent those last bitter months, and all his poetic life, in learning it?—the difference between a poet and a mere dreamer. Had he not utterly rejected dreams? Did he not know that he was a true poet? Was he not proving it at the very moment that he wrote? The first great reason why Keats cancelled the lines and why they must remain cancelled is that they were not true of himself. There was no time and no place for false modesty. To restore those lines is to do him and his thought an injury, in the interests of an apparent logic which he himself rejected.

But what then of the 'sweeping denunciation of the imaginative mind,' as Professor de Selincourt has called it? Keats meant what he said: that it was better for a man not to enter the temple of consciousness, not to become a fever of himself, not to venom all his days. A man who is paying the price, in his body and soul, of being a miserable and mighty poet of the human heart, does not look upon the condition with the same softly approving eye as the dilettante spectator: he envies the simple man, as Tolstoy envied the peasant, and as all supremely conscious souls have envied those who were spared their agonies. Far better, it seems to them, to be a simple doer of good, and never to have been banished from the paradise of unconsciousness.

But still, it may be said, there is no answer to the great question: What good is poetry? No, there is no direct answer. No direct answer is possible. But the full and satisfying answer is in this poem. The revised *Hyperion* is essentially nothing less, and nothing more, than Keats' answer to that question; for it is an account of the manner by which the poet may come to behold the truth face to face, and an example of the way in which he tries to reveal it to the world.

But chief of all reasons why we should not restore the rejected passage is that it does not really supply the answer to the great question which it is supposed to answer. The poet had wondered why he was alone on the height. Were there not others (he had asked Moneta) who felt the misery of the world, and laboured for the love of their fellows? There are, she had replied, but they are not visionaries, not weak dreamers, as you are. They do not come into this temple; they are not poisoned and tortured by this consciousness of life. But neither do they touch the reward of final knowledge: 'standing safe between this statue's knees.' Dreamers in this sense of the word 'dreamer'—one who comes into the pain of a full consciousness of life—all great poets must be; they all must enter the temple of consciousness, all become fevers of themselves and venom all their days. The supreme question

> What benefit canst thou or all thy tribe
> Do the great world?

if it is answered 'None,' condemns them all. They are all of 'the dreamer tribe.' And the cancelled lines—

> The poet and the dreamer are distinct,
> Diverse, sheer opposite, antipodes:
> The one pours out a balm upon the world,
> The other vexes it—

amend nothing: they merely confuse; because the word 'dreamer' now bears an utterly different sense. The 'dreamer' here is the mere romanticist. The true poet is indeed the opposite of the romanticist, for the romanticist is he who eats the fruit, but does not drink the draught, and therefore has never entered the great temple. The true dreamers who enter it, and none save true dreamers enter it except to perish, are by the fact of that entrance separated for ever from the romanticists. 'Wonders are no wonders to them,' any more. And for their pain, they have their ultimate reward. They vex themselves, but they do not vex the world; in so far as the world pays heed to the truth which they discover, it is comforted.

So that the passage which has been unwarrantably restored to the text not only makes Keats do an injustice to himself which he refused to do, but instead of making clear the real nature of his thought it confuses it. The clarity it adds is merely superficial: therefore Keats rejected it.

But why, it may be asked, should Keats have made such a confusion? The answer is simple: that he was in great agony and turmoil of soul. His soul was torn with doubts. Was he, in all that he now saw, being deluded? Was he again a mere dreamer, as he had been in his thoughtless days, or was he the solitary man in his own age marked out to behold the eternal truth? Was he only a dreamer, or a seer? Was he pouring out a balm upon the world or vexing it? Remember the last lines of the induction to this poem,

> Whether the dream now purposed to rehearse
> Be poet's or fanatic's will be known
> When this warm scribe my hand is in the grave.

Out of our knowledge of what has followed we can pour the full content of agony of spirit into those lines; and we can understand why the fever of doubt is sometimes so strangely mingled with the calm of revelation in the second *Hyperion.*

The thought of the poem so far has not been easy. We have been compelled to make long pauses over separate incidents of it in order to be sure of their true interpretation; and during these pauses the main thread of poetic argument may easily have been lost. Therefore it may be well to recapitulate the progress of the poet in his dream.

He begins by entering an earthly paradise, wherein he eats eagerly of a delicious food: then he drinks of a strange liquor and falls into a swoon. (That is the first exhilaration of Maiden Thought, and the subsequent darkening of the mind.) He awakes to find all the beauty of the earthly paradise departed: he is in the great temple of consciousness of life. Here, too, as he sees the mighty image in the West and smells the odour of incense, he is filled with a momentary exhilaration, but for a moment only. An awful voice warns him that he must reach the altar steps before the leaves on the altar are burned, or he will die. He struggles toward them, he passes through the full sensation of death, but his foot touches the altar step, and life returns. He asks the veiled priestess why he has been saved. She answers: Because he has had the power to know what it is to die and live again before his fated hour. The reply is dark to him, and he asks again for enlightenment. She answers: Only those can be thus saved to whom the miseries of the world are misery. He asks again: Why then is he alone? She answers: Only the dreamers enter into the Temple of consciousness: the simple lovers of their fellow-men and doers of good have no thought of entering. But the dreamers who enter are recompensed for their extreme suffering by the justice of the universe; they find safety beneath the statue's knees.

That is the point we have reached. The poet is no better than the simple good man, but in reward for his extreme suffering, and for his power to taste the darkness of death, it is granted to him to reach a height reserved for him alone. That 'sweeping denunciation of the imaginative mind' which has been imputed to Keats is not really there. What he does is not to denounce the poet, but to speak through the lips of Moneta the pitiless truth concerning the life of 'a miserable and mighty poet of the human heart.' There is a great difference between truth and denunciation; and the reason why they have been confused is that Keats could not be sentimental about great poets, because he was one. The evidence that he did not regard Moneta's severity as 'a sweeping denunciation of the imaginative mind' is first, the scope and drift of the whole poem, and more patently, the poet's reply to Moneta that immediately follows:

> That I am favour'd for unworthiness,
> By such propitious parley medicin'd
> In sickness not ignoble, I rejoice,
> Aye, and could weep for love of such award.

Her speech is to him 'propitious'; his own sickness 'not ignoble'; and the award fills him with love. Then he asks for yet more enlightenment: Whose is the temple, whose the image, and who is she, the veiled priestess? The answer comes:

> This temple sad and lone
> Is all spar'd from the thunder of a war
> Foughten long since by giant hierarchy
> Against rebellion: this old image here,
> Whose carved features wrinkled as he fell,
> Is Saturn's; I, Moneta, left supreme,
> Sole priestess of his desolation.

But why, it may be asked, is this temple we have called the temple of the consciousness of life suddenly become the temple of Saturn? The answer is in the account of the first conception of *Hyperion* which has already been given.

In all likelihood, when Keats first began the first *Hyperion*, he had no notion, or but the dimmest notion, that Saturn and Mnemosyne would come to have the significance they finally bore for him. But if we read *Hyperion* carefully in the order in which it was written we can watch the divine figures gradually taking on a deeper and deeper significance. The defeat of the old gods by the new comes to mean the whole vast process of the human universe—'creations and destroyings'; Mnemosyne, who forsakes the fallen Titans to watch over the young Apollo, and thus belongs both to the old order and the new, is as it were the immanent consciousness of this vast process, in whose eyes the whole of human destiny can be read; Apollo, the new-born god, becomes a personification of the poetic mind, and through the pain of reading this destiny in the eyes of Mnemosyne he is re-born into the fullness of poetic power. Meanings so profound as these were certainly not in Keats' mind when he first conceived *Hyperion*; they entered it because he belonged to that high race of poets who cannot be satisfied with making beautiful things. All that they think and feel and know and are must be expressed in their poetry: otherwise it is for them an idle and unworthy game. By the time that Keats finished the first *Hyperion* in April 1819, it had become a parable of the beauty and truth of human life and of the birth of the poetic mind.

The *Hyperion* which Keats finished in April 1819 was a different *Hyperion* from that which he had begun in September 1818. When he took it up again, with months of further knowledge of the poetic nature to express, it was not to continue it. Instead he set himself to make the beginning accord with the end; to make the significance with which he had endowed his primaeval myth plain to those who should care to understand it. And he has done so—not perfectly, perhaps, but sufficiently. He has utterly changed what otherwise might have seemed to be merely a classical legend, into a vision of the nature of the universe and the place and destiny of the poetic mind within it. If it is hard to understand, it is not because of Keats' 'decaying powers,' it is because of their agonized concentration upon a theme which was the highest of all themes.

If this has been made plain, there will be no cause for surprise that the great temple of consciousness should be the temple of Saturn, or that Mnemosyne under her sterner name Moneta should be its priestess. The fate of Saturn is a symbol of the destiny of the world, and Moneta is a symbol of the world made conscious of its own vicissitude. Imagine all humanity from the dark backward and abysm of time to the extreme of the indecipherable future as one single being, then Saturn is its body and Moneta its mind. It is the conscious mind of the world which speaks to the poet:

> The sacrifice is done, but not the less
> Will I be kind to thee for thy good will.
> My power, which to me is still a curse,
> Shall be to thee a wonder; for the scenes
> Still swooning vivid through my globed brain,
> With an electral changing misery,
> Thou shalt with these dull mortal eyes behold
> Free from all pain, if wonder pain thee not.

So the final reward of the dreamer, who has venomed all his days because the miseries of the world will not let him rest, is that he is privileged to behold the creations and destroyings which are human life free from all pain. By his good will he has earned this supreme reward. But Moneta is veiled: the poet hears her voice, he has not yet seen her face.

> As near as an immortal's sphered words
> Could to a mother's soften, were these last:
> And yet I had a terror of her robes,
> And chiefly of the veils, that from her brow
> Hung pale, and curtain'd her in mysteries,
> That made my heart too small to hold its blood.
> This saw that Goddess, and with sacred hand
> Parted the veils.
> Then saw I a wan face
> Not pined by human sorrow, but bright-blanch'd
> By an immortal sickness which kills not;
> It works a constant change, which happy death
> Can put no end to; deathwards progressing
> To no death was that visage; it had past
> The lily and the snow; and beyond these
> I must not think now though I saw that face.
> But for her eyes I should have fled away.
> They held me back with a benignant light,
> Soft mitigated by divinest lids
> Half closed, and visionless entire they seemed
> Of all external things. They saw me not
> But, in blank splendour, beam'd like the mild moon,
> Who comforts those she sees not, who knows not
> What eyes are upward cast.

As I would hardly dare to praise those lines, I hardly dare to try to explain them. They belong, I fear, to that order of poetry, which we either understand intuitively or do not understand at all. They contain a vision of the soul of the world, an apprehension of an ultimate reality. No more perfect or more wonderful symbol of the unspeakable truth has ever been imagined. There is unity, there is calm, there is beauty: it is a vision of a single thing. Yet in that single thing what strange elements are combined? Pain, an eternity of pain; change, an eternity of change; death, an eternity of death; terror, yet no terror; instead, measureless benignity; yet this infinite of love touches no person; it is eternal and impersonal, ' comforting those it sees not.' That, if the word be accepted, is a great poet's vision of God—but of a godhead immanent in the changing and enduring reality of the world. The mortal poet has gained a more perfect vision of that which was revealed to Apollo. Then he had seen through a glass darkly, but now face to face.

He asks to be shown 'what things the hollow brain behind enwombed'—

> what high tragedy
> In the dark secret chambers of her skull
> Was acting, that could give so dread a stress
> To her cold lips, and fill with such a light
> Her planetary eyes, and touch her voice
> With such a sorrow.

It is the high tragedy of life itself, or rather its high mystery, which has become (by the power of Keats' creative comprehension) embodied and visible in Moneta. He sees the fallen Saturn,

> Like to the image pedestall'd so high
> In Saturn's temple; then Moneta's voice
> Came brief upon mine ear—' So Saturn sat
> When he had lost his realms '—whereon there grew
> A power within me of enormous ken
> To see as a god sees, and take the depth
> Of things as nimbly as the outward eye
> Can size and shape pervade. The lofty theme
> Of those few words hung vast before my mind
> With half-unravell'd web. I sat myself
> Upon an eagle's watch, that I might see,
> And seeing ne'er forget.

In a sense it is inevitable that all that follows should be an anticlimax. For we have been watching the progress of the young Apollo; he has become as a god, he has died into life, and what his eyes have seen has been revealed to us. Or, to put it otherwise, we have seen the soul of the world, there remains only to see its body—and this body, which is the story of the Titans in the first *Hyperion*, can never be wholly informed with this soul, for the body was apprehended and created before the soul was apprehended and created. Keats would have needed to rewrite the whole of *Hyperion*, to re-perceive it in the light of his new knowledge. He had no time for that. He had time only to see Thea and Saturn together in the light of Moneta's eyes.

Here is the scene as it stood in the first *Hyperion*. Thea's lament over Saturn, which is substantially the same in both versions, has just ended.

> As when, upon a tranced summer night,
> Those green-rob'd senators of mighty woods,
> Tall oaks, branch-charmed by the earnest stars,
> Dream, and so dream all night without a stir,

Save from one gradual solitary gust
Which comes upon the silence, and dies off,
As if the ebbing air had but one wave;
So came these words and went; the while in tears
She touch'd her fair large forehead to the ground,
Just where her falling hair might be outspread
A soft and silken mat for Saturn's feet.
One moon, with alteration slow, had shed
Her silver seasons four upon the night,
And still these two were postured motionless
Like natural sculpture in cathedral cavern;
The frozen god still couchant on the earth,
And the sad goddess weeping at his feet:
Until at length old Saturn lifted up
His faded eyes and saw his kingdom gone,
And all the gloom and sorrow of the place,
And that fair kneeling Goddess. . . .

That beautiful passage is changed in the second *Hyperion* to this:—

As when upon a tranced summer night
Forests, branch-charmed by the earnest stars,
Dream, and so dream all night without a noise,
Save for one gradual solitary gust
Swelling upon the silence; dying off;
As if the ebbing air had but one wave;
So came these words and went; the while in tears
She press'd her fair large forehead to the earth,
Just where her fallen hair might spread in curls,
A soft and silken mat for Saturn's feet.
Long, long these two were postured motionless
Like sculpture builded up upon the grave
Of their own power. A long awful time
I look'd upon them: still they were the same;
The frozen god still bending to the earth
And the sad Goddess weeping at his feet,
Moneta silent. *Without stay or prop,*
But my own weak mortality, I bore
The load of this eternal quietude,
The unchanging gloom and the three fixed shapes
Ponderous upon my senses, a whole moon;
For by my burning brain I measured sure
Her silver seasons shedded on the night,
And every day by day methought I grew
More gaunt and ghostly. Oftentimes I pray'd
Intense, that death would take me from the vale

And all its burthens; gasping with despair
Of change, hour after hour I curs'd myself;
Until old Saturn raised his faded eyes,
And look'd around and saw his kingdom gone,
And all the gloom and sorrow of the place
And that fair kneeling Goddess at his feet.

The change is a remarkable one. The question whether it makes for more beautiful poetry does not concern us: we are concerned only with Keats' intentions. Moneta's promise to the poet has already been forgotten:

The scenes
Still swooning vivid through my globed brain . . .
Thou shalt with these dull mortal eyes behold
Free from all pain, if wonder pain thee not.

So far from being free from pain while he looks on Thea and Saturn, he endures a ghastly agony, so great that he prayed for death and cursed himself. What has happened thus to distort his purposes?

The answer is that Thea and Saturn did in very truth represent to Keats 'the giant agony of the world,' and they represented chiefly the heaped portion of that agony which he himself had to bear. For a moment he could look upon the pattern of life without pain, and see it mirrored in the benignant light of Moneta's eyes, and know the beauty and accept the necessity that it must be so and not otherwise; but he could not remain at that height of comprehension. His own pain broke through his resolution; and in this new vision of Thea and Saturn he forgets all but his pain, his unendurable pain that yet must be endured. Thea and Saturn are life, they are the life of which Keats' own life was part. And if we care to know something of the price which he paid in agonized contemplation of life for the vision of the eternal harmony which he embodied in Moneta, we have only to read the lines in which he was forced to betray his vision and confess his torment. They are an exact description of what Keats endured in August 1819.

Those terrible lines contain the mood in which he was writing the second *Hyperion*.

Oftentimes I pray'd
Intense, that death would take me from the vale
And all its burthens; gasping with despair
Of change, hour after hour I curs'd myself.

In that mood that poem could not be written. The mood betrays the vision. So profound an inward contradiction Keats, being what he was, could not endure in his poetry. Poetry was a revelation of soul-knowledge, and soul-knowledge was an attitude of the complete being. That, on the highest level, is the cause why Keats abandoned his poem. There are many other levels on which the cause can be as truly stated. He was trying to utter in the abstract, what can only be revealed through the concrete. For to accept is to accept, not to declare that you accept; and, for a poet, to see the identity of truth and beauty is to reveal that identity, not to assert that it is there.

CHAPTER XIII

THE RETURN TO SHAKESPEARE

AT some time between Tuesday, 15th September and Sunday, 19th September 1819, a change took place in Keats which involved his abandoning the second *Hyperion* for ever. He became his true and natural self, and, moved to his depths by the sight of a warm stubble-field on his Sunday walk round Winchester, composed the *Ode to Autumn*—pure Keats, uncontaminated and calm, if ever poem was:

Season of mists and mellow fruitfulness,
  Close bosom-friend of the maturing sun;
Conspiring with him how to load and bless
  With fruit the vines that round the thatch-eves run;
To bend with apples the moss'd cottage-trees,
  And fill all fruit with ripeness to the core;
    To swell the gourd, and plump the hazel shells
  With a sweet kernel; to set budding more,
And still more, later flowers for the bees,
Until they think warm days will never cease,
  For Summer has o'erbrimm'd their clammy cells.

Who hath not seen thee oft amid thy store?
  Sometimes whoever seeks abroad may find
Thee sitting careless on a granary floor,
  Thy hair soft-lifted by the winnowing wind;
Or on a half-reap'd furrow sound asleep,
  Drows'd with the fume of poppies, while thy hook
    Spares the next swath and all its twined flowers:
And sometimes like a gleaner thou dost keep
  Steady thy laden head across a brook;
  Or by a cyder-press, with patient look,
    Thou watchest the last oozings hours by hours.

Where are the songs of Spring? Ay, where are they?
  Think not of them, thou hast thy music too,—
While barred clouds bloom the soft-dying day,
  And touch the stubble-plains with rosy hue;
Then in a wailful choir, the small gnats mourn
  Among the river sallows, borne aloft
    Or sinking as the light wind lives or dies;
And full-grown lambs loud bleat from hilly bourn;

Hedge-crickets sing; and now with treble soft
The red-breast whistles from a garden-croft;
And gathering swallows twitter in the skies.

It need not be pointed out with the finger how deeply Shakespearean that perfect poem is—Shakespearean in its rich and opulent serenity of mood, Shakespearean in its lovely and large periodic movement, like the drawing of a deep, full breath. This is not that majestic marshalling of design which marks the *constructed* period of Milton; this is natural and spontaneous poetic power. And it need not be pointed out with the finger how close and intimate is the relation of the poem to the sonnet with which Keats had emerged from the agony of April. Then, at the moment that he gave up the first *Hyperion*, he wrote:

How fever'd is that man who cannot look
Upon his mortal days with temperate blood;
Who vexes all the leaves of his Life's book
And robs his fair name of its maidenhood.
It is as if the rose should pluck herself
Or the ripe plum finger its misty bloom
As if a clear Lake meddling with itself
Should cloud its pureness with a muddy gloom.
But the rose leaves herself upon the Briar
For winds to kiss and grateful Bees to feed;
And the ripe plumb still wears its dim attire;
The undisturbed Lake has crystal space—
Why then should man, teasing the world for grace,
Spoil his salvation by a fierce miscreed?

At the moment that he finally abandoned the second *Hyperion*, he wrote the *Ode to Autumn*. It is the perfect and unforced utterance of the truth contained in the magic words: ' Ripeness is all.'

To this victory Keats had been brought, it seems, by an addition to his hopeless burden of misery. The chance of making money by Brown's play was lost; his brother was on the verge of ruin. Why the mere multiplication of catastrophe should have led Keats to this inward triumph no man can explain. We should have to go to the New Testament, and there we should find not an explanation but a statement of the mystery. Suffice it that these things are so. But we can declare that a necessary condition of that inward victory was that Keats faced the final disaster alone. Brown was not with him: Brown was not there to urge, by spoken or unspoken word, that he should put Fanny out of his mind and heart; or to tell him that he need not face the world, for he, Brown, would provide—at five per cent. interest, and half-profits.

Keats faced the crisis alone. He touched, for an instant, the bottom of despair: it speaks in his letter to Fanny. Then, alone in Winchester, he emerged out of it—a calm, confident and happy man, secure of his purpose and of himself. In these crucial days of change between 15th September and 19th September, he began a letter to his brother. We can almost watch the change. On 17th September, when he begins to write, the process has already begun. He gives George an account of what he has done towards raising money on his sudden journey to London, and continues:

> We are certainly in a very low estate—I say we, for I am in such a situation, that were it not for the assistance of Brown and Taylor, I must be as badly off as a man can be. I could not raise any sum by the promise of any poem, no, not by the mortgage of my intellect. . . . I have passed my time in reading, writing, and fretting—the last I intend to give up, and stick to the other two. . . . Your wants will be a fresh spur to me. . . . I feel I can bear real ills better than imaginary ones. Whenever I find myself growing vapourish, I rouse myself, wash, put on a clean shirt, brush my hair and clothes, tie my shoe-strings neatly, and in fact adonize as if I were going out. Then, all clean and comfortable, I sit down to write.

On the next day (18th September) his cheerfulness has grown:

> With my inconstant disposition it is no wonder that this morning, amid all our bad times and misfortunes, I should feel so alert and well-spirited. It is because my hopes are ever paramount to my despair. I have been reading over a part of a short poem I have composed lately, called *Lamia*, and I am certain there is that sort of fire in it that must take hold of people in some way.

The conception of 'the poisonous suffrage of the public' is thus completely abandoned; and Keats goes on to give a vivid and beautiful and humorous description of the deserted streets of Winchester at night-time.

On the next day (19th September), he composed the *Ode to Autumn*. On the 20th he copied into his letter *The Eve of St. Mark* which he had evidently been revising. On the 21st he writes:

> Some think I have lost that poetical ardour and fire 'tis said I once had. The fact is, perhaps I have; but, instead of that, I hope I shall substitute a more thoughtful and quiet power. I am more frequently now contented to read and think, but now and then haunted with ambitious thoughts. Quieter in my pulse, improved in my digestion, exerting myself against vexing speculations,

scarcely content to write the best verses for the fever they leave behind. I want to compose without this fever. I hope I one day shall.

Immediately after that he tells of the crucial literary decision involved in the change of being that was taking place within him:

I shall never become attached to a foreign idiom, so as to put it into my writings. The Paradise Lost, though so fine in itself, is a corruption of our language. It should be kept as it is, unique, a curiosity, a beautiful and grand curiosity, the most remarkable production of the world; a northern dialect accommodating itself to Greek and Latin inversions and intonations. The purest English, I think—or what ought to be the purest—is Chatterton's. The language had existed long enough to be entirely incorrupted of Chaucer's Gallicisms, and still the old words are used. Chatterton's language is entirely northern. I prefer the native music of it to Milton's, cut by feet. I have but lately stood on my guard against Milton. Life to him would be death to me. Miltonic verse cannot be written, but is [as?] the verse of art. I wish to devote myself to another verse alone.

At this point Keats broke off his letter to his brother, to tell Reynolds also of his decision:

I have been at different times so happy as not to know what weather it was—No I will not copy a parcel of verses. I always somehow associate Chatterton with autumn. He is the purest writer in the English Language. He has no French idiom or particles, like Chaucer—'tis genuine English idiom in English words. I have given up *Hyperion*—there were too many Miltonic inversions in it—Miltonic verse cannot be written but in an artful, or rather, artist's humour. I wish to give myself up to other sensations. English ought to be kept up. It may be interesting to you to pick out some lines from *Hyperion*, and put a mark + to the false beauty proceeding from art, and one || to the true voice of feeling. Upon my soul 'twas imagination—I cannot make the distinction—Every now and then there is a Miltonic intonation—But I cannot make the distinction properly. The fact is, I must take a walk: for I am writing a long letter to George: and have been employed at it all the morning.

It may seem strange to some, and disconcerting to the main argument of this narrative, that Chatterton should be the hero of these two important passages, and not Shakespeare. The truth of the matter is briefly this: it is possible for a poet to say that he will write Miltonics;

it is not possible for him to say he will write Shakespeareans. It is bound up in the very nature of Shakespeare's poetry that it cannot be imitated. The poetry of Milton can; as Keats said, ' it cannot be written save in an artful, or rather an artist's, humour.' True poetry was to Keats a spontaneous expression of the complete man.

Nevertheless, though the deep thought of his mind was even at this moment upon Shakespeare, as will be made abundantly clear by the sequel, Chatterton was by no means a mere figurehead to Keats. Chatterton did represent the Shakespearean quality to Keats, in a form which he could fairly claim to be his own. The relation in which, for Keats, Chatterton stood to Shakespeare is established beyond doubt by the original dedication to *Endymion*, which Keats suppressed (together with the original preface) on the advice of Reynolds:

INSCRIBED,
WITH EVERY FEELING OF PRIDE AND REGRET
AND WITH ' A BOWED MIND,'
TO THE MEMORY OF
THE MOST ENGLISH OF POETS EXCEPT SHAKESPEARE,
THOMAS CHATTERTON

And the same relation was indicated, even earlier, in the *Epistle to George Felton Matthew.*

> Lend thy aid
> To find a place where I may greet the maid—
> Where we may soft humanity put on
> And sit, and rhyme and think on Chatterton;
> And that warm-hearted Shakespeare sent to meet him
> Four laurelled spirits heavenward to entreat him.

It might be said that Keats regarded Chatterton as his peer, and Chatterton and himself together as fellow-protégés of Shakespeare.

' English must be kept up '—' the most English of poets except Shakespeare.' It is the ' Englishness ' of Chatterton to which Keats now, as ever, does honour. To our modern minds Keats himself is become ' the most English of poets except Shakespeare '; and it is usual to dismiss Chatterton as a sham mediaevalist. Sham mediaevalism, in this exact and philological age, is intolerable; but these scientific prejudices will pass, and Chatterton then be once more recognized for the poet of genius that he was. Let us put the scruples of philology out of our minds and read such lines as these, which may have been vaguely in Keats' mind when he wrote the *Ode to Autumn*, and of which he may have been dreaming when he told Reynolds: ' I always somehow associate Chatterton with Autumn ':

When Autumn black and sun-burned do appear
With his gold hand gilding the falling leaf
Bringing up winter to fulfil the year
Bearing upon his back the riped sheaf;
When all the hills with woody seed is white;
When levin-fires and lemes do meet from far the sight;
When the fair apple, ruddy as even-sky,
Do bend the tree unto the fructile ground:
When juicy pears and berries of black dye
Do dance in air, and call the eyes around;
Then, be the even foul, or even fair,
Methinks my heartes joy is steynced with some care.

Is it not limpid and lovely? Does it not indeed recall, in its golden purity, the early Shakespeare? It is for such things as these—and they are many in Chatterton—that Keats loved Chatterton, and preferred ' his native music to Milton's cut by feet.'

This return to the Shakespearean ideal, which was manifested in the province of pure literature by the abandonment of the second *Hyperion* and the Miltonic influence, was inevitably a movement of Keats' whole being. Without looking for evidence, knowing what we have learned concerning Keats' poetic nature and the nature of his poetry, we could guess that this decision had many repercussions. But we are absolved from conjecture: the evidence exists, and is palpable. On the same day (22nd September) that Keats wrote to his brother that life to Milton would be death to him, and to Reynolds that he had given up the second *Hyperion* because ' there were too many Miltonic inversions in it ' and had written the *Ode to Autumn*, he wrote also to Woodhouse, to Dilke and to Brown. Four of these letters we have complete; of that to Brown we possess only what Brown thought fit to communicate. Nevertheless, the treasure is inestimable. Five letters written on this day of days! It is as though Destiny herself intended that at the supreme moment of his poetic life the whole process of Keats' mind and soul should be plain to posterity.

Let the most ' literary ' be considered first: it is the letter to Woodhouse. On his flying visit to town on 10th September, in order to raise money for George, Keats had called on Woodhouse (who was the friend and literary adviser of Taylor the publisher) to discuss the question whether he could publish a new volume of poems with any prospect of financial success. Woodhouse preserved a faithful note of the conversation. Keats proposed a volume composed of *Lamia* and *The Eve of St. Agnes*. Woodhouse said: ' Why not *Isabella* also? ' Keats replied that he could not bear the poem now, and that he thought it ' mawkish.' After reading *Lamia* to Woodhouse, Keats discussed *The Eve of St. Agnes*, which he had been revising just before, and he shocked Woodhouse by insisting that by the 'solution sweet' he meant that Porphyro and Madeline enjoyed the physical consummation of their love. And he shocked Woodhouse and later critics also by having changed the full romantic closing lines—

> The beadsman, after thousand aves told,
> For aye unsought for slept among his ashes cold—

into the slightly cynical:

> The beadsman stiffen'd twixt a sigh and laugh,
> Ta'en sudden from his beads by one weak little cough.

That the change is so painfully discordant as some critics imagine will scarcely be admitted by those who feel a profound repugnance to the tendency of English criticism to paint Keats *à la Greuze*, and to force him, in defiance of all truth, to remain in that condition of adolescent romanticism out of which he so magnificently fought his way. But, in any case, Keats did well to restore the original, as he did. *The Eve of St. Agnes* was written in a mood of comparatively happy confidence in new-born love: from this mood he had been most tragically driven: but it was better to do as he did, and leave the poem wholly true to the temper in which it was conceived.

It is this conversation with Woodhouse which Keats takes up in his letter to him on 22nd September, after copying the *Ode to Autumn* for him.

> After revolving certain circumstances in my Mind, chiefly connected with the late american letter—I have determined to take up my abode in a cheap Lodging in Town, and get employment in some of our elegant Periodical Works. I will no longer live upon hopes. I shall carry my plan into execution speedily. I shall live in Westminster—from which a walk to the British Museum will be noisy and muddy—but otherwise pleasant enough. I shall inquire of Hazlitt how the figures of the market stand. O that I could do something agrestunal, pleasant, fountain-voic'd—not plague you with unconnected nonsense—But things won't leave me *alone*. I shall be in Town as soon as either of you. I only wait for an answer from Brown: if he receives mine which is now a very moot point.
>
> I will give you a few reasons why I shall persist in not publishing *The Pot of Basil*. It is too smokeable. I can get it smoak'd at the Carpenters shaving chimney much more easily. There is too much inexperience of line,* and simplicity of knowledge in it—which might do very well after one's death, but not while one is alive. There are very few would look to the reality. I intend to use

more finesse with the Public. It is possible to write fine things which cannot be laugh'd at in any way. *Isabella* is what I should call were I a reviewer a weak-sided 'Poem' with an amusing sober-sadness about it. Not that I do not think Reynolds and you are quite right about it—it is enough for me. But this will not do to be public. If I may say so, in my dramatic capacity I enter fully into the feeling; but in Propria Persona I should be apt to quiz it myself. There is no objection of this kind to *Lamia*—A good deal to *St. Agnes Eve*—only not so glaring. Would as I say I could write you something sylvestian. But I have no time to think: I am an otiosus-peroccupatus man.

'A weak-sided poem with an amusing sober-sadness about it.' That is Keats' humorously exaggerated, but sane and mature judgement on what has been strangely declared to be his finest long poem. Keats is adamant in rejecting his own romantic dreams. They belong to the past. *The Eve of St. Agnes* will pass muster, *Lamia* will do. The order in which Keats ranks his own long poems is the order of the life-experience contained in them, it is also the order of their approximation to drama. Whether this judgement of his will commend itself to everyone, is doubtful; yet surely it is beyond challenge. Keats, on this day, when he rejected Milton and returned to Shakespeare, was a man who knew his own business as a poet superlatively well; and I should not care to be included among those who know better than Keats himself the nature of his genius and the excellence of his poetry.

But no less important than this sane and considered judgement of his own poetry, and an integral part of the same act of soul which was expressed in it, is Keats' declared intention to make a living by journalism. He enlarges on this in his letter to Dilke, whom he asks to look for a room for him in Westminster. 'Whatever I take to for the time,' he begins, 'I cannot leave off in a hurry; letter writing is the go now; I have consumed a quire at the least.' Never, so far as we can tell, was there such a letter-writing day as this in all Keats' history: and the letter-writing was necessary. Keats had taken a vital decision which involved, in one way and another, his relations to all his friends.

I have written to Brown on the subject (he says to Dilke) and can but go over the same Ground with you in a very short time. . . . It concerns a resolution I have taken to acquire something by temporary writing in periodical works. You must agree with me how unwise it is to keep feeding upon hopes, which depending so much on the state of temper and imagination, appear gloomy or bright, near or afar off, just as it happens. Now an act has three parts—to act, to do, and to perform—I mean I should *do* something for my immediate welfare. Even if I am swept away like a spider from a drawing-room, I am determined to spin—homespun anything for sale. Yea, I will traffic. Anything but Mortgage my Brain to Blackwood. I am determined not to lie like a dead lump. . . . I would willingly have recourse to other means. I cannot; I am fit for nothing but literature. Wait for the issue of this Tragedy? No—there cannot be greater uncertainties east, west, north or south than concerning dramatic composition. How many months must I wait! Had I not better begin to look about me now? If better events supersede this necessity what harm will be done? I have no trust whatever on Poetry. I don't wonder at it—the marvel is to me how people read so much of it. I think you will see the reasonableness of my plan. To forward it I purpose living in cheap Lodging in Town, that I may be within the reach of books and information, of which there is here a plentiful lack. If I can [find] any place tolerably comfortable, I will settle myself and fag until I can afford to buy Pleasure—which if I never can afford, I must go without. . . .

I ask your opinion and yet I must say to you as to him, Brown, that if you have anything to say against it I shall be as obstinate and heady as a Radical. . . . I hope sincerely I shall be able to put a Mite of help to the Liberal side of the Question before I die. . . . A most extraordinary mischance has befallen two letters I wrote Brown—one from London whither I was obliged to go on business for George; the other from this place since my return. I can't make it out. I am excessively sorry for it. I shall hear from Brown and from you almost together, for I have sent him a Letter to-day. . . .

The decision is clear: Keats is going to accept the world, not by compromising with it, but by doing whatever he can find to do in journalism with a good conscience. But the end of the letter shows clearly that Brown is the most obstinate friend with whom he has to deal. He had written Brown a letter immediately from London, and then a second: now, worried at receiving no reply, he has written yet a third. He supposes the two previous letters have gone astray. One cannot help wondering whether Brown purposely kept silence over a decision which meant that Keats was to live in complete independence of him. At all events, Keats plainly foresaw that the chief difficulties would come from Brown.

Now (says Keats in this third letter to Brown) I am going to enter on the subject of self. It is quite time I should set myself doing something, and live no longer on hopes. I have never yet exerted myself. I am getting into an idle-minded, vicious way of life, almost content to live upon others. In no period of my life have I acted with any self-will but in throwing up the apothecary profession. That I do not repent of. Look at Reynolds, if he was not in the law, he would be acquiring, by his abilities, something towards his support. My occupation is entirely literary: I will do so, too. I will write, on the liberal side of the question, for whoever will pay me. I have not known yet what it is to be diligent. I purpose living in town in a cheap lodging, and endeavouring, for a beginning, to get the theatricals of some paper. When I can afford to compose deliberate poems, I will. I shall be in expectation of an answer to this. Look on my side of the question. I am convinced I am right. . . .

I had got into a habit of looking towards you as a help in all difficulties. This very habit would be the parent of idleness and difficulties. You will see it as a duty I owe myself to break the neck of it. I do nothing for my subsistence—make no exertion. At the end of another year you shall applaud me, not for verses, but for conduct. If you live at Hampstead next winter—I like Fanny Brawne and I cannot help it. On that account I had better not live there. While I have some immediate cash, I had better settle myself quietly, and fag on as others do. . . . I shall be expecting anxiously an answer from you. If it does not arrive in a few days this will have miscarried, and I shall come straight to [Bedhampton?] . . .

We have no authentic record of Brown's answer. If we were to take Brown's word for it, as given many years after to Monckton Milnes, 'he gave every encouragement to these designs, and only remonstrated against the project on account of the pain he would himself suffer from the privation of Keats' society, and from the belief that the scheme of life would not be successful.' Unfortunately, Brown is not quite to be trusted, and the scrap of Keats' fourth letter to him, written on the next day (23rd September), shows that he opposed the project to such an extent that Keats did not post his letter to Dilke. Brown returned to Winchester very shortly after. Keats stood his ground, and on 1st October wrote to Dilke once more, asking him to find rooms for him in Westminster. The opening of this letter to Dilke shows clearly that the previous one to him was never sent.*

In that last week of September, when Brown had returned to Winchester, there must have been obstinate argument between the two friends. But Keats behaved as he had promised Brown in his letter of 22nd September. 'If you have anything to gainsay I shall be even as the deaf adder which stoppeth her ears.' On 1st October he finally confirmed his decision, and wrote post-haste to Dilke to get him rooms.

Yet in all these decisions, which were indeed but one decision—to abandon Miltonics, to make terms with the world, to 'fag as the others do ' in journalism—there must have been implicit a decision concerning his love for Fanny Brawne. Of that decision we have no word, save the one sentence in his letter to Brown: ' I like Fanny Brawne, and I cannot help it.' Therefore, he says, ' I had better not live in Hampstead.' It would call for an almost sublime confidence in one's own powers of penetration to declare positively whether or not Keats meant that argument seriously. His other reasons for leaving Hampstead were peremptory and sufficient. Hampstead was in those days in the country: Keats was to become a working journalist, and therefore had to live in Town. Perhaps it was that he saw an additional advantage in being thus kept away from Fanny; perhaps he saw in it an additional argument for parting from Brown. For my own part, I incline to believe that the separation from Brown and Brown's influence was his preponderant motive, and that Keats felt he must be, at all costs, completely independent.

At the same time he finally admitted to himself that he was in love with Fanny Brawne, and that it was useless to attempt to change the course of nature. He gave up the effort to put her out of his life. He would

> let determined things to destiny
> Hold unbewailed their way.

And perhaps that was all that was in his mind. He seems to have put out of it all thought of what would happen—those were ' the imaginary troubles ' which the real ones had driven out. He had ' given up fretting.' He submitted himself, in regard to his love, to what was to be.

Keats remained in Winchester for a fortnight after all these vital decisions had been taken on 22nd September. We have two letters written during those days of calm: one the continuation of his journal-letter to George, the other to Haydon. In the first we find him clearly re-asserting, in a discussion of Dilke, his Shakespearean ideal of character.

> Brown complained very much in his letter to me of the great alteration the disposition of Dilke has undergone. He thinks of nothing but political justice and his boy. Now, the first political duty a man ought to have a mind to is the happiness of his friends. I wrote Brown a comment on the subject, wherein I explained what I thought of Dilke's character, which resolved itself into this conclusion that Dilke is a man who cannot feel he has a personal identity unless he has made up his mind about everything. The only means of strengthening one's intellect is to make up one's mind about nothing—to let the mind be a thoroughfare for all thoughts, not a select party. The genus is not scarce in population:

> all the stubborn arguers you meet with are of the same brood. They never begin upon a subject they have not preresolved on. They want to hammer their nail into you, and if you turn the point, still they think you wrong. Dilke will never come at the truth as long as he lives, because he is always trying it. He is a Godwin Methodist.

That is an exact re-assertion of the ideal of Negative Capability which Keats had first seized in January 1818 as the central trait of Shakespeare's character; he had seized it in the course of a " disquisition ' with this same Dilke.

His letter to Haydon of 3rd October shows more obviously, yet perhaps less strikingly, the completeness of his return to the Shakespearean ideal.

> I purpose to settle in Town and work my way with the rest. I hope I shall never be so silly as to injure my health and industry for the future by speaking, writing or fretting about my non-estate. I have no quarrel, I assure you, of so weighty a nature with the world, on my own account as I have on yours. I have done nothing—except for the amusement of a few people who refine upon their feelings till anything in the ununderstandable way will go down with them—people predisposed for sentiment. I have no cause to complain because I am certain anything really fine will in these days be felt. I have no doubt that if I had written *Othello* I should have been cheered by as good a mob as Hunt.

The last wall of the tower of ivory has fallen flat. In barely more than a month Keats has moved to the polar opposite of the attitude expressed in his letter to Reynolds of 25th August, when his heart was ' distended with Pride and Obstinacy,' and he passionately ' refused the poisonous suffrage of a public.' Now, ' anything really fine will in these days be felt,' and if he had written *Othello*, he would have been cheered by as good a crowd as that which welcomed the popular hero of the Manchester Martyrs—it was said that 300,000 people took part in that demonstration.

If this letter alone is not enough to convince others that Shakespeare had triumphed in Keats' soul, his next letter dealing with his definite poetic intentions is surely decisive. It was written six weeks later (17th November) to Taylor the publisher. The tone is subdued, for much had happened during those six weeks.

> My dear Taylor—I have come to a determination not to publish anything I have now ready written; but for all that to publish a Poem before long and that I hope to make a fine one. As the marvellous is the most enticing and the surest guarantee of harmonious

numbers, I have been endeavouring to persuade myself to untether Fancy and let her manage for herself. I and myself cannot agree about this at all. Wonders are no wonders to me. I am more at home amongst Men and women. I would rather read Chaucer than Ariosto.* The little dramatic skill I may as yet have however badly it might show in a Drama, would I think be sufficient for a a Poem. I wish to diffuse the colouring of *St. Agnes Eve* throughout a poem in which Character and Sentiment would be the figures to such drapery. Two or three such Poems, if God should spare me, written in the course of the next six years, would be a famous gradus ad Parnassum altissimum. I mean they would nerve me up to the writing of a few fine Plays—my greatest ambition—when I do feel ambitious. I am sorry to say that is very seldom. The subject we have once or twice talked of appears a promising one. The Earl of Leicester's history. I am this morning reading Holingshed's Elizabeth. . . . I will endeavour to set myself selfishly to work on this Poem that is to be.

In the first place, Keats has now made up his mind not to publish anything he has written since *Endymion*—neither *Isabella* nor *The Eve of St. Agnes*, nor the *Odes*, nor *Lamia*, nor *Hyperion*, recast or original. That he did publish most of these, and that in a few weeks' time he was to be busy revising them, is of no account. He published them because he was penniless and needed money, and Taylor was willing to pay him (and pay him generously) for them. Keats was an absolutely honest man; he was completely devoid of the mock modesty of the ordinary author. When, in August 1820, he sent Shelley his *Lamia* volume and told him in the covering letter that 'most of the poems in the volume would never have been published but for the sake of gain,' he was speaking the exact truth. In his nonestate those poems were all he had to sell, and he sold them.

He wanted, he had said in his letters of 22nd September, abandoning Miltonics, 'to devote himself to another verse alone'—'to other sensations.' 'English,' he had also said, 'must be kept up.' In this letter he puts firmly aside the notion of writing yet another romantic tale. His dæmon will not suffer it. Wonders are no wonders to him; there is no romance in the romantic. He is more at home with men and women. He would like to write a drama; but his dramatic skill is not sufficient: so he will content himself with the next best thing, a dramatic poem. And he tries to give Taylor an idea of the kind of dramatic poem he will write.

It is a poem wherein the characters and psychology of real men and women are to be suffused with the rich colouring of *The Eve of St. Agnes*. The hint at Chaucer—'I would rather read Chaucer than Ariosto'—will enable us to make more real to our imagination the poem which Keats has in mind; for Chaucer's *Troilus and*

Cressida has this combination of psychological truth and sensuous colouring. ' Wonders were no wonders ' to Chaucer: the real world of men and women was marvellous and beautiful enough for him. But the most perfect embodiment of the ideal which Keats is trying to describe, is in that yet higher form—the drama—towards which he was steadily aiming: it is Shakespeare's *Antony and Cleopatra.* That play contains, in the highest degree of perfection, the harmony of sensuous opulence and psychological truth which Keats wished to achieve in his dramatic poem. Writing to Haydon a year and a half before (10th April 1818) Keats had said: 'When a Schoolboy the abstract Idea I had of an heroic painting—was what I cannot describe. I saw it somewhat sideways, large, prominent, round and colour'd with magnificence—somewhat like the feel I have of *Anthony and Cleopatra.*' A narrative dramatic poem, coloured with this same magnificence, endued with the same sensuous solidity, and as deeply true to the adult experience of mankind—such was the poem Keats had in mind, two or three of them (if God should spare him) during the next six years, which should nerve him up finally to the writing of a few fine plays.

Lest the phrase, ' the colouring of *St. Agnes Eve,*' should be merely a phrase to us, lest we should have any doubt that, if God had spared him, Keats would have performed what he promised himself, it is as well to have some verses of that poem fresh in our minds.

Then by the bed-side, where the faded moon
Made a dim, silver twilight, soft he set
A table, and, half-anguish'd, threw thereon
A cloth of woven crimson, gold and jet:—
O for some drowsy Morphean amulet!
The boisterous, midnight, festive clarion,
The kettle-drum, and far-heard clarinet,
Affray his ears, though but in dying tone:—
The hall door shuts again, and all the noise is gone.

And still she slept an azure-lidded sleep,
In blanched linen, smooth and lavender'd,
While he from forth the closet brought a heap
Of candied apple, quince, and plum, and gourd;
With jellies soother than the creamy curd,
And lucent syrops, tinct with cinnamon;
Manna and dates, in argosy transferr'd
From Fez; and spiced dainties, every one,
From silken Samarcand to cedar'd Lebanon.

These delicates he heap'd with glowing hand
On golden dishes and in baskets bright

Of wreathed silver: sumptuous they stand
In the retired quiet of the night,
Filling the chilly room with perfume light.—
'And now my love, my seraph fair, awake.
Thou art my heaven, and I thine eremite:
Open thine eyes, for meek St. Agnes' sake,
Or I shall drowse beside thee, so my soul doth ache.'

For harmony of emotional effect, for subtlety of variation, for sensuous opulence, no English narrative poem has ever surpassed *The Eve of St. Agnes*. In a sense it is like *Venus and Adonis*; yet how different! It comes from a maturer being. When Shakespeare had reached a like maturity of being, he had also reached a mastery of dramatic skill. He was not writing narrative poems, but 'fine plays'; he was at the stage where he could coin the natural riches of his soul into a *Midsummer Night's Dream* and a *Much Ado*. Keats was not yet, and knew he was not yet, at such a point; but it seems to me inevitable that he would have attained it.

In the meantime he had made another attempt at drama. The manuscript of the fragment *King Stephen* is dated November 1819; probably the fragment was abandoned just before he wrote the letter to Taylor, and was Keats' own proof to himself that his dramatic skill would 'show poorly in a drama.' These 170 lines of an abandoned play are more like the Shakespearean parts of those early histories that indiscriminately bear his name, than anything ever written by another hand than Shakespeare's. Listen to these various lines:

Now we may lift our bruisèd vizors up
And take the flattering freshness of the air. . . .

the fortunate star
Of boisterous Chester whose fell truncheon now
Points level to the goal of victory. . . .

He shames our victory. His valour still
Keeps elbow-room amid our eager swords
And holds our bladed falchions all aloof. . . .

What weapons has the lion but himself?

Come on! Farewell, my kingdom, and all hail
Thou superb, plum'd and helmeted renown,
All hail! I would not truck this brilliant day
To rule in Pylos with a Nestor's beard.

In the last the precise critic would detect reminiscences both of *Othello* and *Henry V*; it is more important to recognize the indefinable vigour and vividness which justifies reminiscence, and the evident ease with which a scene so full of movement was written. Nevertheless, Keats abandoned *King Stephen*. It was not so much that his dramatic skill would have failed him, as that Keats in his own inward life had passed far beyond the phase at which Shakespeare was touching up historical plays. Keats had been plunged, at an age when men are just leaving the university, into a life-experience akin to that of Shakespeare's tragic period. If he was to write plays, they would have needed to be plays of the order of *Hamlet*, *Othello*, *Macbeth* and *Lear*. That was impossible. Keats had not yet such command of language, and he had not yet (as he frankly told Taylor) enough dramatic skill. Therefore, pending the acquisition of such skill, he proposed to write a dramatic poem, 'and that a fine one.'

The poem was not written; probably it was not even begun. There was no time. The rest of this year 1819 was chiefly occupied in revising his rejected poems for the press. Keats had had to accept Taylor's offer, for his plan of making a living by journalism had collapsed.

Almost immediately after returning to London, Keats went to Hampstead to see Fanny Brawne. He saw her, and on the day following he wrote her this:

> My sweet Girl,
>
> I am living to-day in yesterday: I was in a complete fascination all day. I feel myself at your mercy. Write me ever so few lines and tell me you will never for ever be less kind to me than yesterday.—You dazzled me. There is nothing in the world so bright and delicate. When Brown came out with that seemingly true story against me last night, I felt it would be death to me if you ever had believed it—though against anyone else I would muster up my obstinacy. Before I knew Brown could disprove it I was for the moment more miserable. When shall we pass a day alone? I have had a thousand kisses, for which with my whole soul I thank love—but if you should deny me the thousand and first—'twould put me to the proof how great a misery I could live through. If you should ever carry your threat yesterday into execution—believe me 'tis not my pride, my vanity, or any petty passion would torment me—really 'twould hurt my heart—I could not bear it....

At this moment he wrote the sonnet:

> The day is gone, and all its sweets are gone!
> Sweet voice, sweet lips, soft hand and softer breast,
> Warm breath, tranced whisper, tender semi-tone,

Bright eyes, accomplish'd shape, and langu'rous waist!
Vanish'd unseasonably at shut of eve,
When the dusk holiday—or holinight
Of fragrant-curtain'd love begins to weave
The woof of darkness thick, for hid delight;
Faded the flower and all its budded charms,
Faded the sight of beauty from my eyes,
Faded the shape of beauty from my arms,
Faded the voice, warmth, whiteness, paradise—
But as I've read love's missal through to-day,
He'll let me sleep, seeing I fast and pray.

But the precarious happiness lasted only for a brief space. Keats loved, but he could not trust, Fanny Brawne; he could not live without her, but he felt that she could live without him. On 13th October he wrote to her that he could not go on with his work for thinking of her. He must write to her in order to get her out of his mind.

> Upon my Soul I can think of nothing else. The time is passed when I had power to advise and warn you against the unpromising morning of my life. My love has made me selfish. I cannot exist without you. I am forgetful of everything but seeing you again—my Life seems to stop there—I see no further. You have absorb'd me. I have a sensation at the present moment as though I were dissolving—I should be exquisitely miserable without the hope of soon seeing you. I should be afraid to separate myself far from you. My sweet Fanny, will your heart never change? My love, will it? . . . Do not threat me even in jest. I have been astonished that Men could die Martyrs for religion—I have shudder'd at it. I shudder no more—I could be martyr'd for my Religion—Love is my religion—I could die for that. . . . You have ravish'd me away by a Power I cannot resist; and yet I could resist till I saw you; and even since I have seen you I have endeavoured often 'to reason against the reasons of my Love.' I can do that no more—the pain would be too great. My love is selfish. I cannot breathe without you. . . .

Yet it was not wholly true that he could resist his love until he saw her again. He had resisted, to the very utmost of his power, until the tension of his being became unbearable: until he knew that, if he resisted any more, all that he was, as man and poet, would die. At the same moment he that knew 'life to Milton would be death to him,' he knew also that 'he liked Fanny Brawne and could not help it.' His Heart had to be his Mind's Bible. When he came to London, he came to accept his destiny, and his destiny was love and death. To live, he had to love, and by loving he died.

On 19th October the inevitable decision was taken. He wrote to tell Fanny that he was coming to live in Hampstead.

> I must impose chains on myself. I shall be able to do nothing. I should like to cast the die for Love or death. I have no Patience with anything else—if you ever intend to be cruel to me as you say in jest now but perhaps may sometimes be in earnest, be so now—and I will—my mind is in a tremble, and I cannot tell what I am writing.

If I have failed to make it clear that those who say Keats should have resisted this love, are saying nothing else than that Keats should have resisted his deepest and truest being, and that he should have denied his own genius and betrayed his own ideal, I have failed in everything. Keats, in order to be Keats, and not some futile phantasm of our romantic imagination, *had* to submit to this love. That was his destiny as a man and as a poet. He was of such a kind that he could not refuse it. He accepted it; he passed a year of agony, and he died.

Whether he need have died, who can say? Who can say whether other great men, who have followed the deepest truth within them to agony and the grave, need have died? They died; and their destinies, and the splendour and beauty and terror of their destinies is manifest in their deaths. Not otherwise with Keats. As surely as any hero of humanity, he died for the truth that was in him.

Fanny Brawne could have saved him? Perhaps she could. But only by being other than she was. The agonized sonnet which Keats wrote to her at this time contains the truth:

> I cry your mercy—pity—love!—aye, love!
> Merciful love that tantalises not,
> One-thoughted, never-wandering, guileless love,
> Unmask'd, and being seen without a blot!
> O! let me have thee whole,—all—all—be mine!
> That shape, that fairness, that sweet minor zest
> Of love, your kiss,—those hands, those eyes divine,
> That warm, white, lucent, million-pleasured breast,—
> Yourself—your soul—in pity give me all,
> Withhold no atom's atom or I die,
> Or living on, perhaps, your wretched thrall,
> Forget, in the mist of idle misery,
> Life's purposes,—the palate of my mind
> Losing its gust, and my ambition blind.

'Withhold no atom's atom or I die.' Had Fanny Brawne given herself to love as Keats gave himself, wholly and for ever, Keats' history would have been different. Doubtless, he would have died young, but five or six, ten or a dozen years might have been added to his life—another poetic life-time at the least. But now he burned out like a rush-light; he was utterly consumed. His agony of spirit made smooth the way for the devastation of his body.

Fanny Brawne killed him. That is true; but it is a partial truth. Fanny Brawne was what she was, and what she was Keats knew. He had tried to cut her out of his heart, and that had come near to killing his soul; so he opened his heart to her again, and his body was killed. It was better, far better, that Keats should have suffered his body to die than his soul. Keats had the courage of the great man that he was: he bore his destiny to the end. And for that act of heroism a perfection of beauty and truth shines out of his life for ever.

Τά γε μὰν λίνα πάντα λελοίπει
Ἐκ Μοιρᾶν, χὡ Δάφνις ἔβα ῥόον· ἔκλυσε δίνα
Τὸν Μοίσαις φίλον ἄνδρα, τὸν οὐ Νύμφαισιν ἀπεχθῆ. *

CHAPTER XIV

THE END

EARLY in February 1820 came the haemorrhage which was the beginning of the end. It was not inevitable, in any ordinary sense of inevitability. Keats' body was weakened by the torments he had endured since his return to London. The seeds of disease had been there for many months; in this well-prepared land they sprouted and flourished. Keats wrote to his old friend, Jem Rice, shortly after the haemorrhage, a letter describing his moods since his return to London in October:

> I cannot answer you on your own ground with respect to those haunting and deformed thoughts and feelings you speak of. When I have been, or supposed myself in health, I have had my share of them, especially within the last year. I may say, that for six months before I was taken ill I had not passed a tranquil day. Either that gloom overspread me, or I was suffering under some passionate feeling, or if I turned to versify, that acerbated the poison of either sensation. The beauties of nature had lost their power over me.

Such had been Keats' temper since his return to London. And now his poetic life was over. Never, save for fitful moments, after the haemorrhage does he seem to have believed he would recover; it was impossible for him to write poetry, for he had finally discarded the only kind of poetry that could be written in such agony as his. From the time of his return to London until his death, Keats was to all intents and purposes silent as a poet. Besides the fragment of *King Stephen*, and the two sonnets which were quoted in the last chapter, there remain of Keats' own work only the lines *To* ——, the fragment written on the margin of *The Cap and Bells*, and perhaps the *Ode to Fanny*.* Five intensely personal poems, and a semi-satirical extravanganza written in collaboration with Brown. The dramatic poem was never begun.

It is the fashion to deplore and dismiss *The Cap and Bells*. It has the inevitable defects of all that Keats wrote in collaboration with Brown; but it has what is in the eyes of traditional criticism of Keats the more serious defect of being utterly anti-romantic. *The Cap and Bells* is not a masterpiece, but Keats' own contributions to it, which are easy to distinguish, have often a bitter-sweet enchantment. Keats is engaged in deriding his own romanticism.

Criticism generally has followed Rossetti in declaring *The Cap and Bells* ' the only unworthy thing Keats ever wrote.' The verdict is preposterous; but it springs very naturally from the reluctance of those who are determined to have a romantic Keats, at whatever expense of truth, to look at the reality. In *The Cap and Bells* Keats quite deliberately makes fun of *The Eve of St. Mark,* which Rossetti had declared to be ' the choicest example of Keats' maturing manner.' Naturally, that attitude of Keats towards what Rossetti thought his masterpiece was intolerable to Rossetti, as it has been intolerable to a whole succession of critics who have embraced the Pre-Raphaelite misconception of Keats.

The Eve of St. Mark was almost the last piece of romantic poetry Keats wrote. When he became, with the *Odes,* a great poet, he discarded the attitude for ever. In the second *Hyperion* he denounced it pitilessly; in *The Cap and Bells* he merely laughed, rather bitterly, at it. What is remarkable is that the bitterness of the poem should be so little, seeing that it was written during weeks of utter despair. Here, for instance, is Crafticanto's description of Bellanaine's arrival at Elfinan's capital.

> As flowers turn their faces to the sun,
> So on our flight with hungry eyes they gaze,
> And, as we shaped our course, this, that way run,
> With mad-cap pleasure or hand-clasp'd amaze;
> Sweet in the air a mild-toned music plays,
> And progresses through its own labyrinth;
> Buds gathered from the green spring's middle days
> They scatter'd—daisy, primrose, hyacinth,—
> Or round white columns wreath'd from capital to plinth.
>
> Onward we floated o'er the panting streets
> That seem'd throughout with upheld faces paved;
> Look where we will, our bird's-eye vision meets
> Legions of holiday; bright standards waved
> And fluttering ensigns emulously craved
> Our minute's glance; a busy thunderous roar,
> From square to square among the buildings raved,
> As when the sea, at flow, gluts up once more
> The craggy hollowness of a wild reefed shore.

It would be far too crude to call this a parody by Keats of his own romantic narrative verse; the thing itself is too delicate, and parody did not lie within Keats' intention. What he felt about his romantic narratives was that they were ' unreal,' the work of a fanciful invention rather than of an imaginative comprehension. We have only to remember his words to Taylor, written most probably while he was actually composing *The Cap and Bells*: ' I have been endeavouring to persuade myself to untether Fancy and let her manage for herself. I and myself cannot agree about this at all. Wonders are no wonders to me. I am more at home amongst Men and women.' Possibly he had *The Cap and Bells* itself in his mind; but it is more likely that he was thinking of a continuation of *The Eve of St. Mark*. And he found that his heart was not in the business. In *The Cap and Bells* he is, as it were, ' placing ' romantic verse to his own satisfaction, by assigning it to a wholly fantastic kingdom, and making its unreality the adornment of world of the unreal. Instead of continuing *The Eve of St. Mark*, with a wry smile he proceeds to make its heroine the mistress of Prince Elfinan, that is to say, he turns upon her the light of his fuller and less comfortable knowledge, and banishes her to a world of fairy-land. Thereby he gives pain to admirers of *The Eve of St. Mark*. They do wrong to be pained. We need not admire *The Eve of St. Mark* the less, because we understand and approve of Keats' attitude towards it. He considered it a dream: and it is a dream. He had learned that he could not live by dreams, and he was determined to make that which he did live by the stuff of his poetry. Keats was no sentimentalist—no ' pet-lamb in a sentimental farce '—he was far more severe towards himself than we can suffer ourselves to be towards him. But if our sentimentalism is pained by his severity we have no right to condemn him. The truth remains that he is right and we are wrong.

If we cannot accommodate ourselves to the spectacle of Keats laughing a little bitterly at his own romanticism, we must give up the effort to understand him. After all, there is no overwhelming reason why we should not be allowed to prefer our own Keats to Keats himself, save that it seems disloyal to a great spirit not to accept him as he was. To take from him what pleases us, and to reject the rest, is permissible, but only if we frankly recognize what we are doing. We are mere pleasure-seekers, who choose the sweet fruit and refuse the sour, though they come from the same tree. The attitude is legitimate: but, in honesty, we ought not glorify this attitude into one of justice to Keats. We are studying our own comfort, as we have every right to do; but we ought not subtly persuade ourselves that we are being righteous by foisting our own standards of perfection on to a great poet whose whole life was a struggle against them. To work ourselves into the belief that when Keats is not pleasing us, he is not expressing himself, that when he rejects work that we admire he is morbid and unbalanced, is an insidious kind of hypocrisy. The truly great man cannot be judged by our standards, he must be judged by his own. The inward compulsion which we feel to judge a man by himself, in relation to his own being and the ideals which his being drives upward into his consciousness, is the surest evidence that we are confronted with a great man.*

P

At the most critical moment in his life, this great man rejected the beauty and beatitude of dreams. No one had dreamed more beautifully and beatifically than he; no one can ever have felt greater pain than he at having to cut out the desire for loveliness alone from his own heart. But he obeyed the necessity of his destiny; he could not turn aside from the path of his search after truth. ' I would rather fail,' he had said months before, ' than not be among the greatest '; and the greatest, he knew, did not invent beauty, they discovered and conquered and revealed it. They did not dream; they saw and understood. But it was not by their example, but by the compulsion of his own soul, that he put away what now he saw to be childish things. He followed the greatest, not as a disciple, but as one compelled by his own nature to tread the same path. Probably he had learned to know his own nature more fully by following it out in Shakespeare, by ' understanding Shakespeare to his depths '; but life itself conspired to urge him on to reach at twenty-three a point which Shakespeare did not reach till many years later. Life prodigally heaped upon him the miseries of the world, for he was her beloved son.

Save for *The Cap and Bells* and the fragment of *King Stephen*, Keats wrote but five poems after the *Ode to Autumn*. Two of these were the sonnets: *The Day is gone and all its Sweets are gone* and *I cry your mercy, pity, love—aye love!* One is a sonnet of momentary happiness at seeing Fanny Brawne again; the other an expression of the enduring agony which he suffered henceforward to the end of his life. The other two poems were likewise addressed to Fanny Brawne: they are the lines *To* —— and the *Ode to Fanny*. Like the sonnet *I cry your mercy*, they are intensely personal poems of torment and despair. There is besides the fragment of blank verse, also written to Fanny Brawne, which Keats wrote on the margin of *Cap and Bells*.

These poems cannot be dated precisely, for the simple reason that they are of such a kind that Keats would make no reference to them in his letters. What he was enduring was a secret between himself and his soul: sometimes the sheer extremity of pain drew from him a cry of agony addressed to his mistress. But of his poems he speaks not at all. After the letter of 17th November to Taylor, in which he speaks of his intention to write a narrative dramatic poem, ' and that a fine one,' there is no more mention of his poetic purposes in his letters. He was involved in a struggle, which was hardly even a struggle, against death.

Only once, and that in a letter to Fanny herself, does Keats mention a poem that he has in his head. It is in August, six months after his haemorrhage, on the eve of that journey to Italy which, because it would separate him from her for ever, he knew would be fatal to him.

If my health would bear it (he says), I could write a Poem which I have in my head, which would be a consolation for people in such a situation as mine. I would show someone in Love as I am, with a person living in such Liberty as you do. Shakespeare always sums up matters in the most sovereign manner. Hamlet's heart was full of such Misery as mine is when he said to Ophelia: 'Go to a Nunnery, go, go!'

The reference to Shakespeare as his precursor in the misery and mightiness of a poet of the human heart has by this time become inevitable. Keats felt that he was suffering what Shakespeare alone had suffered before him. But the poem to express this suffering was not written, because Keats had not the strength to write it. Nevertheless, one of the three remaining poems of Keats does utter something of this particular intensity of pain. It is certainly not the poem which Keats had in his head; but it is an approximation to it. *The Ode to Fanny* may have been written somewhere about January 1820, when Fanny Brawne had resumed her parties, her flirtations, and her stylishness.

Physician Nature! let my spirit blood!
O ease my heart of verse and let me rest;
Throw me upon thy Tripod, till the flood
Of stifling numbers ebbs from my full breast.
A theme! a theme! great nature! give a theme;
    Let me begin my dream.
I come—I see thee, as thou standest there,
Beckon me not into the wintry air.

Ah! dearest love, sweet home of all my fears
And hopes and joys, and panting miseries,—
To-night, if I may guess, thy beauty wears
    A smile of such delight,
    As brilliant and as bright,
As when with ravish'd, aching, vassal eyes,
    Lost in soft amaze,
    I gaze, I gaze!

Who now with greedy looks, eats up my feast?
What stare outfaces now my silver moon?
Ah! keep that hand unravish'd at the least;
    Let, let the amorous burn—
    But, pr'ythee, do not turn
The current of your heart from me so soon.
    O save, in charity,
    The quickest pulse for me.

Save it for me, sweet love! though music breathe
Voluptuous visions into the warm air,
Though swimming through the dance's dangerous wreath;
    Be like an April day,
    Smiling and cold and gay,
A temperate lily, temperate as fair;
    Then, Heaven! there will be
    A warmer June for me.

Why, this—you'll say, my Fanny! is not true:
Put your soft hand upon your snowy side,
Where the heart beats: confess—'tis nothing new—
    Must not a woman be
    A feather on the sea,
Sway'd to and fro by every wind and tide?
    Of as uncertain speed
    As blowball from the mead.

I know it—and to know it is despair
To one who loves you as I love, sweet Fanny!
Whose heart goes flutt'ring for you every where,
    Nor, when away you roam,
    Dare keep its wretched home.
Love, Love alone, has pains severe and many:
    When loneliest, keep me free
    From torturing jealousy.

Ah! if you prize my subdued soul above
The poor, the fading, brief pride of an hour;
Let none profane my Holy See of Love,
    Or with a rude hand break
    The sacramental cake:
Let none else touch the just new-budded flower.
    If not—may my eyes close,
    Love! on their last repose.

In that poem the agony is far from its extremity. But it is the same agony that was devouring him when in August he recalled Hamlet's words to Ophelia, and continued his letter thus:

Indeed, I should like to give up the matter at once—I should like to die. I am sickened at the brute world you are smiling with. I hate men, and women more. I see nothing but thorns for the future—wherever I may be next winter—in Italy or nowhere, Brown will be living near you with his indecencies. I see no prospect of any rest. Suppose me in Rome—well, I should there see you as in a magic glass going to and from town at all hours—I wish you could infuse a little confidence of human nature into my heart. I cannot muster any—the world is too brutal for me. . . .

Keats' was, if we please to call it so, a jealous love; it would be truer to say that it was a complete and impassioned love. The lover made an entire surrender of himself to his beloved and demanded an entire surrender in return. This was not peculiar to Keats, nor did it derive its quality from his sickness. It may be a rare thing in this world of ours; but its rarity, like that of poetic genius itself, is not the rarity of a sick and morbid thing, but of a precious and wonderful thing. To call it 'a grotesque and humiliating passion' is to be guilty of a grotesque and humiliating insensitiveness.

I have heard you say (Keats wrote to Fanny on 5th July 1820) that it was not unpleasant to wait a few years—you have amusement—your mind is away—you have not brooded over one idea as I have—and how should you? You are to me an object intensely desirable—the air I breathe in a room empty of you is unhealthy. I am not the same to you—no—you can wait—you have a thousand activities—you can be happy without me. Any party, any thing to fill up the day has been enough. How have you pass'd this month? Who have you smiled with? All this may seem savage in me. You do not feel as I do—you do not know what it is to love—one day you may—your time is not come. Ask yourself how many unhappy hours Keats has caused you in Loneliness. For myself, I have been a Martyr the whole time, and for this reason I speak; the confession is forc'd from me by the torture. I appeal to you by the blood of that Christ you believe in: Do not write to me if you have done anything this month which it would have pained me to have seen. You may have altered—if you have not—if you still behave in dancing rooms and other societies as I have seen you—I do not want to live—if you have done so I wish this coming night may be my last. I cannot live without you, and not only you, but *chaste you, virtuous you*. The Sun rises and sets, the day passes, and you follow the bent of your inclination to a certain extent—you have no conception of the quantity of miserable feeling that passes through me in a day— Be serious! Love is not a plaything—and again: do not write unless you can do it with a crystal conscience. I would sooner die for want of you than——

Yours for ever,

J. KEATS.

I do not propose to follow the bitter story to the end. 'I cannot live without you, and not only you, but chaste you, virtuous you,' Keats cried in his pain. It was the simple truth. 'Withhold no atom's atom, or I die '; Fanny Brawne withheld many atoms, and Keats did die. She is not to be blamed. She could not understand Keats' passion; if she had understood it she would have felt the like passion herself. She is not to be blamed for not understanding: she was a mere girl. Yet how many of the grown men who have written about Keats have understood more than she? It seems that mankind is divided into those who understand love of that kind and those who do not; between the two classes of men there is a great gulf fixed, and the effort to bridge it would be in vain. But those who cannot understand Keats' love, will never understand his poetry, for these two things spring from a single source.

Keats' life as a poet was over: a bare handful of scarcely endurable poems to Fanny is all that remains after his great decision of 22nd September. He submitted himself to life, and life accepted the sacrifice: he returned to Shakespeare, and drank the same bitter cup to the very dregs. For Shakespeare also reached a point in his life when he could find no other than direct speech for his agony; when his natural expression in the drama, to which he had been apprenticed since his youth up, and which he had learned to handle as no one has handled it before or since, was disturbed and troubled. He lost grip of his own art under the stress of suffering that appears to have come to him through such a passion as Keats'. The plays of the *Hamlet* period—*Measure for Measure*, *Troilus and Cressida*, *All's Well* and *Hamlet* itself—are incoherent with an inexpressible pain. Their dramatic purport is muddied and unclear: what we can learn from them beyond a doubt is that a sensuous and passionate love has suffered shipwreck. They are, if we are to judge them objectively, bad plays, but there enters with them into Shakespeare's drama a new intensity of profound experience which he was thenceforward to obey, to rebel against, to obey and to follow to its appointed consummation at the last verge of human experience. This baptism into the giant agony of the world caused Shakespeare also to utter himself in a handful of scarcely endurable sonnets.

Where Shakespeare could not express himself dramatically, although he was older than Keats by a dozen years, although he was, unlike Keats, under no menace of imminent death, although he had become a master of his art, are we to wonder if Keats, scarcely more than a boy in years, should have found it impossible, even had 'his health been able to bear it '? Keats had returned to Shakespeare; and his own poetic silence is the measure of the completeness of that return.

If the main contention of this book concerning Keats has been accepted, that his greatest poetry actually was, as he wished it to be, a spontaneous utterance of the complete being, and for that reason is the only English poetry which is truly *like* Shakespeare's, it will be obvious that the re-establishment of Shakespeare's drama as the formal ideal must have been the outward expression of a more intimate victory of Shakespeare. The victory of Shakespeare the poet —if this unreal distinction may be made for a moment—depends upon the victory of Shakespeare the man. This twofold acceptance of Shakespeare was a single act. I have failed in everything if I have not made it palpable that Keats' rejection of Milton was an integral part of a movement of Keats' whole being; and that this must of necessity have been so, because a poet of Keats' kind is a complete man who cannot suffer a divorce between his heart and mind and soul to endure. Milton is the great master of the poetry which is created out of that divorcement. Milton's poetry is a magnificent thing, but in the final judgement it is a lifeless and sterile thing. Keats' words when he rejected Milton were: 'Life to him would be death to me.' Was it not almost death to Milton himself? Compare *Samson Agonistes* with *The Tempest*. The difference between them is between a dead art and a living one; between a poetry of which the inward springs are petrified and pure poetry that remains obedient to the fullness of life within.

The poetry of Shakespeare reveals the beauty of life *in* life. Truth is beauty, it says, and shows that truth *is* beauty. It accepts the world of men and women, accepts all things, accepts them in many moods, from loathing and disgust to exaltation and serenity, but always and for ever it makes the fundamental act of acceptance, which is to make 'the Heart the Mind's Bible,' to submit to experience and not to turn away. No matter what his mood, Shakespeare was loyal to the world of men and women. As he saw it, so he represented it, faithful always, so far as human mind can tell, to his own deepest experience and his own organic being—a pure poet from first to last, following the destiny of a pure poet, submitting to life that life may be glorified through him.

To Shakespeare the poet Keats returned. Therefore he returned to Shakespeare the man. These two acts are impossible to separate. How impossible it may already have appeared from the letter in which Keats told Fanny of the poem he had in mind. 'Shakespeare always sums up matters in the most sovereign manner. Hamlet's heart was full of such misery as mine is when he said to Ophelia: "Go to a nunnery, go, go!"' Nor will it have been forgotten that in the letter in which he coined for Shakespeare the phrase 'the miserable and mighty poet of the human heart,' he had said: 'The middle age of Shakespeare was all clouded over; his days were not more happy than Hamlet's, who is perhaps more like Shakespeare himself in his common everyday life than any other of his characters.' The conception of that dramatic poem of which he told Fanny Brawne, and his appeal to Shakespeare as his forerunner in suffering and in knowledge, are a single movement of the soul. And if we desire to penetrate to something of the actual life-experience which inspires and colours *Hamlet*, the letters of Keats during this last year of his life are the master-key. Whether Keats actually did 'understand Shakespeare to his depths' when he wrote those words two years before may perhaps be doubted by those who cannot palate the notion of a prophetic understanding of one soul by another. Assuredly he understood him now.

The return of Keats to Shakespeare the man as his sole companion and secret-sharer, though it is implicit and necessary in the development of Keats' life, can fortunately be made almost palpable to the sense. The immitigable evidence of the letters is there. About three weeks after the fatal haemorrhage, Keats wrote to Fanny that he had been glancing through the *Nouvelle Heloise*.

> I have been turning over two volumes of letters written between Rousseau and two Ladies in the perplexed strain of mingled finesse and sentiment in which the Ladies and gentlemen of those days were so clever, and which is still prevalent among Ladies of this country who still live in a state of reasoning Romance. . . .
>
> What would Rousseau have said at seeing our little correspondence! What would his Ladies have said! I don't care much —I would sooner have Shakespeare's opinion about the matter. The common gossiping of washerwomen must be less disgusting than the continual and eternal fence and attack of Rousseau and these sublime Petticoats. . . . Thank God, I am born in England with our own great Men before my eyes. Thank God that you are fair and can love me without being letter-written and sentimentalized into it.

Than this no more intimate appeal could be made to Shakespeare. Shakespeare is a living presence to Keats, speaking encouragement and approval to him. He would understand Keats' love-letters; he would know that the direct utterance of an all-absorbing passion of body and mind and soul was natural and right and true; he would have no truck with that sickly romanticising and falsification of passion in which Jean-Jacques, for all his gifts, indulged. And on no single point does the profound difference between a false and a true romanticism emerge than on this very point of love. True Romanticism is true individualism—a self-creation of the soul by means of the Mind's faithful interpretation of the Heart. It is essential to it that the consciousness should be utterly loyal to the unconsciousness, and that there should be no veil of heart-inwoven lies interposed. Rousseau was, for all his vision, a liar; he betrayed his own knowledge, and mankind has had to pay for his treachery, because it has not been able to distinguish between the true and the false in him.

Keats was a true romantic, Shakespeare was a true romantic; and they both made the essential act of a true romanticism. They put away from themselves as degrading the lie of romance. Truth, truth at all costs, even though he dies for his loyalty to it, is written on the heart of a true romantic; and as Keats declared in the second *Hyperion*, he does indeed have to pass through a living death to reach the truth.

But the most moving of all Keats' appeals to Shakespeare his forerunner and secret-sharer is contained in a letter to Fanny written late in July 1820, at a moment when his agony of suffering through his doubt of her loyalty was extreme.

> Upon my soul (he says) I have loved you to the extreme. . . . You complain of my ill-treating you in thought, word and deed. I am sorry—at times I feel bitterly sorry that I ever made you unhappy—my excuse is that those words have been wrung from me by the sharpness of my feelings. At all events, and in any case, I have been wrong; could I believe that I did it without any cause, I should be the most sincere of Penitents. I could give way to my repentant feelings now, I could recant all my suspicions, I could mingle with you heart and Soul though absent, were it not for some parts of your Letters. . . .

He regrets that he has pained her, he will even acknowledge that he was wrong to have pained her: but not that what he thought or said was wrong.

> My friends laugh at you! (he goes on) I know some of them—when I know them all I shall never think of them again as friends or even acquaintance. My friends have behaved well to me in every instance but one, and there they have become tattlers, and inquisitors into my conduct: spying upon a secret I would rather die than share it with anybody's confidence. For this I cannot wish them well, I care not to see any of them again. If I am the Theme, I will not be the Friend, of idle Gossips. Good gods, what a shame it is our loves should be so put into the microscope of a Coterie. . . . These Laughers, who do not like you, who envy you for your Beauty, who would have God-bless'd me from you for ever: who were plying me with disencouragements with respect to you eternally. People are revengeful—do not mind them—do nothing but love me—if I knew that for certain, life and health will in such event be a heaven, and death itself will be less painful. I long to believe in immortality. I shall never be able to bid you an entire farewell . . .
>
> [If] after reading my letter you even then wish to see me—I am strong enough to walk over—but I dare not. I shall feel so much pain in parting with you again. My dearest love, I am afraid to see you; I am strong, but not strong enough to see you. Will my

> arm ever be round you again, and if so shall I be obliged to leave you again? My sweet Love! I am happy whilst I believe your first Letter. Let me be but certain that you are mine heart and soul, and I could die more happily than I could otherwise live. If you think me cruel—if you think I have sleighted you—do muse over it again and see into my heart. My love to you is ' true as truth's simplicity and simpler than the infancy of truth.' . . . I will be as patient in illness and as believing in Love as I am able.

It is mistrust, a justified and unconquerable mistrust, of Fanny Brawne's loyalty that is eating Keats' heart away. And to describe the loyalty of his own love he used lines from Shakespeare. Those lines come from *Troilus and Cressida*—one of the three plays which precede *Hamlet*, and together with *Hamlet* mark the period when Shakespeare also

> forgot in mist of idle misery
> Life's purposes, the palate of his mind
> Losing its gust, and his ambition blind.

Keats was suffering the self-same agony as Shakespeare suffered in this period and expressed (or rather could not express) in *Troilus and Cressida*. He wanted to spare Fanny, he did not want to make her unhappy: therefore he refrained from quoting the full passage of Shakespeare. Here it is: the loyal Troilus speaks to the disloyal Cressida.

> O, that I thought it could be in a woman—
> As, if it can, I will presume in you—
> To feed for aye her lamp and flames of love;
> To keep her constancy in plight and youth,
> Outliving beauty's outward, with a mind
> That doth renew swifter than blood decays!
> Or that persuasion could but thus convince me,
> That my integrity and truth to you
> Might be affronted with the match and weight
> Of such a winnow'd purity in love—
> How were I then uplifted! but, alas!
> I am as true as truth's simplicity
> And simpler than the infancy of truth.

Keats had that speech by heart. His reading, as we can tell from the marginal notes on the one of his copies of Shakespeare which has come down to us, was much on *Troilus and Cressida*.* ' I will be as believing in love as I am able,' Keats' letter had ended; it is the exact phrase to describe the feeling of Troilus' mistrustful heart. But indeed I believe that Keats during this last year of his life, when he was silent as a poet, read little else than Shakespeare. That is, in the nature of things, only a conjecture; but I believe it to be a true one. In his letters during this last year he quotes no one but Shakespeare; he was reading Shakespeare on the boat that took him on his death-voyage to Italy; it was in his Shakespeare that he copied out for Severn the sonnet *Bright Star*.

Shakespeare the poet his ideal, Shakespeare the man his secret-sharer. Of those fine plays, wherein the grim knowledge of his heart and mind should have been illumined by the knowledge of his soul, and the truth of his deepest experience uttered in poetry that should come ' as naturally as the leaves to a tree '—of ' that other verse alone ' to which he would have devoted himself if God had spared him, we have nothing. Or rather, we had nothing until some few years ago seven and a half lines of blank verse were found written on the margin of the manuscript of *The Cap and Bells*. They have been quoted already; I quote them again as a fragment of one of those unwritten plays, and an example of that other verse:

> This living hand, now warm, now capable
> Of earnest grasping, would, if it were cold,
> And in the icy silence of the tomb,
> So haunt thy days and chill thy dreaming nights
> That thou wouldst wish thine own heart dry of blood
> So in my veins red life might stream again
> And thou be conscience-calm'd—see, here it is—
> I hold it towards you.

. . . .

I cannot tell whether I have been successful in my purpose, which was, so far as I can define it at all, to show through the living reality of Keats, what a pure poet is and what he does. What he is is a mystery; what he does is a mystery. No man can tell whether he has been successful in revealing a mystery. Probably he cannot, by the nature of things, achieve success in such a task. It is enough that he should not have betrayed it.

It will have been betrayed, if I have in any way forced the facts to suit my purpose. I believe I should have been conscious of such a treachery if it had been committed; and I am conscious of none, unless it be in the very fact that I have spoken of revealing a mystery.

Let me say then that my purpose has been to vindicate more completely than it has been vindicated before Matthew Arnold's sentence concerning Keats; that I have been trying to show that it was inevitable that Keats should be ' with Shakespeare,' and how and why it was inevitable. Let me put it thus: Keats had gone a long way, a very long way, upon a predestined path—upon the path of the individual soul which is, in Wordsworth's phrase, gifted with far ‘ more than ordinary organic sensibility,’ and which is by nature compelled to be loyal to its own experience. After a time that path of the individual soul, exploring the universe in search of truth, and governed in its search by loyalty to its own deepest knowledge, becomes a lonely one indeed. Soon all the familiar landmarks and all the familiar faces disappear from the sight of the pioneer; and then even those figures which once seemed great to him also fade away. Something which he has felt and known, they deny or do not admit; therefore he must leave them behind. Only those whose experience has been co-extensive with his own remains; their words alone can satisfy him. At last, if the pioneer be a Keats, there is left only Shakespeare. And Matthew Arnold’s sentence, because it is true, is true in deeper senses than Arnold himself intended: ‘ I think I shall be with the English poets at my death! He is, he is with Shakespeare.’ There was nobody else for him to be with; nobody else who could be with him. In the life of a pure poet is a secret fitness, because to be a pure poet demands that a man should make himself the faithful servant and obedient instrument of the unseen harmony which is in the universe. This harmony is manifested through and in him. When Keats began *Endymion*, that is, when he took the first great step on the path of poetry and decided wholly to dedicate himself to its mysterious purposes, he wrote to Haydon:

> I hope for the support of a High Power while I climb this little eminence, and especially in my Years of more momentous Labor. I remember your saying that you had notions of a good Genius presiding over you. I have of late had the same thought, for things which I do half at random are afterwards confirmed by my judgment in a dozen features of Propriety. Is it too daring to fancy Shakespeare this Presider?

Was it too daring? There are more things in heaven and earth than are dreamed of in our philosophy.

NOTES

CHAPTER I, *p.* 10.

I do not think the comment alone does show precisely *that*; though taken together with Keats' omission of the poem from his 1820 volume, it does. What it does show is something which is more important and can never be too stubbornly insisted upon, namely, that 'romantic' poetry, even in its most exquisite form, and even when deeply coloured as was *La Belle Dame sans Merci* with life-experience, was to Keats always a diversion from the true goal of poetry—namely, the objectivity of the drama.

CHAPTER I, *p.* 10.

The 'general power' of Keats' mind will have been sufficiently demonstrated by the whole tenour of the narrative. But I cannot refrain from bringing to the reader's notice one instance of its curious swiftness. It occurs in Keats' manuscript notes on Burton's Anatomy. The sentence of Burton runs thus:

'And to advance the common cause, undergo any miseries, turn traytors, assassinates, *pseudo-martyrs*. . . .'

Against the last word Keats writes 'The most biggotted word ever met with.'

CHAPTER II, *p.* 15.

Mr. Sydney Cockerell tells me that Mr. Thomas Hardy has suggested that this odd word 'jar' should be read 'tiar' (tiara). 'Tiar' is a Keats word; and the emendation seems to me excellent.

CHAPTER II, *p.* 17.

Perhaps that praise would be given more truly to Richard Woodhouse, the friend and literary adviser of Taylor the publisher, and to a certain extent Keats' friend also. But Woodhouse was not an active man of letters.

CHAPTER III, *p.* 31.

'Intensity' and 'intense' are two of Keats' peculiar and personal words, like 'identity,' and 'sensation,' and 'philosophy.' In order to follow Keats' thought exactly, his use of such words should be closely studied. I suggest such a study to anyone who desires to do a valuable piece of literary research.

Some of these uses of words have been hastily described as vulgarisms by those who have made no attempt to discover what Keats means by them. They are for the most part nothing of the kind. Keats had a private and personal vocabulary for his highly individual thoughts. It is because his thoughts could not be expressed in the common language of discourse that he had recourse to these private words. The most superficial study of them will reveal, first, that he is very consistent in his use of them, and secondly and more importantly that they are the vehicle of some of his most intimate thinking. Certain of these words I have tried to explain in the course of my narrative; but there is real need of a much more comprehensive examination of them.

Intense and *intensity* cannot be paraphrased. Perhaps, the closest approximation to their meaning is *ecstatic* and *ecstasy*. But those words and the condition generally understood by them are alien to Keats' vocabulary and his nature. *Intensity* is rather a heightened consciousness than an abrogation of it. Consider these examples, which will show at least how necessary some understanding of the words is to an understanding of Keats' thought.

> I went next morning to see 'Death on the Pale Horse.' It is a wonderful picture, when West's age is considered; but there is nothing to be *intense* upon, no women one feels mad to kiss, no face swelling into reality. The excellence of every art is its *intensity*, capable of making all disagreeables evaporate from their being in close relationship with Beauty and Truth. Examine *King Lear*, and you will find this exemplified throughout: but in this picture we have unpleasantness without any momentous depth of speculation excited, in which to bury its repulsiveness. . . . (*Letter of 28th December* 1817.)

And again:

> Verse, fame, and Beauty are *intense* indeed,
> But Death *intenser*—Death is Life's high meed.
> (*Why did I laugh to-night*?)

It is evident that *intensity* in the true work of art excites *intensity* in the man who truly understands it, and this *intensity* is not ecstatic. Far from it: it is a condition of 'momentous depth of speculation.' And again, Poetry, Fame, and Beauty excite this *intensity;* but Death far more than they. *Intensity* is a state of comprehension.

CHAPTER III, *p.* 31.

One would perhaps most naturally compare with this the speech of Diotima in Plato's 'Symposium'. But Mr. F. M. Cornford has supplied me with a less familiar reference to Plato's letters (Epistle vii, 341 B—E) and a translation of the passage. The italics are my own.

> This much, however, I am able to affirm concerning all that have written or shall hereafter write, claiming knowledge of the things I study, whether as having learnt from me or from others or as having made discoveries of their own: it is, in my judgement,

impossible that they should understand anything of the matter. There is not, nor shall there ever be, any writing of mine on this subject. *It is altogether beyond such means of expression as exist in other departments of knowledge; rather, after long dwelling upon the thing itself and living with it, suddenly, as from a leaping spark, a light is kindled, which, when it has arisen in the soul, thenceforward feeds itself.* And yet of this I am sure: that if these things were to be written down or expressed in words, I could express them better than anyone; I know too that, if they were set down in writing badly, I should be the person to suffer most. And if I thought they could be adequately expressed to the world in speech or writing, in what nobler business could I have spent my life than in writing a work of great service to mankind and revealing Nature to all eyes under the light of day? But I do not think that what passes for an ' attempt ' in this field is a good thing for men, unless it be for the very few who can be enabled by a slight indication to make the discovery for themselves. Of the rest, some would be puffed up with an entirely offensive spirit of false superiority, others with a lofty and presumptuous conceit of understanding some grand mystery.

CHAPTER IV, *p.* 33.

This portrait of Shakespeare reappears in Keats' letters several times. His beloved sister-in-law, Georgiana Wylie—

> Nymph of the downward smile, and sidelong glance,
> In what diviner moments of the day
> Art thou most lovely?—

made, or knitted, some *tassels* for it. And the portrait, tassels and all, seems to have been taken about by Keats to his various lodgings. The tassels served to remind him of a woman who, in spite of her knitting tassels for Shakespeare, seems to have been as lovely in heart as she was in feature.

This portrait of Shakespeare with the tassels is an oddly precious memory of Keats. Somehow it combines, as it were in a single symbol, all Keats' loyalty and affection. I am quite sure that, however preposterous he may have come to feel the tassels were, he would not have taken them off for any man on earth. He would have fought legions of butcher boys and ' literary fashionables ' on behalf of those tassels, in the sure knowledge that though no one else could understand them, Shakespeare would.

I have never seen tassels on pictures; but I seem to remember some in Cruikshank's illustrations to Dickens. They were, if I remember rightly, rather like the little bags which are put on horse's ears in summer to save them from flies.

CHAPTER IV, *p.* 36.

For what some would call the 'superstitious' feeling of Keats about Shakespeare at the moment of beginning *Endymion*, which was his deliberate dedication of himself to poetry, we should compare with his surmise to Haydon the conclusion of his letter to Reynolds of 18th April 1817.

> I'll tell you what—on the 23d was Shakespeare born. Now, if I should receive a letter from you, and another from my Brothers on that day 'twould be a parlous good thing. Whenever you write say a word or two on some Passage in Shakespeare that may have come rather new to you, which must be continually happening, notwithstanding that we read the same Play forty times—for instance, the following from the *Tempest* never struck me so forcibly as at present,
>
> 'Urchins
> *Shall, for the vast of night that they may work,*
> All exercise on thee——'
>
> How can I help bringing to your mind the line—
>
> '*In the dark backward and abysm of time.*'

Surely it was at this strange moment of his career—the true and conscious beginning of his full life as a poet, that passages of Shakespeare became for Keats on the level of 'Sun, Moon and Stars,' of the highest order of 'ethereal' realities [see p. 56.]

CHAPTER IV, *p.* 37.

I had conjectured that 'Timotheus,' of whom I could remember nothing, concealed 'Tim. Athens'—or 'Timon of Athens,' and that the reference was to

> Timon hath built his everlasting mansion
> Upon the beached verge of the salt sea. . . .

However, the publication of a letter in *The Times Literary Supplement*—a letter in which, it is fair to say, this conjecture was incidental—led to my being informed most gently, by Professor Garrod, that this 'Timotheus' is a familiar figure. He appears in Dryden's Ode in honour of St. Cecilia's Day.

CHAPTER IV, *p.* 38.

It is pertinent to add that Bailey records that during this stay at Oxford he and Keats made a pilgrimage in early October to Stratford-on-Avon, where Keats was profoundly impressed by the lifelike quality of the coloured bust of Shakespeare in the Parish Church. Anyone who has had the experience of coming unprepared upon that startling portrait of Shakespeare will guess from his own experience what Keats felt in beholding it.

CHAPTER IV, *p.* 47.

Bailey appears, through Keats' letters, an unattractive person. It is amusing and not uninstructive to remember that this Man of Principle, this Man of Character, behaved in such a way when in search of a wife that even the tolerant and charming Jem Rice—one of the most attractive of all the minor figures in Keats' letters, a man oddly like Charles Lamb, whom would to heaven Keats had been able to know a little better across the chasm of a generation—after 'examining the whole for and against minutely,' abandoned Bailey entirely.

Keats' account of the whole story is in the Journal-Letter to George of February 1819. The affair, like all the affairs which Keats took to heart, had an immediate effect upon his thought. In his letter to George he thinks over *l'affaire* Bailey aloud:

> The great thing to be considered is—whether it is want of delicacy and principle or want of knowledge and polite experience. And again weakness—yes, that is it; and the want of a Wife—yes, that is it—and then Mariane [Reynolds] made great Bones of him although her Mother and Sister have teased her very much about it. Her conduct has been very upright throughout the whole affair—She liked Bailey as a Brother but not as a Husband—especially as he used to woo her with the Bible and Jeremy Taylor under his arm—they walked in no grove but Jeremy Taylor's. Mariane's obstinacy is some excuse—but his so quickly taking to Miss Gleig can have no excuse—except that of a Ploughman who wants a wife. . . . All this I am not supposed by the Reynoldses to have any hint of. It will be a good lesson to the Mother and the Daughters—nothing would serve but Bailey. If you mentioned the word Teapot some one of them came out with an *à propos* about Bailey—noble fellow—fine fellow! was always in their mouths—. This may teach them that the man who ridicules romance is the most romantic of Men—that he who abuses women and slights them loves them the most [the reference is plainly to Keats himself, see p. 96]—that he who talks of roasting a Man alive would not do it when it came to the push—and above all, that they are very shallow people who take everything literally. A Man's life of any worth is a continual allegory. . . .

There follows the passage concerning Shakespeare's 'life of allegory' quoted in the half-title and in the text (see p. 115).

That was one of Keats' deepest thoughts to which Bailey's behaviour gave the occasion. But immediate connection of another is more curious. Some days later in the same letter occurs the famous passage which I have quoted and upon which I have commented on pp. 118-119. It is Keats' vision of the truth of human life as a thing of beauty.

The greater part of Men make their way with the same instinctiveness, the same unwandering eye from their purposes, the same animal eagerness as the Hawk. The Hawk wants a Mate, so does the Man—look at them both, they set about it and procure one in the same manner.

It seems highly probable that Bailey was the occasion of this part of Keats' vision. Bailey's behaviour had been taken to heart and included and accepted. Since Keats thus accepted it, and to such exquisite purpose, I have no doubt done wrong in calling Bailey 'a pietistic sensualist.' But I could no other; the thought of him irritates me still, though none rejoices more than I at the truly poetic justice by which this Man of Principle—this embryo Archdeacon of Colombo, and thorough-paced 'Wordsworthian'—who cut Haydon on principle, was cut by Keats and Jem Rice, not on principle at all. But Keats forgave him: Keats forgave everybody—even a 'Wordsworthian.' We cannot very well do less.

CHAPTER IV, *p.* 48.

Anton Tchehov, perhaps the greatest of all pure poets in the latter days of the nineteenth century, naturally possessed this quality to a high degree. I am not sufficiently familiar with the Russian language to know whether he found or created a single word for the condition. But no more beautiful *phrase* for it could be found than his: 'And all things are forgiven, and it would be strange not to forgive.' That little sentence is as lovely in translation as it could possibly be in the original. It belongs to the same order as the sayings of Christ. Moreover, it puts the distinction within the sameness most purely. This condition is a forgiveness of things rather than of persons. And perhaps in that distinction and that sameness can be found the relation and the difference between the highest moral beauty, typified in the figure of Christ, and the highest spiritual beauty, typified (for me at least) in the purest of all pure poets, William Shakespeare.

CHAPTER IV, *p.* 51.

How dearly loved let witness the charming early sonnet *To My Brothers*, written on Tom's birthday, 18th November 1816.

Small busy flames play through the fresh laid coals
  And their faint cracklings o'er our silence creep
  Like whispers of the household gods that keep
A gentle empire o'er fraternal souls.
And while, for rhymes, I search around the poles,
  Your eyes are fix'd, as in poetic sleep,
  Upon the lore so voluble and deep
That aye at fall of night our care condoles.

> This is your birth-day, Tom, and I rejoice
> That thus it passes smoothly, quietly.
> Many such eves of gently whisp'ring noise
> May we together pass, and calmly try
> What are this world's true joys,—ere the great voice,
> From its fair face, shall bid our spirits fly.

CHAPTER IV, *p.* 51.

In fact something very like the phrase occurs, also at this period, at the beginning of Keats' Journal-Letter to George of December 1818. 'Suppose Brown or Haslam or any one whom I understand in the next degree to what I do you, were in America, they would be so much the farther from me in proportion *as their identity was less impressed upon me*'. The phrase has lost its suffocating intensity; and the reason for this mitigation is that the phase of Keats' experience is at an end. Tom is dead: and the love for Fanny Brawne is beginning.

Since the above paragraph was written a missing fragment of Keats' Journal-Letter to George of February-May 1819 has been published by Miss Lowell ('John Keats': Vol. II, p. 607). It also contains a form of the key-phrase in the following interesting passage dated 17th March 1819:

> There is a great difference between an easy and an uneasy indolence. An indolent day fill'd with speculations even of an unpleasant colour is bearable and even pleasant doing when one's thoughts cannot find out anything better in the world . . . but to have nothing to do, and to be surrounded with unpleasant human identities; who press upon one just enough to prevent one getting into a lazy position; and not enough to interest or rouse one; is a capital punishment of a capital crime: for is not giving up, through good nature, one's time to people who have no light and shade a capital crime?

It is curious that the phrase should thus recur at a moment when his depression and despair reached the nadir; and those who follow the narrative of the early months of 1819 will understand that the quite unexpected re-emergence of the phrase on 17th March 1819, is to me a confirmation both of the importance I attach to the phrase and of my interpretation of Keats' condition of soul in March 1819.

CHAPTER V, *p.* 59.

There is an interesting parallelism between this magnificent description by Keats of his own art of poetry, and Tolstoy's description of art in *What is Art?* Tolstoy says:

> Art is differentiated from activity of the understanding . . . by the fact that it acts on people independently of their state of

> development and education, that the charm of a picture, of sounds, or of forms, infects any man whatever his plane of development. The business of art lies just in this: to make that understood and felt which in the form of an argument might be incomprehensible and inaccessible. Usually it seems to the recipient of a truly artistic impression that he knew the thing before, but had been unable to express it.

The measure of Keats' genius is apparent in the fact that Tolstoy, where they agree, is right, and where they differ, wrong. Tolstoy plunges into the age-old fallacy concerning the ' natural ' man. Keats knows well that the natural man who takes natural delight in the highest poetry is not man ' in the state of nature '—it is man momentarily awakened to the highest degree of spiritual development, or man momentarily in contact with his soul. Spiritual development is, indeed, not the same as intellectual development. It is a higher and more difficult achievement; it does not consist, as Tolstoy persuaded himself, in the mere absence of intellectual development. It is a necessary supersession of the intellect by the soul. This condition is natural to man, as his highest aptitude (of which the mysterious response to great art is premonitory) must be natural to him; but he is not born with it, only with the capacity for it.

CHAPTER V, *p.* 62.

' From a knowledge of what is to be aimed at '. Perhaps the best commentary upon Keats' thought in this sentence is the following passage from Walter Pater's essay on Wordsworth:

> For most of us the conception of means and ends covers the whole of life, and is the exclusive type or figure under which we represent our lives to ourselves. Such a figure, reducing all things to machinery, though it has on its side the authority of that old Greek moralist who has fixed for succeeding generations the outline of the theory of right living, is too like a mere description or picture of men's lives as we actually find them, to be the basis of the higher ethics. It covers the meanness of men's daily lives, and much of the dexterity with which they pursue what may seem to them the good of themselves or others; but not the intangible perfection of those whose ideal is rather in *being* than in *doing*—not those *manners* which are, in the deepest as in the simplest sense, *morals*, and without which we cannot so much as offer a cup of water to a poor man without offence.

CHAPTER V, *p.* 66.

In his note on Keats' ' philosophy ' in the Memorial Volume, Professor Bradley suggests that the phrase ' the love of good and ill' should be read 'the lore of good and ill.' This is an unacceptable suggestion. I refer to it because I have found Professor Bradley the only critic who has written with real penetration of Keats' *thought*. The change he proposes is a drastic one, and he proposes it because he considers that the ideal goal of 'loving good and ill' is foreign to Keats. To acquiesce in good and ill was an ideal of Keats, but to 'love good and ill' was not.

This, it seems to me, is a curious instance of what I have called Professor Bradley's 'instinctive avoidance' of the conclusion to which, I believe, one is forced by a study of Keats' poems and letters —that his goal was indeed to know the universe of human experience as a harmony, and that he did come to know it as such and love it. To have a soul-knowledge of the universe as a harmony is to 'love good and ill.' It is beyond that *amor intellectualis Dei* which Spinoza achieved, though that also was certainly a love of good and ill. The vision of Moneta in the second *Hyperion* is a sublime poetical expression of Spinoza's *amor intellectualis Dei:* but Keats passed beyond that, to a condition wherein the tension of that intellectual love of God was relaxed. The *Ode to Autumn* is the voice of an absolute and supra-intellectual acceptance.

It is remarkable that Professor Bradley's instinctive avoidance of this 'mystical' conclusion should lead him so far as to suggest that we should actually alter the wording of a phrase so crucial. It is an additional evidence that Professor Bradley alone has really penetrated Keats' thought. Keats took the *salto mortale*. Professor Bradley will not follow him. But he feels the phrase is crucial, and rather than let it go by in silence, he would change it. It is a fine example of critical integrity.

Finally, this 'love of good and ill' is, as Keats well knew, the peculiar gift of the pure poet. In its most conscious form it is the love of the immanent reality of God; in its most instinctive it is that protean element in the character of the pure, and therefore objective, poet,—a character which, as Keats told Woodhouse (27th October 1818), 'has as much delight in conceiving an Iago as an Imogen.' These forms are forms of the same essence.

CHAPTER V, *p.* 76.

There may be some who will demur to my declaring, *sans phrase*, that 'the ambition of my intellect' has nothing to do with rational thought. I can well imagine the temptation of the sceptical critic to turn on me with: 'Mr. Murry insists that Keats means what he says, but when Keats says something that does not fit with Mr. Murry's theory, he has no compunction in declaring that Keats means the very opposite of what he says.' I am afraid that the very nature of my attempt in this book makes it impossible to safeguard myself against such criticism, and I am certain that there are many other passages in my narrative which are open to the same attack.

In general I would say this—and the grounds for my assertion are implicit in my whole narrative—Keats means what he says always when he is being a pure poet. When he is using the language of discourse he cannot always mean what he says, for the simple reason that he cannot always say what he means. He has to use words that were not made for his purposes. Just as his 'philosophy' is almost the direct opposite of philosophy in the ordinary sense, so here 'intellectual' ambition is unintellectual. If authority for such an interpretation is required, I should refer to such a passage as this (24th September 1819: to George):

> The only means of strengthening one's intellect is to make up one's mind about nothing—to let the mind be a thoroughfare for all thoughts, not a select party.

That is to say for Keats the only means of strengthening the intellect is what the rationalist would consider a complete abnegation of intellect.

I believe that I could produce similar authority for every interpretation of Keats that I have made. I have not attempted to do so, not so much because it would make an already difficult narrative more cumbersome, as because my story of Keats will stand or fall on other grounds than these.

CHAPTER VII, *p.* 82.

In the Woodhouse transcript, the last lines are thus given:

> and lo from all his limbs
> Celestial glory dawned: he was a god!

That was probably a subsequent amendment. The existence of Keats' own MS. of the first *Hyperion* was not known or even suspected until quite recently. Whichever was the ending finally contemplated by Keats, the poem was complete.

CHAPTER VIII, *p.* 97.

People who should know better have a strange habit of talking as though psychology were a new invention of the nineteenth century, because the word and the study came into vogue at that time. Someday they may awake to the simple fact that literary creators like Shakespeare and Keats had forgotten more psychology than the most advanced psycho-analyst ever knew. Psychology is either true knowledge concerning the spiritual nature of man or it is moonshine and abracadabra: perhaps, when we are a little nearer the millennium, the psychologists will take it into their heads to go for the elements of their science to the past-masters of it—those creative writers whose productions are recognized by the consensus of generations to be 'just representations of human nature.'

CHAPTER VIII, *p.* 101.

The 'you' of this sentence is, of course, his 'dear sister', Georgiana Keats (*née* Wylie), not his brother George. Keats had a delightful trick of turning from one to the other in his letters to America.

CHAPTER VIII, *p.* 104.

'She is not seventeen,' should be, according to Mr. Buxton Forman, whose authority in such matters is unimpeachable, 'She is not nineteen.' It is very odd that Keats should not have known. But eighteen is much more appropriate than sixteen to what Fanny Brawne was.

CHAPTER IX, *p.* 123.

I am glad to have Professor Bradley's corroboration of this reading of a sonnet, which like many other of Keats' most significant poems, is neglected by the commentators. 'In *Why did I laugh?*' he writes in his essay in the Memorial Volume, 'there is a very sharp contrast between the *aching ignorance* of the opening lines and the accent of complete certainty at the close.'

CHAPTER IX, *p.* 125.

'Plumb'—The spelling reminds one of Charles Lamb's letter to Joseph Hume:

> 'I always spell plumb-pudding with a *b*, p-l-u-m-*b*,—I think it reads fatter and more suetty.'

In the case of Keats' sonnet, it reads richer and riper.

CHAPTER IX, *p.* 126.

For a reason which seems to be intimately connected with his reason for declaring *Isabella* the finest of all Keats' long poems, Sir Sidney Colvin declares that what to me is the inferior of two sonnets on Fame which Keats sent to his brother George on 30th April 1819 is 'the finer.' He quotes the second and not the first in his *Life of Keats*. Here are the two for purposes of comparison. I give the revised version of the first, as I have given the original version in the text.

ON FAME

You cannot eat your cake and have it too.—Proverb.

How fever'd is the man, who cannot look
  Upon his mortal days with temperate blood,
Who vexes all the leaves of his life's book,
  And robs his fair name of its maidenhood.
It is as if the rose should pluck herself
  Or the ripe plum finger its misty bloom,
As if a Naiad like a meddling elf
  Should darken her pure grot with muddy gloom;

But the rose leaves herself upon the briar,
For winds to kiss and grateful bees to feed,
And the ripe plum still wears its dim attire;
The undisturbed lake has crystal space;
Why then should man, teasing the world for grace,
Spoil his salvation for a fierce miscreed?

Another on Fame

Fame, like a wayward girl, will still be coy
To those who woo her with too slavish knees,
But makes surrender to some thoughtless boy
And dotes the more upon a heart at ease;
She is a Gipsy will not speak to those
Who have not learnt to be content without her;
A Jilt, whose ear was never whisper'd close,
Who thinks they scandal her who talk about her;
A very Gipsy is she, Nilus-born,
Sister-in-law to jealous Potiphar;
Ye love-sick Bards! repay her scorn for scorn;
Ye Artists lovelorn! madmen that ye are!
Make your best bow to her and bid adieu,
Then, if she likes it, she will follow you.

The second of these sonnets may be the more perfect technically: but it is a much slighter thing. The first is like the sonnet of March 1818, *Four Seasons fill the measure of the year*, a vaunt-courier of *The Ode to Autumn*, whereas the second belongs almost to the class of Keats' *vers de société*.

Moreover, Sir Sidney Colvin and Professor de Selincourt both state positively that the two sonnets were written on 30th April 1819. It *may* have been so; but there is no certain evidence for it, and the internal probabilities are against it. The following is the passage from Keats' letter on which the statement is based.

> Friday—30th April—Brown has been here rummaging up some of my old sins—that is to say sonnets. I do not think you will remember them so I will copy them out as well as two or three lately written. I have just written one on Fame—which Brown is transcribing and he has his book and mine. I must employ myself perhaps in a sonnet on the same subject——

There follows the first of these sonnets in a form which shows that it was composed there and then. The second sonnet is the one ' he has just written.' Whether ' just written ' means that it was written on that day, or, as I should naturally suppose, is equivalent to the previous ' lately written '—no one can positively say. What is certain is that they are the expression of two very different moods, of which one is profoundly Keats' own, while the other has more than a touch of the 'man of the world' cynicism which Keats derived from Brown.

But, as I have tried to show, the first sonnet 'to Fame' has not very much to do with the Fame that is the subject of the second sonnet, or indeed with anything that ordinary mortals understand by the word Fame, and this manifest discrepancy between the title and the poem itself may have had some influence on Sir Sidney's judgement.

CHAPTER IX, *p*. 130.

While I was correcting the proofs of this book I read in 'Q's' otherwise delightful 'Charles Dickens and Other Victorians' the following passage. It shows how stubbornly rooted in the finest critical minds is the misunderstanding of these lines of Keats. If this book should succeed in its aim of eradicating once for all this universal misconception, I shall die happy.

> Turn now to Keats and you are returned upon *mere* poetry, in the Latin sense of *mere*. Keats has no politics, no philosophy of statecraft: he is a young apostle of poetry for poetry's sake.
>
> 'Beauty is truth, truth beauty'—that is all
> Ye know on earth, and all ye need to know.
>
> But, of course, to put it solidly, that is a vague observation—to anyone whom life has taught to face facts and define his terms, actually an *uneducated* conclusion, albeit most pardonable in one so young and art. . . .

There we have it—the old familiar note of condescending patronage. I wonder who, of all the innumerable critics who have taken this tone towards Keats, has 'faced facts' as Keats had faced them before he rose to the victory in those lines. 'An uneducated conclusion'? So were the conclusions of 'the world's ransom, blessed Mary's son.'

CHAPTER X, *p*. 135.

And yet it seems to be true that in the process of the supremely rational thought of metaphysics or science, a moment always comes when the mind in its effort towards an exacter comprehension of reality is compelled, apparently by the nature of things, to make an irrational movement. In metaphysics this abnegation by the rational mind of its own nature in order to reach a further stage of comprehension is, for a literary critic, not impossible to detect. In the more arduous sciences, for which the training of the specialist is necessary, this act of detection is difficult, if not impossible, for the layman: and very few scientific minds are sufficiently self-conscious to be aware of the nature of their own activity. But, though I speak with all diffidence in this matter, it does appear to me that the highest kind of scientific discovery is achieved by thought of the same order as that by which the highest poetic discovery is achieved. Suddenly, and often without the man of science being aware of it, his assumption changes: he assumes no longer that reality is rational, but that it is harmonious. By an act of intuition he sees that it is harmonious, and this harmony is for him a truth. There is, in the old assumption not the slightest ground for his belief that this discovered harmony is a truth. A new assumption, and with it a new kind of thought, has supervened.

By the necessities of exposition I am forced here and elsewhere to present the non-rational thought of pure poetry and the rational thought which reaches its absolute perfection in mathematics as exclusive of each other. This is not the truth. The non-rational thought of pure poetry and the rational thought of pure mathematics are set in a true opposition. That is, they are complementary to, rather than exclusive of, each other. They present the fundamental harmony under its two real aspects; and as I have tried to indicate in my text the thought of pure mathematics at its highest is also non-rational.

To discuss this question would carry me into a region of exalted metaphysic where, perhaps, my wings would melt. But I may say this: the supremely rational thought of pure mathematics is concerned with *structure*; the non-rational thought of pure poetry is concerned with *being*. In its most elementary form the rational thought of mathematics is concerned with structure at the point when it is least essential. $2+2=4$ is the least important of all truths about any pair of two objects. The progress of mathematical thought is governed by the attempt to approach ever more closely to the *essential structure* of the universe. At the last this essential structure must become identical with *being*. I believe that every advance of mathematical thought in this process of approximation is marked by an act of non-rational perception. The nature of these advances is frequently disguised from the mathematician himself because he works in abstract symbols. First, for example, Minus quantities enter his calculations—he does consider their implications—then what he himself calls irrationals, e.g. $\sqrt{-1}$—he does not consider their implications—then at the modern end of the long evolution, Quanta—he does not consider their implications.

CHAPTER X, *p.* 138.

Perhaps no more striking analogy to Keats' process of soul at the moment of writing the 'indolent' letter, and no more illuminating commentary on the whole mystery of Soul-making, can be found than the following brief quotation from the third sermon of Meister Eckhart. (Trans. C. de B. Evans: p. 17):

What the active intellect does for the natural man that and far more does God do for the solitary soul: he turns out active intellect, and installing himself in its stead he himself assumes the duties of the active intellect.

When a man is quite idle, when his intellect is at rest within him, then God takes up the work: he himself is the agent who produces himself in the passive intellect. What happens is this. The active intellect cannot give what it has not got: it cannot have two ideas together, but first one and then the other. What though light and air show multitudes of forms and colours all at once, thou canst only observe them one after the other. And so with thy active intellect, which resembles the eye. But when God acts in lieu of thy active intellect, he engenders many images together in one point. . . .

CHAPTER X, *p.* 138.

Once more the appropriate commentary upon this mysterious statement is a passage from Meister Eckhart. 'The eye with which I see God is the same eye with which he sees me.' Doubtless others of the great mystics, with whom I am unfamiliar, would provide analogies equally striking.

CHAPTER X, *p.* 139.

I have lately come across a remarkable, though difficult, discussion of this very point in a book called 'Cosmic Anatomy,' by 'M.B. (Oxon)'. This book deals with many matters clean beyond my comprehension. It contains many of those strange 'borderline' speculations which are almost invariably dismissed as 'mystical.' I have never seen any reference to the book in print. But I think it is an important piece of work, and one which deserves to be studied carefully by those—they are not plentiful—who can approach without prejudice the efforts of a very original and serious mind towards the truth. The book is published by Mr. J. M. Watkins, Cecil Court, W.C.2.

CHAPTER XII, *p.* 170.

It is impossible to interrupt the narrative (and run the risk of mystifying the reader) by insisting once more upon what I believe to be true—namely, that the second *Hyperion* could not have been completed *as that poem.* It must necessarily have changed into something quite different. The visions and actions of the deified Apollo could have been none other than the visions and actions of the future Keats—that is to say, his unwritten poems and plays. This may be called a transcendental criticism: the name is unimportant, provided the criticism is a true one.

CHAPTER XII, *p.* 172.

Sir Sidney Colvin dismisses this prelude completely with the words—' The preamble or induction he had finished; and this, *if we leave out the futile first eighteen lines*, with which it begins, contains much lofty thought conveyed in noble imagery. . . . .' 'Life of John Keats,' 2nd ed., p. 450.

CHAPTER XIII, *p.* 194.

' Inexperience of line.'—I find it hard to believe that Keats used this phrase. Yet Miss Lowell, to whom the letter belongs, has thus transcribed it in *The Memorial Volume*. (And in her own 'John Keats,' Vol. II.) I cannot call to mind any similar phrase in Keats' letters. The context seems to call for ' inexperience of life.' Possibly Keats wrote—for his spelling was peculiar—' inexperience of live,' which is still, after all, a common slip of the pen. And Miss Lowell's poetical theories would have inclined her to read it *line*.

CHAPTER XIII, *p.* 197.

The details of the evidence concerning Brown's attitude and Keats' decision, though fascinating to those who care to make an exact study of Keats' biography, do not lend themselves to treatment in the main narrative: the facts are briefly these.

Of the two letters to Brown there remain only such fragments as Brown himself thought fit to make public, and these only in the form of copies made by Brown for Monckton Milnes. I am afraid he did some judicious scissors-and-paste work in order to make the letters square with, or at least not flagrantly contradict, his own account of the affair to Monckton Milnes.

In the first place, he gave a wrong date to the letter of 22nd September. He dated it 23rd September. That may have been and probably was mere inadvertence. At all events, I can see no motive for it. On any other day than this of 22nd September one would not hesitate to say the mistake was Keats', who was extremely vague about dates in general. But on this day his letters happen to be very precisely dated. Keats was writing so many that he could not have made the mistake; and he says quite definitely in his letter to Dilke: ' I shall hear from Brown and you almost together, for I have sent him a letter to-day.' This was his third letter to Brown.

Before he had posted his letter to Dilke, Keats received from Brown a reply to one, or both, of his two previous letters to him—one written from London, one after his return to Winchester. To this Keats immediately replied in a fourth letter. Brown transcribed a fragment of this fourth letter for Milnes, dating it 23rd September. He was however careless enough to include the following passage in his transcript:

> I ought (Keats wrote) to have waited for your answer to my last [i.e. Keats' third letter, of 22nd September] before I wrote this.

I feel, however, compelled to make a rejoinder to yours. I had written to Dilke on the subject of my last, I scarcely know whether I shall send my letter now. I think he would approve of my plan; it is so evident. Nay, I am convinced out and out, that by proving for a while in periodical works I may maintain myself decently.

It is to be noted, first, that Brown completely suppresses 'the rejoinder.' But it is obvious that he had objected; and that he had objected in such a fashion that Keats did not send his letter of 22nd September to Dilke is proved by Keats' letter to Dilke on 1st October, which begins:

My dear Dilke,
For sundry reasons which I will explain to you when I come to Town, I have to request you will do me a great favour, as I must call it knowing how great a Bore it is. That your imagination may not have time to take too great an alarm, I state immediately that I want you to hire me a couple of rooms (a Sitting Room and bed room for myself alone) in Westminster. . . .

Thus it is clear that Keats' letter to Dilke of 22nd September was not sent, because of Brown's objection to the plan.

I have suggested in my narrative that Brown purposely delayed replying to Keats' first two letters. The suggestion can be justified. Writing to his brother George on Friday, 24th September, Keats says:

Brown, who was at Bedhampton, went thence to Chichester, and I am still directing my letters Bedhampton. There arose a misunderstanding. I began to suspect my letters had been stopped from curiosity. However, yesterday Brown had four letters from me in a lump, and the matter is cleared up. . . .

Was it cleared up? Keats *had* written, and had sent, four letters to Brown. But Brown cannot have received them 'in a lump.' For immediately after writing letter No. 3 to Brown, Keats received an answer to Nos. 1 and 2, as we have seen. Keats, who was not so suspicious of Charles Brown as I have become, accepted Brown's word that the four letters had arrived 'in a lump', without thinking, as a trustful friend would do. But there is something incurably 'fishy' about Brown's manœuvres at this time, as there is about his manipulation of the letters for Milnes, and about his account of his own conduct towards Keats given to Milnes—an account against which Dilke vehemently protested. Dilke's protest will be found in the memoir of Brown prefixed to the Buxton Forman edition of the Poems and Letters.

It may be said that I ought, in fairness, to have given Keats' warm and generous words in praise of Brown, which Brown did most diligently copy for Milnes' edification.

> Here I will take an opportunity (says Keats) of making a remark or two on our friendship, and on all your good offices to me. I have a natural timidity of mind in these matters; liking better to take the feeling between us for granted, than to speak of it. But, good God! what a short while you have known me! I feel it a sort of duty thus to recapitulate, however unpleasant it may be to you. You have been living for others more than any man I know. This is a vexation to me, because it has been depriving you, in the very prime of life, of pleasures which it was your duty to procure. As I am speaking in general terms, this may appear nonsense; you, perhaps, will not understand it; but if you can go over, day by day, any month of the last year, you will know what I mean. . . .

These are noble and generous words. Keats meant them. But whether they were altogether true of Brown is another matter. Keats' own unselfishness was such that he would never have dreamed of imputing even mildly interested motives to Brown. That his own society, that the chance of collaborating with himself, might be precious to Brown, never struck him. Brown was not a hero; he was a decent ordinary man, *l'homme moyen sensuel*, who liked Keats well enough to lend him enough to live on, but not disinterestedly enough to let Keats go his own independent way without trying to prevent him.

And, in suggesting that Brown was disingenuous in his behaviour at this moment in September, I am not trying to make him out a villain. I am merely anxious to discover what he was up to. Very likely it was nothing worse than a very real, and intelligible, reluctance to consider Keats' plan and to make it real to his own imagination, as he would have had to do had he answered Keats' letters. So he pretended he had not received them: it would have been impossible to admit that he had received them and not replied, because Keats had been anxiously awaiting an answer. So he made up the story of having received the four letters ' in a lump,' which, seen through the cold light of an intervening century, will not square with the facts.

The interest of the point is the additional evidence it gives of Brown's opposition to Keats' plan, and the rather odd sidelight it throws on the rather odd character of Brown, who played a more considerable part in Keats' life than the innocuous and romanticized conception of himself as ' a retired Russia Merchant and the generous friend and protector of Keats ' would suggest.

Since the above was written, Miss Lowell, in her second volume, on the authority apparently of the memoir of Brown's life by his son, has declared that Brown's ostensible visit to Bedhampton (at which place Keats wrote to him in vain) concealed a visit to Ireland to marry Abigail Donohue. But even that will not explain the discrepancy in Brown's story of the letters.

CHAPTER XIII, *p.* 200.

'I would rather read Chaucer than Ariosto.' It is perhaps worth remarking two things: first, that there is a good deal of the Ariosto influence in *The Cap and Bells*, on which Keats was at this time (November) engaged in collaboration with Brown; and that Brown was a great admirer, and I believe also a translator, of Ariosto.

CHAPTER XIII, *p.* 206.

'For the last Thread of Destiny was spent, and Daphnis went down the stream. The torrent whirled away the man whom the Muses loved, and whom the Nymphs held dear.'

CHAPTER XIV, *p.* 207.

The date assigned to the *Ode to Fanny* by Sir Sidney Colvin and Professor de Selincourt (and now by Miss Amy Lowell) is the beginning of 1819. 'It carries,' says Sir Sidney, 'internal evidence of having been written before the winter was out in the lines,

> I come, I see thee as thou standest there,
> Beckon me not into the wintry air.

But that evidence is just as conclusive for the winter of 1820 as for the winter of 1819.

I have assumed that the poem was written early in 1820, though I feel no positive conviction about the date. I am only too willing to admit that it *may* have been written during the two months of 'idle fever' which followed mid-February 1819. The lines

> O ease my heart of verse and let me rest . . .
> A theme! a theme! great nature! give a theme;

would fit well with his period of 'as it were moulting'; and the whole tenour of the poem, the pitiful appeal to Fanny not to be unfaithful to him by her behaviour at a dance to which he himself cannot go, would fit well with the moment at which a fortnight after asking his sister to teach him 'a few common dancing steps' (27th February 1819), he told her: 'I went lately to the only dance I have been to these twelve months or shall go to for twelve months again (13th March). [See pp. 112 sq.]

But, I think, it would fit a little better in, say, January 1820. The poem, it seems to me, is by a nuance more agonized than we should expect in February 1819. However, I attach no importance to the choice one way or the other. It is merely for convenience of exposition that I have assigned it to the later date, because it expresses that mistrust of Fanny felt by Keats towards Fanny which, although permanent, became more agonizing in his last year.

CHAPTER XIV, *p.* 209.

How remote still from a real understanding of Keats are some of the most gifted modern minds is strikingly revealed by Mr. Bernard Shaw's remarks upon him in the 'Memorial Volume.' Mr. Shaw speaks of the 'purely literary poet,' and continues:

> The other sort of poet is one for whom poetry is only a means to an end, the end being to deliver a message which clamours to be revealed through him. So he secures a hearing for it by clothing it with word-garments of such beauty, authority and eternal memorableness that the world must needs listen to it. These are prophets rather than poets; and for the sake of being poets alone would not take the trouble to rhyme love and dove, or bliss and kiss.
>
> It often happens that a prophet-poet begins as a literary poet, the prophet instinctively training himself by literary exercises for his future work. Thus you have Morris exercising himself in his youth in rewriting all the old stories in very lovely verses, but conscientiously stating at the beginning that he is only 'the idle singer of an empty day.' Later on he finds his destiny as the busy singer of a bursting day. Now, if Morris had lived no longer than Keats, he would have been an even more exclusively literary poet. . . .

The conception of Keats as an immature William Morris is extraordinary. But Mr. Shaw's words are altogether remarkable. They give one the uncomfortable feeling that he really meant it when he said 'Better than Shakespeare.'

CHAPTER XIV, *p.* 218.

'Keats' reading was much on *Troilus and Cressida.*' Not unnaturally, seeing that he told Fanny Brawne (February 1820): 'My greatest torment since I have known you has been the fear of you being a little inclined to the Cressid.' Of the nine manuscript notes in the only one of Keats' two copies of Shakespeare which is now known, no less than five are on *Troilus and Cressida*. One of them is the following:

Sith every action that hath gone before
Whereof we have Record, Triall did draw
Bias and thwart, not answering the ayme:
And that unbodied figure of the thought
That gave't surmised shape. [Act I, Scene 3].

'The genius of Shakespeare was an innate universality—wherefore he had the utmost achievement of human intellect prostrate beneath his indolent and kingly gaze. He could do easily Man's utmost. His plans of tasks to come were not of this world—if what he proposed to do hereafter would not in his own Idea " answer the aim " how tremendous must have been his Conception of Ultimates.'

APPENDIX: THE COMPOSITION OF *HYPERION*

MISS LOWELL, in the second volume of her 'John Keats' (pp. 339-345), which appeared while this book was in the press, makes the extraordinary statement that the second *Hyperion* was written before the first. I call the statement extraordinary because it is Miss Lowell herself who possesses and first published the letter to Woodhouse on 22nd September 1819, which, I had thought, finally settled the problem of the two Hyperions. Miss Lowell speaks of her 'startling discovery': but it is not easy to see wherein the discovery consists. That the second *Hyperion* was written before the first is scarcely a discovery; it is a theory, and a demonstrably mistaken one. In arguing a matter so vital, however, one cannot appeal to internal evidence, though it is quite conclusive to me. I find it significant, nevertheless, that Miss Lowell gives no consideration to either *Hyperion* as a poem. She is content to say that she agrees with Keats that they were both failures. But *all* Keats' poems were failures in his own eyes.

The problem of the two *Hyperions* is complicated. Until Miss Lowell published the letter of 22nd September to Woodhouse, it was strictly insoluble by external evidence. Previous to that publication, the only external evidence had been Brown's statements to Monckton Milnes (1) that *Hyperion* was begun at Wentworth Place, i.e. after Tom Keats' death; (2) that in the evenings of November and December 1819 Keats was remodelling *Hyperion* into the form of a dream. Brown's memory, twenty odd years after the event, was naturally unreliable in detail. The psychological probabilities are that he would have been less likely to be mistaken in statement (2) than in statement (1). And in fact statement (1) is demonstrably wrong.

For the moment, however, it is desirable to leave Brown's statements out of account entirely, and begin with the letter to Woodhouse, which must be read together with Keats' letter of the same day to Reynolds, who was staying with Woodhouse in Dorset. The first lines of the letter to Woodhouse show that Keats expected each to read the other's letter. To Reynolds Keats says: 'I have given up *Hyperion*: there were too many Miltonic inversions in it.' His last letter to Reynolds had been written on 25th August: in it he had said 'The Paradise Lost becomes a greater wonder.' From that one may reasonably conclude that in mid-August Keats was engaged upon *Hyperion*; and this is proved by his letter to Bailey of 15th August, in which he says, 'I have also been writing parts of my *Hyperion* and completed four acts of a tragedy.'

That evidence, I think, *proves* that from some time before 15th August till some time before 22nd September Keats was engaged in 'writing parts of *Hyperion*' (whatever that phrase may mean), and that he suddenly abandoned it on or about 20th September.

To prove what the phrase means there are two pieces of evidence. There is (1) the statement of Woodhouse that in April Keats had given the MS. of *Hyperion* to him to read, that Keats said he would not go on with it, and that the MS. consisted of about 900 lines. The first *Hyperion* consists of 883 lines—and the actual MS. which Woodhouse read is in the British Museum. It is the MS. of the first *Hyperion*, and, I should guess, a fair copy for the first two books, and a first draft for the third book. However that may be, the statement of Woodhouse—his statements, as Keats students know, are far more reliable than Brown's—proves that the *Hyperion* on which Keats was engaged in August and September 1918 was not the first *Hyperion*.

There is (2) the letter to Woodhouse. 'I will give you a few lines from *Hyperion* on account of a word in the last line of a fine sound,' Keats says, and he quotes the first five lines of Canto II of the second *Hyperion*. (The word is *legend-laden*.) Then he says: 'I think you will like the following description of the Temple and Saturn' and he quotes from the middle of Canto I 'I look'd around . . . shut against the sunrise evermore.' Finally, he says: 'Here is what I had written for a sort of induction,' and quotes the first ten and a half lines of Canto I. Miss Lowell, strangely, finds a hidden meaning in '*had* written'. It is to her 'pretty conclusive proof that the lines were old work.' I am afraid it proves nothing of the kind. Keats has just said he has given up *Hyperion*; the letter proves that the *Hyperion* he had given up was the second *Hyperion*. What more natural than that he should say of the induction which he has abandoned with the rest of the poem: 'This is what I *had* written'?

So that we may take it as proved that when Keats told Bailey on 15th August that he was writing parts of his *Hyperion*, he meant he was writing the second *Hyperion*. Of course to Keats himself it was not the *second Hyperion*. It was the same poem—simply *Hyperion*. Nor does the fact that he had written at least as far as the beginning of Canto II of the second *Hyperion* nullify Brown's statement that Keats was engaged in November-December 1819 in recasting *Hyperion* into the form of a dream. He may very well have been trying to make his two attempts a single whole for publication. I think (for reasons given in the narrative) it went against the grain to publish the first *Hyperion* alone, even though Keats saw its superiority as achieved poetry.

It is extremely difficult to understand on what evidence Miss Lowell bases her theory that the second *Hyperion* was a first attempt written in September-November 1818. If the letter to Woodhouse implies anything, it implies that the passages from the second *Hyperion* which it contains had been lately written. The fact that Keats did not mention to George that he had made a new beginning to *Hyperion* is surely no evidence at all. He did not begin writing to George till 17th September, by which time most probably he was already at the point of abandoning the second *Hyperion*: and why tell him of a new beginning already abandoned? He had never told George very much about *Hyperion* at any time. He never copied a single line even of the first *Hyperion* for him.

There is not the least necessity for such a theory as Miss Lowell's; there is no external evidence at all for it; and on the internal evidence, it is absolutely impossible. All things are possible, of course, in a certain sense. The value of Miss Lowell's theory can, however, be forcibly presented by saying that there is precisely the same reason for believing that *The Ode on a Grecian Urn* was written in October 1817 (or any other month and year) as there is for believing that the second *Hyperion* was written in September-November 1818.

We may now regard Miss Lowell's 'startling discovery' as disposed of, and turn to the more interesting question of when the first *Hyperion* was written. The second *Hyperion*, it is clear, was substantially written in August and September 1819.

The first *Hyperion* was finished in its present form in April 1819. That is the principal fact we know 'beyond a peradventure' about it. The rest we have to deduce from indications in Keats' letters. The foundation-stone of the edifice we have to build is the following passage, dated simply 'Friday' in Keats' Journal-letter of December-January 1818-19 to George. The Friday was probably Friday, 18th December.

> I think you knew before you left England that my next subject would be 'the fall of Hyperion.' I went on with it a little last night, but it will take some time to get into the vein again. I will not give you any extracts, because I wish the whole to make an impression. . . .

That passage immediately follows this, written (it seems certain) on the previous day:

> I am passing a quiet day—which I have not done for a long while—and if I do continue so, I feel I must begin again with my poetry. . . . I live under an everlasting restraint—never relieved except when I am composing—so I will write away.

From those two passages in their order it is clear that on an evening in mid-December (? 17th December) Keats took up *Hyperion* again, and found it difficult to get back into the vein; and that his work on the poem had been interrupted for a long while. I think that there is no reasonable doubt that the interruption had lasted since Tom's death on 1st December, after which Keats had removed from Well Walk to Brown's house at Wentworth Place. He is on this day (17th December ?) only just settling in properly, for he mentions Bentley the postman's bringing along his books in a clothes basket. Thus we are taken back to the end of November. We have but two short notes of Keats' during November, to Fanny Keats and Jem Rice, neither of which mentions or is likely to mention his writing. For the end of October, however, we have two letters, one to Woodhouse (27th October), and one to George. The following lines from the letter to Woodhouse are a clear clue:

> If then he [the poet] has no self, and if I am a poet, where is the wonder that I should say I would write no more? Might I not at that very instant have been cogitating on the Characters of Saturn and Ops?

That shows that Keats has been lately engaged, and that Woodhouse knew he had been engaged, on *Hyperion;* and that in a moment of depression (for which there was cause enough) he had said he would not write any more. [In passing, I should be inclined to conjecture that the story of his own quick-mindedness told to Rice on 24th November:

> And again, 'Keats,' says a friend, 'when will you come to town again? 'I will,' says I, 'let you have the MS. next week,'

concerns Woodhouse and a request from him for the MS. of *Hyperion,* in which I believe Keats had at that time got to about the end of Book II. Quite likely it is the fair copy of those two books made for Woodhouse that we now have in the British Museum. But this is, of course, mere conjecture.]

The obvious connection of the letter to Woodhouse of 27th October with *Hyperion* is corroborated by a passage in his letter to George, written about the same day.

> No sooner am I alone than shapes of epic greatness are stationed about me and serve my Spirit the office which is equivalent to a King's body-guard.

Hyperion, it is worth remembering, was an 'epic' poem to Keats.

Thus we are taken back to the end of October, when Keats, in alternating moods, was busy on *Hyperion.*

The next probable, if not certain references, take us back a month further. Keats wrote to Dilke on 21st September:

> I wish I could say Tom was any better. His identity presses upon me so all day that I am obliged to go out—and although I

> intended to have given some time to study alone, I am obliged to write and plunge into abstract images to ease myself of his countenance, his voice, his feebleness—so that I live now in a continual fever. . . .

On the same day, or the day after, he wrote to Reynolds:

> . . . The voice and shape of a woman has haunted me these two days—at such a time when the relief, the feverous relief of Poetry, seems a much less crime. This morning Poetry has conquered—I have relapsed into those abstractions which are my only life. . . .

There is, I think, no reasonable doubt that the 'abstract images' and the 'abstractions' refer to *Hyperion*. Not only is there no other poem of Keats' to which such phrases could apply, but the evidence which shows him busily engaged upon *Hyperion* at the end of October gives unmistakable meaning to these phrases.

The search cannot be taken further back. Keats had only arrived back from Scotland in mid-August. The probabilities are that he began *Hyperion* about the beginning of September, and worked steadily at it until Tom's death. In this belief I have Sir Sidney Colvin's weighty support. Had it not been for Miss Lowell's strange theory, it would indeed have been hardly necessary to restate the evidence for a generally accepted conclusion.

In dealing with the progress of *Hyperion* after mid-December, I have to part company with Sir Sidney Colvin. But it is as well to be clear. What can be regarded as definitely established upon external evidence is that Keats began the first *Hyperion* in September 1818 and worked on it till the end of November. Then came the interruption of Tom's death. Keats made an effort to resume the poem in mid-December, but found it hard to get into the vein. The poem was abandoned, or as I prefer to say, finished, and the MS. given to Woodhouse in April 1819.

In my narrative there is a definite and detailed theory of what happened to *Hyperion* between mid-December and April. It is, in one sense, only a theory. But it must be remembered that nothing but theory is possible. The external evidence is almost *nil*. What there is, I submit, bears out my theory exactly.

There is an interval of some days after the first attempt to resume *Hyperion* (17th December?). Just before Christmas, for which Brown had gone to Chichester, Keats says: 'Just now I took out my poem to go on with it—but the thought of my writing so little to you came upon me and I could not get on. . . .' Then comes another long interval, probably of about a week. He says: 'I will not give any extracts from my large poem which is scarce begun.' A few days later (2nd January) he says: 'I have no thought pervading me so constantly and frequently as that of you—my Poem cannot frequently drive it away—you will retard it much more than you could by taking up my time if you were in England.'

Whether or no the student of Keats is persuaded by my account of the reasons why Keats could make no headway with *Hyperion*, the fact of his inability is clear.

Between 7th and 14th January Keats wrote to Haydon: 'I have been writing a little now and then lately: but nothing to speak of, being discontented and as it were moulting.' A few days later he went down to Chichester and wrote at least the first draft of *The Eve of St. Agnes* and *The Eve of St. Mark*. On 8th March comes a definite reference to *Hyperion* in a letter to Haydon: 'You must be wondering where I am and what I am about! I am mostly at Hampstead and about nothing; being in a sort of *qui bono* temper, not exactly on the road to an epic poem.' And somewhere towards the end of February he had written to George: 'I have not gone on with *Hyperion* lately, for to tell the truth, I have not been in great cue for writing lately.'

That brings the account for *Hyperion* down to 8th March. Evidently little or nothing of it had been written since Tom's death—at most a few lines with effort. Any work on it had been definitely interrupted in January by the composition of *The Eve of St. Agnes* and *The Eve of St. Mark*, both of which were written, or at least drafted, during Keats' stay at Bedhampton near Chichester: both bear the marks of inspiration drawn from that cathedral city. Woodhouse states that *The Eve of St. Mark* was written on 13-17th February.

Exactly two months later (13th April) Keats wrote to Haydon, who had been again pestering him about money: 'Now you have maimed me again; I was whole, I had begun reading again—when your note came I was engaged in a book. I dread as much as a plague the idle fever of two months more without any fruit.' That exactly covers the whole period from the writing of the fair copy of *The Eve of St. Mark* dated by Woodhouse. On the same day Keats wrote to Fanny Keats: 'My idleness of late has been indeed growing so that it will require a great shake to get rid of it. I have written nothing, and almost read nothing, but I must turn over a new leaf.' And two days later (15th April) he wrote to George: 'I am still at a standstill in versifying. I cannot do it yet with any pleasure. I mean, however, to look round on my resources and means and see what I can do without poetry. . . .'

That means, I take it, that Keats had been trying to write—in vain. These efforts, which he considered abortive, certainly included the sonnet *Why did I laugh to-night?* But it is impossible to say with certainty whether *As Hermes once* and *La Belle Dame sans Merci* also belong to them. The letter to George is without dates at the critical moment. But the probabilities are heavy that both these poems belong to the few days following 15th April.

At some time in those same few days Keats finished, or brought to an end, the first *Hyperion*. He had written but a handful of lines with effort between 1st December and 15th April; before the end of April Woodhouse had the MS. complete in his hands. With the end of 'the idle fever' necessarily came a rush of inspiration concerning the destiny of Apollo. The greater part of the third book was written in a sudden burst of activity about the third week in April. When *Hyperion* was finished, the *Odes* began.

The last three sentences were based on the internal evidence that is fully developed in the main narrative. Since they were written Miss Lowell has supplied a quite unexpected piece of external evidence to corroborate the theory. She herself is sublimely uninterested in both the first and the second *Hyperions*: therefore she makes no use of it. It is indeed difficult to see what use she could make of it with her perverse notion that the second *Hyperion* was written before the first: and her lack of interest accounts for the lamentable hiatus in her transcription of Woodhouse's precious words on Keats' methods of composition. This is the form in which she gives them ('John Keats,' Vol. I, p. 501):

> He (Keats) has said that he has often not been aware of the beauty of some thought or expression until after he had composed and written it down.—It has then struck him with astonishment and seemed rather the production of another person than his own. This was the case with the description of Apollo in the third book of *Hyperion*. . . . It seemed to come by chance or magic—to be as it were something given to him.

This external and unexpected evidence gives a valuable support to my interpretation. Readers of the main narrative will understand in what a peculiar sense that description of Apollo was 'something given' to Keats.

KEATS
AND
SHAKE-
SPEARE

*

MURRY

*

OXFORD

b